BORDER TRADE

NORTH-EAST INDIA AND NEIGHBOURING COUNTRIES

Edited by

GURUDAS DAS

R.K. PURKAYASTHA

AKANSHA PUBLISHING HOUSE

NEW DELHI-1100 59 (INDIA)

AKANSHA PUBLISHING HOUSE
R-37-B, Vani Vihar
Uttam Nagar
New Delhi-110059

Border Trade

First Edition, 2000

ISBN 81-87606-02-9

[Responsibility for the opinion expressed, facts stated and conclusion reached is entirely that of the respective authors. The Publishers bear no responsibility for them.]

PRINTED IN INDIA

Published by M.P. Misra for Akansha Publishing House, New Delhi and Printed at Tarun Offset Press, Delhi

Contents

CONTEMPORARY TRADE: NORTH-EASTERN REGION AND BANGLADESH

BORDER TRADE PROSPECT IN ARUNACHAL PRADESH

INDO-NEPAL TRADE

Foreword

North East India is surrounded by Bangladesh, Myanmar, China, and Bhutan. It is connected with the mainland through what is known as chickens neck, a very narrow strip of land with the width of 33 km only. Given this peculiar geo-political location, cross-border markets are likely to be more cost-effective for North East India's surplus production than the distant national markets.

Although no reliable estimates are available on border trade, the potential for Indian exports to neighbouring countries is immense and calls for an introspection with regard to trade policies. The official trade statistics seem to reveal a fraction of the actual volume of border trade. It is of utmost interest to map out the traditional trade routes, important trading centres and the nature of trade taking place between us and the neighbours. Our trade with countries is handicapped by the non-existence of infrastructural facilities at different trade routes.

Border trade and economic development in border areas are interdependent, as border trade leads to economic development which through secondary effects increases border trade many folds. The process of Globalisation and Liberalisation has opened up the economy of North East India. As a result, our trade relation with the neighbouring countries will grow and diversify. How to gain from this development without losing control over North East India resources and how to promote reinvestment of profits within the regions for social and economic development will be the challenge facing North East India. A large part of international border between North East India and the Neighbouring countries is unmanned and badly demarcated. Border trade cannot flourish without good border management.

North East India Council for Social Science Research held on 14-15 December 1998 a seminar on Border Trade in North East India—Prespective, Issues and Problems. It was inaugurated by Mr. S.C. Marak, Chairman, State Planning Board, Meghalaya. The Valedictory address was delivered by Professor B. Pakem, Vide-Chancellor, North Eastern Hill University. The four academic sessions were presided over by Professor Indad Hussain, Mr. Gautam Sen, Professor K.S. Singh and Dr. Archana Sharma.

We take this opportunity to thank North Eastern Council and Indian Council of Social Science Research for their support to NEICSSR for holding this seminar of vital importance to the country. Dr. Gurudas Das and Dr. Rakhal Kumar Purakayastha, editors of the volume deserve special mention. I would like to thank profusely a large number of unnamed scholars and colleagues who provided the infrastructural support and made this seminar a total success.

B. Datta Ray

Secretary, NEICSSR

Editors' Note

This volume is the outcome of a seminar on "Border Trade in North-East India: Perspective, Issues and problems," held on 14-15 December, 1998, organised by North East India Council for Social Science Research, Shillong.

This issue has recently caught in the imagination of the policy makers of our country as one of the panacea of underdevelopment of the north-eastern region (NER). "Border trade" is now increasingly being viewed as one of the means to generate growth impulse in the stagnant economy of the NER. As the region is surrounded by four neighbouring countries, viz., Bangladesh, Bhutan, China and Myanmar, with whom it shares 98 per cent of its border, it is only natural that closed borders will rob her avenues to grow.

Prior to 90s, political integration and concerns for the security of north-eastern borders had been given more importance in the 'state centric view' adopted by the Centre towards the development of the NER. Neither the role of border trade in easing out the suffocation of the people living in the border areas nor its instrumental value in enhancing production, consumption and industrialisation could be visualised in a hostile political relationship with the neighbouring countries.

It is only after normalisation of India's relationship with the neighbouring Bangladesh and China as well as initiation of the programmes of globalisation of the national economy in the 90s that the idea to situate. The NER within the larger context of South Asia has received greater attention. As the main centres of national market are far away, the cross-border markets are viewed as potential vents for the region's surplus produce and unutilised resources.

Already the demand for coal and limestone in Bangladesh has led to hectic mining activities in the southern belt of Meghalaya. Similarly, the demand for ginger and other horticultural products in markets of Bangladesh has led to their extensive cultivation in the hills of north-east. As the resource base particularly of the hills of NER is complementary to that of the adjacent plains of Bangladesh, there exists a tremendous scope for cross-border trade between these two regions.

In contrast to NER-Bangladesh trade, the resource base of NER and Myanmar largely appears to be competitive. As a result, a mind of transit trade particularly in manufactures produced outside NER as well as Myanmar has developed along NER-Myanmar border.

Although the size of the market in Bhutan is quite small, a significant part of it is supplied from India through NER-Bhutan border. Like NER-Myanmar trade, NER-Bhutan border is also basically used as transit route for exporting goods produced elsewhere in India.

The volume of informal/unofficial trade carried out through all the transit points along NER-Bangladesh as well as NER-Myanmar borders is far more higher than that of their formal/official counterparts. There is an urgent need to direct this trade through legal channel. This calls for an intensive study of the commodity structure of this trade for further trade liberalisation between the bordering countries.

The seminar, that has produced this volume, has perhaps been the first attempt to look into the various facets of the border trade between NER and the neighbouring countries directly. As the authors were handicapped by non-availability of reliable data, emphasis was given on the generation of primary data—both quantitative and factual—so that at least the composition and direction of border trade can be analysed. A few scholars have taken the trouble of visiting the different transit points in order to report the ground realities of our borders and border trade. Most of the papers, as a result, are narratives as not much theorisation is possible at this stage. It is quite perplexing to note that even uniform official data is not available on the length of our borders with the neighbouring countries. The data on border length vary with their sources. Obviously this is reflected in this volume too.

We are grateful to NEICSSR and its secretary Dr. B. Datta Ray for giving us the opportunity to associate ourselves with this volume. Our thanks to Dr. H. Srikanth, Dr. C.J. Thomas and Dr. Uday Chand Das for helping us in various ways while editing this volume. Finally, we are grateful to Mr. M.P. Misra for taking up the responsibility of publication of this volume.

St. Anthony's College
Shillong

Gurudas Das
R.K. Purkayastha

Inaugural Address

S.C. Marka

At the outset, let me compliment the North East India Council for Social Science Research for organising this seminar on Perspective Issues and Problems of Border Trade in the North East India. It is only through such positive initiatives and constructive deliberations that not only awareness is created about the potential of the region in such a crucial sector but also provides a forum for knowledgeable people to discuss on the issues and problems facing this sector which despite its immense potential has not actualised to the desired level in view of various handicaps and constraints. I am certain that such deliberations would throw up specific solutions as also evolve strategy / action plan which will not only help the State Governments of this region in evolving suitable policies but also guide the private sector.

In recent years there have been remarkable changes in the international economy. We are no longer left with the concept of nation states in the economic sphere. In the recent decade the world has been increasingly shrinking; international borders are losing their rigidity, where there is an interplay of global forces through the dynamics brought about through transport, trade and communications. We have virtually seen the world been reduced to a large economic global village. We are witnessing the emergence of a free market scenario and globalisation of economic zones. The world economy is crucially hinging on trade and commerce which has assumed unique significance in the economic strategies of all countries. This is all the more relevant in the North Eastern Region which is bound on virtually all sides with international borders.

Often, we have talked of the isolation of the North Eastern Region which has resulted in its economic backwardness and its alienation from the mainstream. Time has come for us to convert this geographical handicap into an opportunity. Such can only take place if the North Eastern Region takes the conscious policy to improve and augment border trade and above all to look outwards. Our strength lies in the international borders and beyond; we should look outward towards neighbouring countries rather than only viewing inwards to marketing with the rest of the country. This is so because of our unique geographical location.

Unemployment is a burning problem in the North Eastern Region. We are faced not only with increasing number of unemployment but also lack of adequate opportunities to remedy the same. Such an unemployment can only be solved through economic development of the Region. Economic development will necessarily imply a flow of investment which can be made viable through border trade with neighbouring countries. The market for our products lies in that direction and hence, we should exploit this to the maximum extent possible. At present, the goods which we have been exporting are mainly primary minerals like coal, limestone etc. as well as some horticultural products like oranges, etc. Our efforts should be to diversify the export basket of foodgrains and other horticultural products specially in processed form so as to realise higher per unit value and consequently enable the farmers of the region, specially in the border areas, to earn better prices for their products.

We are having marketable surplus in various agricultural/horticultural products like potato, ginger, turmeric, oranges etc. If even a part of this surplus of agricultural/horticultural sector could be exported specially in processed forms it would boost our economy tremendously. Herein, I would like to make a few specific suggestions. There is need for greater collaboration with our neighbouring countries so as to accelerate the momentum in this direction. We can consider setting up joint ventures in processing vegetables, fruits with our neighbouring countries which would benefit all of us. We should also try to set up processing units for oranges, pineapples, ginger dehydration etc. as also cement projects in the joint sector.

There is another unique institution of this region which needs to be revived for promotion of better economic relations with neighbouring countries and that is the concept of border Hats. Since the days of pre-Independent India, when Meghalaya was under the composite state of Assam and Bangladesh was then known as East Pakistan, people used to exchange different products ranging from rice, fish, limestone to miscellaneous materials like spices, fruits etc. Both these regions even had free access of trade to Burma now known as Myanamar. In view of these facilities of free access the farmers on both sides had ready market for their produce. But after India attained Independence those facilities were withdrawn and this led to the discontentment of the people living in the border areas, discouraging them from increasing and expanding their trade operations. Under these circumstances some people also resorted to smuggling activities in the area. Therefore, in order to safeguard the border people from perpetual disillusionment and vicious circle of poverty; to reap fruits of economic development and to provide both physical and emotional security to them, there is a need to allow and strengthen border trade.

Promotion of Border Trade through local Markets (Haats) with Bangladesh is of importance to improve the economic conditions of the people of this region living in the areas adjoining Bangladesh. The sudden closure of local and traditional markets with the people across the border has caused great economic hardships especially for those people who have been mostly dependent on trade.

Trade on some items like limestone, timber and wood,

tezpata, fresh and dried fruits, between the people of Meghalaya and the people of Bangladesh had been continuing for some time in the small scale and in identified areas. But, after closure of the Border trade through the Haats, it has been found that people living in border areas of the state have not been able to arrange for marketing their products satisfactorily. Further, because of the hilly terrain and absence of communications to most areas of the border adjoining Bangladesh, arrangements for transport of their products had become difficult, costly and unremunerative.

It is therefore felt that resumption of border trade through local markets (Haats) with Bangladesh on a larger scale would go a long way in alleviating multifarious problems.

The basic economic strategy in the North Eastern Region will be to encourage trade and investment resulting in overall economic development. It is a life and death question involving the destiny of thousands of men and women. Individually and with collaborative efforts, the states of the North Eastern Region have to review and formulate their economic policies so as to promote such trade and investment and take advantage of the geographical opportunities offered to this region through our common border with so many countries. Unless we move fast, unemployment frustration and tension would increase.

I look forward to the deliberations in the present seminar so as to evolve strategy and action plan towards this direction which will augment the border trade of the region and thereby promote economic development.

With these words I inaugurate the seminar.

PART I

HISTORICAL PERSPECTIVE: TRADE AND TRADE ROUTES

1

The Border Trade in North-East India: The Historical Perspective

—B.B. Kumar

The North-East India was a very important part of the country as far as the border trade is concerned. The region had many important trade centres. The articles produced in the region were in great demand elsewhere. Many items were imported through North-East India and were exported through our ports to other countries.

The North-East India had trade links with Tibet and Burma through land routes. There was an ancient land route from Peshwar to Parvatipur (now in Bangladesh) passing through Vazirabad, Lahour, Jalandhar, Saharanpur, Lucknow, Tirhut and Katihar. It extended further to Assam[1] from Parvatipur.[2] It mostly passed keeping Ganges to the south. A southern route from Lahour to Bhagalpur through Raivind, Firozepur, Bhatinda, Delhi, Allahabad, Varanasi, and Patna, branched off to Ganga Sagar (Calcutta) from Patna. The route extended from Bhagalpur to Kajangal in Rajmahal and then to Calcutta.[3] Another route branched off from this southern route to Kamarupa from Kajangal by crossing Ganges at that point. It may be mentioned that Bhaskara Varman, the king of Kamarupa and Chinese traveller, Yuan Chuang met the emperor, Harsha Vardhana at Kajangala[4], and they must have used the same route for travelling to that place from the Kamarupa. The two monarchs marched towards Kanauj with their armies from that place. Harsha Vardhana proceeded along the southern route and Bhaskara Varman followed the northern one.[5] The route to Kamarupa extended upto the Yunnan province of China.[6] Kamarupa formed an important part of this trade route. An alternative trade route from India to China passed through Chumbi valley in Sikkim and Tibet. The ancient silk route passed through the north and the north-west.

A proposal was made in the early part of the last century to open up Patkai trade route.[7] That, however, could not materialise due to various reasons. That was, perhaps, to follow the ancient route linking Brahmaputra valley to the South-East Asia and Yunnan province of China. One of the reasons of not restoring the ancient trade routes through Brahmaputra Valley towards the east was the higher cost of road construction. The interests of the British owned Steam-Navigation Companies operating in the rivers of Burma were supposed to be adversely effected by such land routes and their opposition certainly played crucial role in this case.

The Brahmaputra valley was linked up with Burma through Manipur also. But, one or two routes linking the valley with Manipur were most difficult.[8] This route was not an important one for border trade between Assam and Burma due to difficult terrain.

The human movement between India and Burma through Surma valley and Manipur started in the remote past. According to Sir A. Phayre, "The route by which Kahatriya princes arrived (in Burma) is indicated in the traditions as being through Manipur..."[9] According to Capt. Dun, "There can be no reasonable doubt that a great Aryan wave of very pure blood passed through Manipur into Burma in pre-historic times."[10] Johnstone has mentioned:

> "In the days when the Indian branch of the Aryan race was still in its progressive and colonising

stage, this district (Manipur) was repeatedly passed over by one wave after another of invaders intent on penetrating into the remotest part of Burma."[11]

It may be mentioned that there were regular routes between Burma and India which were used by the traders, colonisers and the Buddhist Missionaries. D.G.E. Hall mentions about one such road linking Lower Burma and India via the bank of the Irrawady, the bank of the Chindwin and the Manipur.[12] K.M. Pannikar has mentioned about another route through these hills to China.[13] It is obvious that the existence of such land routes facilitated the trade between North-East India with Tibet and Burma on one hand and Bangladesh on the other. The land routes through Manipur continued to operate upto the present day. There were atleast three routes connecting Surma valley with the Manipur Valley and two connecting the latter with the Kabaw Valley in the Chindwin river valley in the present day Burma.[14] There were many minor routes connecting Brahmaputra valley with Tibet which were used for the trade.

North-East India produced many items which were marketed outside the region. *Mahabharata,*[15] *Harshacharit,*[16] etc., mention about the products of Kamarupa. Silk clothes, ivory products, etc. from Kamarupa continued to be appreciated outside the region. Many items were imported from China, Tibet and Burma through this region and exported outside India from this country. One of the routes of the import of Chinese clothes was through Yannan and Assam;[17] and the same was sent to the Bay of Bengal through Brahmaputra. It may be mentioned here that Brahmaputra was navigable from Gwalando in Bangladesh (the confluence of the Ganges and Brahmaputra) to Dibrugarh, and upto Sadiya during the floods.[18] Cinnamon was exported from China, Tibet and Burma. The route of its import and of many other products was through Assam.

There were many minor trade-route linking the region

with the foreign countries through which considerable trade was carried. Considerable trade was also carried between the villagers of both sides of the international border. Such trade, though illegal and called smuggling, still continues. The tribes inhabiting Indo-Tibet and Indo-Burma border had trade links with their neighbours across the border. Some of the tribes of Arunachal Pradesh used to be expert traders. The Monpas, the Sherdukpens, the Boris, the Ramos, the Bokars, the Pailibos continued to have trade links with the Tibetans. The Boris used to visit Nayi Lube market in Tibet and barter their raw hides, and chillies for rock salt, woolen clothes, raw wool, Tibetan swords, Tibetan vessels, ear-rings and brass bangles. They used to barter salt, iron and utensils brought from Tibet with the other groups of the Adis."[19] The bokars exchanged their surplus chillies, butter, hides, tamen (a creeper used for dyeing) for the cattle, sheep and goats, swords and woolen goods in the Tibetan markets.[20] The Shimongs and Ashings used to carry their clothes to the Tibetan markets and exchanged them for salt, beads, etc.[21]

It may be pointed out that two principal trade routes out of the several important ones in the Siang district pass through the Bori and the Bokar countries to the Tibetan plateau.[23] The Tibetans used to come down through the Kepung La Pass to the Ashing area of Arunachal Pradesh and further down upto Pasighat for exchanging the rock-salt, iron, hand-woven clothes, swords, musk, imitation turquoise necklaces, blue porcelain beads, yarn of different colours, snuff, china silver and wooden bowls and metal pots for mithuns, raw hides, deer horns, and white and red rice.[24] These trading activities reportedly continued in large scale upto the sixth decade of this country, as reported by Sachin Roy.

Gait has reported about the hectic trade between the Assam and Bengal.[25] and also between Assam and Tibet.[26] According to Gait, Rudra Singh "is said to have received the submission of all the hill tribes, and to have established an extensive trade with Tibet."[27] This clearly indicates that the border trade also depended on the law and order situation of the country concerned. The quantum of trade might have varied from time to time, but it continued uninterrupted on our northern border in the past. Mackenzie has also reported about the border trade with Tibet. He quote from Hamilton's description of the trade between Assam and Tibet based on the Pemberton's Report.

> "Tibetan caravans conducted by 20 persons used to come down annually to a mart of Chouna on the Assam border after two months journey from Lassa and conveyed silver bullion to the amount of about one lakh of rupees, and a considerable quantity of rock salt for sale to the Assam merchants at Geegunshur four miles away. The large quantities of rice brought by the merchants at the latter place were purchased and imported into Tibet from Assam by the Tibetan merchants. Tussa silk cloth, iron and lac found in Assam, skins, buffalo horns, pearls, and corals, first imported from Bengal were traded by the Assamese merchants. The Tibetan merchants brought woolens, gold dust, salt, musk, horses, Chinese silk, etc. The annual fair was temporarily stopped due to Burmese occupation. Attempt was made to revive it in 1833. The fair was started at Udalguri later on."[28]

Marts are regularly held (daily, biweekly, weekly or annual) at the foot-hills-of the Himalayas throughout the country and also at the foot-hills bordering Bangladesh, Burma and Tibet. The border trade of Assam, Meghalay, Mizoram and Tripura was mostly carried through such marts. R.M. Nath has written about the trade of the Garos with Bangladesh:

> "The Garos living in the areas bordering Goalpara, Mymensing and Rangpur districts as also the Garos of the interior came down to the plains to sell their

> cotton and chillies and purchase paddy, salt, cloth and other necessities; and rulers of the states exacted taxes from them. To deal with the Garos, each ruler used to appoint a Laskar—at every pass of duar. Often times the fraudulent tactics of the merchants and the officers of the states, were retaliated by the Garos by chopping off their head which were sold at high premium in the hills—the price varying according to the wealth and position of the merchant or the officer."[29]

The Khasis and the Jaintiyas used to visit the marts of Bangladesh in the south and that of the Assam in the north. The Khasis used to visit the marts upto the central part of the Nowgong. Iron was manufactured in the hills and exported in the shape of hoes to the Assam valley and in lumps of pig iron to the Surma valley, where it was used for clamps by the boatbuilders. An estimated 20,000 maunds of iron were exported from the hills in 1853.[30]

The ancient trade routes and the marts played important roles in the internal and border trade in the North-East region. The discussion about them provides insights in the historical perspective. The importance of the trade routes and the marts for the people may be understood from the fact that the British authorities used to close down the trade routes and prevent the marauding tribes from attending the marts to force them to behave. Mackenzie has described such closures and the impacts of the same. He wrote:

> "In April 1861 the dwars were closed to Naga traders by order of the Commissioner of Assam, in consequence of the murder of one Tonoo Cachari in the Geleki Dwar, used by the Namsang and the neighbouring clans. In the February following, the Nangota Abor Nagas, who were not known to us to be the guilty tribe, surrendered five of their number as those who had committed the murder.

This surrender, it appeared, they made under pressure brought to bear on them by the Boree Nagas of Tabloong, Jaktoong, Kamsang, and Namsang, who being such distressed by the closure of the Dwars threatened to attack the Nangotas if they did not give up the offenders."[31]

Mackenzie further observed:

"In November 1867 the Geleki guard-house was again attacked at night........ The Dwars were at any rate closed to trade; the out-posts strengthened; and neglected stockades hastily repaired. The stoppage of trade again proved a successful policy. The Tabloong, Namsang, and other Nagas who were carrying on a most profitable traffic with the tea gardens, which they could not afford to loss, speedily combined, and in a few months' time they succeeded in tracing out the raiders, and arresting by force or strategy two of their leaders, who were delivered over to the British authorities for punishment. These men proved to belong to the Yungia Abor Nagas, a remote clan in the upper hills, who actuated by a love of plunder and a craving for skulls had led a stealthy war party through the trackless jungles to the plains below; and had, as they said attacked the police-station under the notion that it was a settlement of ryots — a mistake not very creditable to the discipline of the post."[32]

The remarks made above underline the importance of trade including the border trade, for the people of this region. Some points emerging from the above-mentioned facts needs to be kept in mind, which are:

i) The North-East India was not the closed corner of the country; it has wider trade links. The region was linked up across the border through major and minor trade routes.

ii) The region continued to have flourishing trade with the neighbouring countries.

iii) The trade flourished whenever the law and order situation was sound and suffered at the time of anarchy.

iv) The quantum of illegal border trade is almost the same as that of the actual trade with its neighbours; the border trade potential is really very high.

The partition of India created unnatural border and the age-old trade ties with the part of Bengal called East Pakistan (now Bangladesh) were snapped. The trade with Tibet received severe jolt after the occupation of Tibet by China, and specially after the Indo-Chinese border conflict in 1962. Situation on both sides of the Indo-Myanmar border remained fluid. This, border trade highly decreased after independence of India, and specially after the sixth decade of the century. The situation further aggravated due to the lack of roads and the speedier modes of communication. The costs of bringing in the locally needed items, and that of exporting the local produce became prohibitively high. The production of many agricultural and horticultural items, such as, potato, orange, pineapple, ginger, and other perishable products in the southern border areas of Meghalaya, became non-economic. The people suffered. In this background, the steps envisaged by the Central Government to facilitate trade with Bangladesh and Bhutan generate optimism. The border trade with Tibet and Myanmar should also be encouraged.

The economy of the border areas is always of supplementary and complementary nature and this aspect of economy should always be kept in mind while promoting the border trade. Only such border trade shall make the economy healthy. Appropriate steps should, however, be taken to prevent the flow of narcotics and the arms between the neighbours. The trade of the items produced in the third country, such as, the Korea and Japan, should also be discouraged in this case.

NOTES & REFERENCES

1. Dr. Motichandra, *Sarthavaha*, p. 12; Patna, 1953.
2. *Ibid.*
3. *Ibid.*
4. Vasu, N.N., *Social History of Kamarupa*, vol. I, p. 151.
5. *Ibid.*
6. Motichandra, *op. cit.*, p. 127.
7. Mackenzie, A., *The North-East Frontier of India*, Reprint, Delhi, 1981, p. 64.
8. Singh, R.K. Jhaljit, *A Short history of Manipur*, Imphal, 1965; p. 3.
9. Phayre, A., *History of Burma*, p. 3.
10. Dun, *Gazetteer of Manipur*, p. 6, foot-note.
11. Johnstone, James, *My Experience in Manipur and Naga Hills*, p. 280.
12. Hall, D.G.E., *History of South-East Asia*, p. 121.
13. Pannikar, K.M., *India and China*, p. 17.
14. Singh, R.K. Jhaljit, *op. cit.*, p. 3.
15. *Maha.*
16. Agarwal, Dr. Vasudevasharan, *Harsh Charit: Ek Samskritik Adhyayan*, pp. 170-72.
17. Motichandra, *op. cit.*, p. 127.
18. *Ibid.*, p. 12.
19. *Ibid.*, p. 127.
20. Roy, Sachin, *Aspects of Padam Minyong Culture*, p. 32
21. *Ibid.*, pp. 32-33.
22. *Ibid.*, p. 33
23. *Ibid.*, p. 32.
24. *Ibid.*, p. 33.
25. Gait, Edward, *A History of Assam*, Reprint, Guwahati, 1994, p. 285.
26. *Ibid.*, p. 171.
27. *Ibid.*.
28. Mackenzie, *op. cit.*, p. 15.
29. Nath, R.M., *The Background of Assamese Culture*, p. 111.
30. Gurdon, P.R.T., *The Khasis*, Reprint, Delhi, 1990, p. 58.
31. Mackenzie, *op. cit.*, p. 97.
32. *Ibid.*, pp. 97-98.

2

The Modus Operandi of Trade Between the Eastern Himalayan Subregion and Assam in the Pre-Colonial and Colonial Periods

—J.B. Ganguly

I

In the pre-colonial period there was a long tradition of brisk trade flow between the Himalayan mountainous sub-region comprising Bhutan, Tibet (Autonomous Region of China), North-Eastern Hills of India and Burma (Myanmar) and Assam. This trade flow was stimulated by the facts that by exchanging one group's surplus produces with that of the other both the groups could expand their respective areas of choices for satisfaction of needs. Therefore transmountain trade flow was a boon for the peoples involved in such economic transactions. Benefits were not limited to exchange of required goods alone; trade relations promoted cultural exchanges, transmission of technology and learning of arts of turning out new manufactures.

The *duars* or passes served as the highway of commerce across transmountain territories. Through the *duars* on the Assam-Bhutan border every winter traders from Bhutan, Tawang and the neighbouring areas came down to the foothills in Assam with their merchandise, such as, rock-salt, gold-dust, musk, woollens, blankets, yak-tails, ponies, Chinese silk, etc. to barter for cloths, raw-silk, yarn, rice, dried fish and the like. Markets were located at the *duars* where the traders from the uplands and the plains met and exchanged each other's wares on a barter basis. Transactions continued for over three months.

Annual fairs were also held at some important *duars*, namely Udalgiri, Doimara, etc. Udalgiri fair accounted for almost the entire volume of trade between Assam and Tibet.

Some of the tribal communities of the north-eastern hills, namely the Khampas, Nishis, Mishings, Mishmis, Khamptis, Singphos, *et al.* acted as intermediaries between the different groups of traders. This system enabled Assam to procure goods produced in Tibet, China and Burma by bartering its exportable surpluses. There were a network of markets in the foothills of Assam bordering the Khasi, Jaintyla and Garo Hills, Naga Hills, Mizo Hills, Karbi Anglong and North Cachar Hills. In these markets the hillmen and the Assamese exchanged their respective surplus produces and stock of goods. Through this system some quantities of goods that came from Bhutan, Tibet and China also reached the dwellers of Assam's neighbouring hills. Similarly the goods offered by Assam at the *duars* markets and annual fair included some produces of these hillmen. The Meiteis of Manipur, the Mizos and some Naga communities had direct trade relations with Myanmar and neighbouring states.

While mules and ponies were mostly used for transporting gods in the hilly region, bullock carts were more commonly used in Assam plains for transporting goods to the *duars* markets and fairs. Besides, in the Assam hills and plains goods were also carried by human on their backs or heads.

Free flow of transmountain trade was often disrupted by some tribal peoples living in the hills adjacent to the *duars* who raided the markets and villages in the nearby foothills and looted goods and even took away villagers for using them as their slaves. To tackle this problem the Ahom rulers introduced the system of *posa,* that is, payment of an annual grant in kind to the chiefs of the concerned tribes as a *quid pro quo* for the latter's undertaking of preventing such raids and maintaining peace in the duars. The Ahom Rulers conferred official positions on some of these chiefs. Also officers called *duaries* were appointed by the Raja for the management of the *duars.* Duties levied on goods transacted at the *duars* yielded substantial amounts of revenues to the Ahom government.

II

During the colonial rule over Assam and the adjoining areas the mode of operation of trans-Himalayan trade took a new turn. After annexing Assam and getting Gambhir Singh, an ally of the British installed as the king of Manipur in the wake of the Burmese withdrawal from Assam and Manipur under the Treaty of Yandabo of 1826, the East India Company started exploring different alternative trade routes to Yunnan, the South-West province of China bordering Tibet and Burma. At that time the East India Company enjoyed the monopoly of British trade in China. And their main item of trade was opium. Even as in 1800 China prohibited import of opium in any form into China, the foreign traders cladestinely smuggled opium into China by bribing the officials. And it was a very profitable trade for the East India Company. The dispute over trading in opium in China ultimately resulted in the waging of opium war of 1840-42. Under the Treaty of Nanking of 1842 China agreed to open five ports—Canton, Shanghai, Amoy, Ningpo and Fooshow—to foreign trade. At that time foreign trade actually stood for opium trade. By that time more foreign powers, such as, United States and France also made commercial treaties with China for enjoying the privilege of trading with that country. Following the Chinese defeat in the second China War of 1858 in the hands of the British and the French more ports were opened for foreign trade.

In this context the British commercial interests were earnestly trying to open overland trade routes from North-East Indian Frontier to China via Burma (district of Bamo) along which they could export opium besides their growing industrial products to that country. Opening of such commercial routes would have placed them at an advantageous position over their competitors, such as, the French and the Americans, in capturing the vast Chinese market. At that time Burma was vassal state of the Chinese empire and there were regular trade transactions between the two countries. The British were keen on cultivating close relations with Burma. They went so far as prevailing upon Manipur to reluctantly acquiesce in the transfer of Kabow valley to Burma in 1835 in lieu of payment of an annual compensation of six thousand rupees by the British to the Raja of Manipur. But Burma was not helpful in extending transit and trade facilities to the British traders. No wonder, the British waged two more wars with Burma on one or other pretext and finally annexed Burma to the British Indian Empire by 1885. While annexing Burma the British agreed to pay the customary tribute to China. Even after all such efforts flow of British manufactures to China across Burma was not encouraging because of Chinese aversion and resistance.

Attempts were also made at opening of trade routes to Tibet through the north-eastern frontier hills. The tribal peoples of these hill areas had trade connection with the Tibetans and the Chinese. Some of the tribes acted as the middlemen between the Tibetans and the people of Assam to facilitate the exchange of their products with each other.

The British encountered resistance from the Mishmis, Adis, Singhphoes, et al in opening trade routes through their respective areas. They, therefore, initially followed the policy of fostering friendship with these tribal groups. They continued the Ahom system of paying *posa,* but in cash, to several tribes. Regular markets were established in the foothill areas where the people of Assam plains and the professional commercial class, such as, the Marwaris could take part in exchanging goods with those brought by the hill-dwellers.

Annual fairs were organised in places like Sadiya, Udalgiri (in Mangaldai sub-division of Darrang district) and Doimara. The Monpas from Tawang, Bhutias and Tibetans came to Udalgiri with their merchandise for trade. The Doimara fair was located at further north of Udalgiri beyond the Assam border. The Sherdukpens in large numbers took part in trade deals in this fair. The Sadiya fair catered to the needs of the Adis, Mishmis, Singhphos, Khamptis and other neighbouring tribes. The items offered by the Tibetans, Bhutias and these tribesmen for sale in these fairs included pony, sheep, yak's tail, rock salt, blanket, musk, pepper, spice, dye, lac, wax, ivory, rubber, madder, Mishmi teeta, Mishmi cloth, Addi cloth, spear, *dao*, basket, bag, mat, amber, honey, rhinocerous horn, rug, etc. Goods purchased by the highlanders from the fairs included paddy, rice, ericloth, cotton cloth, brasspot, betel leaf, betelnut, molasses, dried fish, tobacco, rapeseed, iron, silver, muslin, broad cloth, opium, buffalo, bell metal pots, cotton yarn, eri yarn, English yarn, Assamese *gamocha* (napkin), American drill, tea, sugar, cambric, teacup, etc. Some of the items brought by the tribesmen for sale were not produced by them but procured from the Tibetan and Chinese traders in exchange of goods obtained from the trade marts. In this manner trans-Himalayan trade flow still continued though of a much reduced volume.

The system of exchanges of goods for money gradually picked up, although transactions by barter exchange system was also there. The cash in the hands of the tribesmen came from *posa* received from the British, direct sale of some items against cash and advances made by the Indian traders, such as, the Marwaris to the tribals for sale of some of their farm and forest products.

Business meets of the people from the plains and those

from the hills in the trade fairs and established markets and payment of *posa* to the tribes notwithstanding, several tribal groups from highlands did not desist from conducting depredating raids occasionally on the villages in the foothills located in Assam. They also violently interfered with the entry of the British explorers, missionaries and the Trigonometric Survey party into their territories. The British responded by mounting military expeditions on the north-eastern hills to subdue the tribes and extend their political control over them up to the undemarcated Tibetan border. That was reckoned as the "Outer Line" up to which the British sovereignty was claimed. But no direct administrative structure was built up. Under the Regulation of 1875 the "Inner Line" was drawn along the boundary between the administered areas of Assam and the North-Eastern Hills. No British subject was allowed to cross the Inner Line without a 'pass' issued by the appropriate authority.

In the closing decades of the nineteenth century Russia started nurturing close friendship with Tibet while China continued to vigorously assert her claim over Tibet as a part of that country. Being alarmed by the turn of events the British became active in upholding Tibet as the buffer between the Russian Empire and India and later that between China and India. In the wake of such international moves and counter-moves the British plan of opening overland trade routes to Tibet and China lost its importance. The trade fairs also gradually ceased to attract the traders from Bhutan, Tibet and China and even the north-eastern hills. Three important happenings accounted for the decay of the trade fairs. Demand for Tibetan rock salt which was a key item of transaction in the fair declined as cheaper Bengal salt became available. Secondly some permanent markets were established in several places on the south bank and a few on the north bank of the Brahmaputra where the tribal people came for shopping and disposing of their surplus produce. In course of time some Indian businessmen, mostly the Marwaris, obtained Inner Line pass to establish shops and business houses in areas beyond the Inner Line. Those became the outlets of selling British and Indian industrial products, tea, salt, and other provisions to the local people who sold their handloom products, handicrafts, a few cash crops like Mishmi teeta, madder, etc. and several forest products. These developments almost choked the trans-Himalayan trade flow into and out of Assam.

Assam's trade relations with Manipur, however, got a boost in the mid-nineteenth century. With the appointment of the Political Agent by the British in Manipur in 1835 Anglo-Manipur relations entered into a new phase. One of the important tasks performed by the Political Agent was to prevail upon the Manipur Raja to ease restrictions and reduce duties levied on imports of goods from and export of goods to India. After 1891 British control over Manipur became more direct and extensive. The British took initiative in building too vital road links—one from Cachar to Imphal and further cast up to the border of Burma and the other from Imphal to Mao on the Manipur—Naga Hill border and onward to Dimapur via Kohima. Completion of these two roads greatly augmented the volume of trade flow between Assam and Manipur and between Manipur and Burma.

REFERENCES

1. Barpujari, H.K. (ed.), *The Comprehensive History of Assam*, Vols. III and V, 1993, Publication Board Assam, Guwahati.
2. Bhattacharjee, J.B., (Ed.), *Studies in the Economic History of North-East India*, 1994, Har-Anand Publications, New Delhi.
3. Brown, R., *Statistical Account of Manipur*, reprint 1975, Sanskaran Prakashak, Delhi.
4. Chowdhury, J.N., *Arunachal Pradesh*, Cosmo Publications, New Delhi 1983.
5. Elwin, V., (Ed.), *India's North-East Frontier in the Nineteenth Century*, third Impression, 1972, Oxford Univ. Press, Madras.
6. Hunter, W., *Imperial Gazetteer of India*, Vol. VIII, New Edition, 1908, Oxford at the Clarendon Press.

7. Hodson, T.C., *The Meitheis*, Third reprint, 1984, Neeraj Publishing House, Delhi.
8. Mackenzie, A., *The North-East Frontier of India*, Reprint, 1995, Mittal Publications New Delhi.
9. Pemberton, R.B., *Report on Manipur 1835*, reprinted in Savajaoba, N. (Ed.), *Manipur: Treaties and Documents*, Vol. I, 1993, Mittal Publications, New Delhi.
10. Nehru, Jawaharlal, *Glimpses of World History*, Jawaharlal Nehru Memorial Fund, Oxf. Univ. Press, New Delhi, Sixth Impression, 1989.

PART II

CONTEMPORARY TRADE: NORTH EASTERN REGION AND THE NEIGHBOURING COUNTRIES

3

Trade Between the North-Eastern Region and Neighbouring Countries: Structures and Implications for Development

—Gurudas Das*

The trade between North-Eastern Region (NER) and the neighbouring countries (NC), i.e., Bangladesh, Bhutan, China and Myanmar may conveniently be classified into two types: official and unofficial (illegal). While the volume of official trade is recorded at different levels, it is almost impossible to quantify the volume of unofficial trade. The official trade flows both directly and indirectly. Direct trade flows through the Land Custom Stations (LCS)/custom check posts along the international borders between NER and NC. Hence the items of trade, quantity and value — all are recorded at LCS. However, in case of indirect trade, it is very difficult to estimate the contribution of the NER as the goods produced in the region are exported from places outside the region, after value addition in the process of production of exportables. Moreover, even in case of direct trade, no records of flows of goods, either inflows or outflows, is available for 'border

* I am grateful to Shri P. Sikdar, superintendent, Office of the Commissioner of Customs; Debasish Choudhuri, Principal, Women's College; F.D. Rynja, DDG, DRI; R.K. Bose, G.M., KLMC; Shillong, to name a few, and others, for the support and cooperation rendered by them without which the ideas expressed in this paper would have not been possible.

trade'. As a result, for any objective analysis, based on empirical data, of trade between NER and NC, one has to bank on only custom data on direct official trade which is only a part (sometimes insignificant) of the total volume of trade.

Moreover, the official trade statistics emanating from different agencies, operating at different levels, lack in comparability. Even the data supplied by customs, in some cases, suffer from inconsistency. Thus the lack of reliable trade statistics has been a major problem for any objective analysis of trade between NER and NC. This paper is also largely suffers from this drawback.

However, on the basis of both empirical and factual data as well as discussions with different enforcing authorities and exporters, an attempt is made here to comprehend the issues like:

i) Of the NC, who are the significant trade partners of our country in general and the NER in particular?
ii) What is the commodity structure of NER's exports to the NC ?
iii) Is there any basis for trade between NER and the NC, and,
iv) What are the implications of this trade for the society and economy of NER ?

I

NEIGHBOURS IN THE NORTH EAST AS TRADE PARTNERS

India is having a land border of about 15000 kms of which about 4600 kms, i.e., about 31 per cent run along the border between NER and the NC.[1] The region shares only about 2 per cent of her border with the mainland of the country and the rest 98 per cent is linked with international border. Hence the cross border markets in the NC may act as vents for region's surplus rather than far away national market. In fact, the destiny of the region largely depends on the relationship between India and her neighbours in the north east. Let us first find out who, among the neighbours, are our significant trade partners?

Indo-Bangladesh Trade

Bangladesh, among all the countries having land border with India, is the most important trade partner. During 1997-98, Bangladesh ranked 11th position with 2.25 per cent of India's total export to that country. It may be noted that besides USA, Hong Kong, Russia and Netherlands, Bangladesh is one of the important destinations of India's exports where India is having surplus trade balance all along 1991-92 to 1997-98. As a result. inspite of being one of the least developed countries in the world. Bangladesh occupies an important position as far as India's export trade is concerned.

The north-eastern region shares about 1500 kms border with Bangladesh that touches Assam. Meghalaya. Mizoram and Tripura (Table 3.1). The region has age-old socio- economic ties with Bangladesh from time immemorial. Although the partition has disrupted the structure of age-old flow of goods and services between these two areas, even then the communication channels are not completely abandoned. The old road links and water ways are being used in many places for export-import trade between Bangladesh and the north-eastern region. In fact, the land borders between Bangladesh and the NER are more accessible and cost effective than the borders with other neighbouring countries. i.e.. China, Bhutan and Myanmar. Moreover, so far as existing infrastructural linkage is concerned, the region is having better transportation linkage is terms of both surface transport as well as water ways with Bangladesh than the other NC. Furthermore, the accessibility of Indian exports is more in Bangladesh than the other NC, perhaps, because of the fact that the system of governance and Exim policy in Bangladesh are more liberal than the centrally controlled China, Bhutan and Myanmar. Perhaps, these largely explain as to why India's as well as north-eastern region's export performance is far better in case of Bangladesh compared to other NC.

Indo-Bhutan Trade

The volume of Indian exports to Bhutan, 'the land of the thunder dragon' is negligible. Bhutan having a population of less than 2 millions, of which the share of urban population is only 7 per cent ,is one of the poorest among the least developed countries in the world. In 1997-98, the percentage share of India's total export that has gone to Bhutan , as per a rough estimate, comes around below 0.02 per cent. It may be noted that although the lion's share of Bhutan's imports comes from India. It is not the inaccessibility of Indian exports into Bhutan but the very low import demand that has made Indian export performance in Bhutan negligible.

The NER and Bhutan share a common border of about 650 kms . Principal exports from the NER to Bhutan consist of coal, limestone, rice and wheat whereas the region mainly imports woods. The trade between the two areas primarily runs through Assam-Bhutan borders. Of course the volume of trade is not very significant. As Bhutan enjoys free trade status, detail trade statistics are not recorded at the land custom stations along the Assam-Bhutan borders.

Indo-China Trade

Although China is having one of the biggest market in the world, the volume of official Indo-China export-import trade is abysmally low. During 1997-98, China has absorbed only 2 per cent of India's total export which is even less than that of Bangladesh (2.25 per cent). In fact, China occupied the 14th position in terms of share of absorption of India's exports during 1997-98. It may be noted that the percentage share of India's total export to China during the reference year has been the highest since 1991-92 (Table 3.2 & 3.3). And since 1993-94 India's exports failed to pay her imports and the country is having a deficit trade balance so far the Indo-China trade is concerned. The causes of very low volume of trade between these two neighbouring countries may well be seen in their strained mutual political relationship.

However, inspite of the fact that the region is having about 1000 kms. common land border with China, the volume of direct trade between the region and southern provinces of China is almost negligible. Besides strained political relationship. the land border between the NER & China runs through inaccessible hilly terrains which stand against the natural growth of trading activities across the border.

Indo-Myanmar Trade

Myanmar, the rice bowl of the far East,' had for long been a major supplier of rice to the growing Indian population until the 60s. Although India's import demand for rice has gradually declined with her attainment of self sufficiency in rice production following the green revolution, the major official imports from Myanmar now consist of pulses, and wood and wood products. In spite of having a long trade relations, India has failed to create any sizeable market for her exportables in Myanmar. In fact, India is having persistent deficit trade balance with Myanmar in most of the years since Independence (Table 3.6). The usual explanation that the restrictive import policy of the Myanmar Government has been the prime cause of India's poor export performance in that country does not reveal the incompetence of the India's export sector to compete with its counterpart in China, Japan and other South East Asian Countries. In fact the rice economy of Myanmar with a population of 46.8 million,[2] 25 per cent of which live in urban areas, where the agriculture contributes 63 per cent to GDP and manufacturing sector contributes only 7 per cent,[3] has to import bulk of its demand for non-agricultural goods. The lion's share of this import comes from Japan, China, Thailand and Singapore. While Japan contributes 21% of the total import of Myanmar. China's contribution is 17%, Thailand's 15%, Singapore's 12% and Malaysia supplies 7%, whereas India's share is below 3 per cent .[4] Many of the manufacturing goods that are coming into Myanmar from China and other South-East Asian economies also unofficially find their way into Indian market through Indo-Myanmar border.

The Indo-Myanmar border runs along the four states of the north eastern region, viz., Arunachal Pradesh, Manipur, Mizoram and Nagaland. Together they share about 1450 kms., border with Myanmar. Much of the land border trade between the NER and Myanmar runs through Moreh sector of Manipur because of relatively better infrastructural support. Besides Moreh, a significant level of trade also takes place through Champhai border in Mizoram and Lungwa border in Nagaland.

Borders and Authorised Trade Outlets

As per 1994 Government of India notification[5] the country is having a total of 138 authorised land custom stations along her land borders with the neighbouring countries. Of them, 100 LCS are with the neighbouring Bangladesh, Bhutan, China and Myanmar. Out of these 100, 90 LCS are only with Bangladesh which indicates the importance of Indo-Bangladesh border trade.

However, about 63 per cent of the LCS along Indo-Bangladesh border fall along the stretch of West-Bengal-Bangladesh. The states of NER having border with Bangladesh, i.e., Assam, Meghalaya, Mizoram and Tripura. together are having only 32 LCS. While both Assam and Meghalaya each share 400 kms of common border with Bangladesh, Mizoram and Tripura each share about 350 kms border with Bangladesh.

Table- B indicates that Meghalaya-Bangladesh Trade is more extensive compared to other states of NER.

TABLE A

The Distribution of LCS in India

Country	*No. of LCS*
Afganistan	3
Bangladesh	90
Bhutan*	5
China	2
Myanmar	3
Nepal	22
Pakistan	13
Total	138

*Note: 2 LCS were officially declared in 1997.

Along the Indo-Myanmar border, out of the 3 LCS one each in Manipur (Moreh), Mizoram (Champhai) and Arunachal Pradesh (Nampong), only Moreh sector has been officially opened for trade following the Indo-Myanmar Border Trade agreement on January 21,1994.

Along the Indo-China border, the NER does not have any authorised trade outlets. Of the two LCS along the Indo-China border (Table-A), one each comes along the stretches of U.P.-China and Himachal Pradesh-China borders.

Out of the 5 LCS with Bhutan, 3 are located along Assam-Bhutan border and 2 along West-Bengal-Bhutan border. The volume of trade between Bhutan and the NER is insignificant.

Thus, of the four neighbouring countries, NER is having sizeable volume of trade only with Bangladesh and Myanmar. The next section will deal with the structure and volume of exports to these two countries.

TABLE B

LCS along NER-Bangladesh Border

States	*No. of LCS*	*Functioning*	*Non-Functioning*
Assam	14	4	10
Meghalaya	10	6	4
Mizoram	1	—	1
Tripura	7	3	4
Total	32	13	19

Note: Functioning LCS are those where regular trading take. place.

Source for column 2: GOl, Ministry of Finance, Dept. of Revenue, notification no. 63/94- Customs (NT). Column 3 and 4 Office of the Commissioner of Customs, Shillong

II

COMMODITY STRUCTURE OF EXPORTS FROM NER

It is difficult to make any accurate assessment of the export performance of the NER as the state-wise export figures are not available. Moreover, the inter-state input output linkages hardly allow us to have any precise state-wise export estimates for different commodities. For example, it is difficult to calculate the share of NER in the export of jute products from the country because the jute produced in the region is used mostly for blending with other varieties in the manufacture of such products in jute mills in West Bengal. Similar is the case for wood products, cotton, ginger products, paper and a host of other products. As a result, for the commodities for which raw materials are procured from NER and processed elsewhere for value-addition and then are being exported—any realistic assessment of the share of NER to total export from the country is very difficult to arrive at.

However, goods that are produced in the region and exported, directly or indirectly, without any value addition elsewhere, for them records are available. But the export figures for such goods involve two short comings. Firstly, they do not represent the true nature of the trade as, in most cases, the volume of unofficial trade (unrecorded) is much higher than official (recorded) trade. Secondly, even in case of official trade, the export figures differ from agency to agency. Of course. the extent of variation does not deter us in identifying the major characteristics and trends of NER' s exports to NC.

In a recent report jointly prepared by the Ministry of Commerce, Government of India, and Indian Institute of Foreign Trade on the 'Industrial Development and Export Potential of the North-Eastern Region,'[6], exports from NER have been classified into three categories, viz.,. (i) products of NER but exported primarily from outside the region like tea, jute, silk, handloom and handicraft products, (ii) items produced in NER and exported through the customs check post-located at the borders within the region, and (iii) products produced and procured from outside the NER and exported to the NC.

All the three categories together contributed to a total of Rs. 836.66 crores export from NER in 1996-97 which is about 7 per cent of the total export of the country in that year, The contribution of tea alone, first category products, amounts to 82.79 per cent. The contribution of mineral products to total export from NER amounts to a little more than 10 per cent. Agro-forest based products contributed 6.93 per cent of the total export from NER. It may be noted that except tea, the traditional export item ,the region is exporting only primary products. The contribution of the manufacturing sector to the export market is negligible.

However, in this section we shall only consider the official exports from NER to Bangladesh and Myanmar through the custom check posts or land custom stations (LCS) along the borders between the NER & these two NC. This will help us in understanding the nature and characteristics of direct export from the region. Hence the indirect exports of the products of the region from other parts of the country as well as direct export of the products of the region to other parts of the world except the neighbouring Bangladesh and Myanmar are not under the purview of this paper. We also exclude the exports from the region, if any, that are not routed through the Land-Custom Stations of the region.

TABLE C

Exports From NER: 1996-97

Product Group	*Value (Rs. in Crores)*
Tea	692.66 (82.79)
Mineral Products	84.62 (10.11)
Agro Forest Based Products	57.98(6.93)
Others	*1.4 (0.17)*
Total	836.66(100)

Source: Ministry of Commerce and IIFT, Executive Summary, Industrial Development and Export Potential of the NER.

Commodity Structure of Exports from NER and of Imports of Bangladesh: The Basis of Trade

It has already been pointed out in the previous section that one of the important destination of Indian exports is Bangladesh. Trade between India and Bangladesh is carried out as per the Indo-Bangladesh Trade Agreement which provides for the "Most favoured Nation" treatment accorded to goods and services of both the countries. India's total export to Bangladesh during 1996-97 was Rs. 3084.80 crores. The share of NER estimated at Rs. 103.67 Crores. i.e.. 3.36 per cent of the total Indian exports (Table 3.7) in that year. Of the total exports from NER, Meghalaya contributed 83.04 per cent, Assam 16.80 per cent and Tripura 0.16 per cent.

As many of the commodities exported through Assam's Sutarkandi and Karimganj Ferryghat custom check posts are produced in Meghalaya, the contribution of the state appears

TABLE D

Exports from NER to Bangladesh: 1996-97

State	*Value (Rs in Lakh)*
Assam	1742.22
Meghalaya	8608.70
Tripura	16.16
Total	10367.08

to be not less than 90 percent of the total export from NER to Bangladesh. Thus, while the exports from Meghalaya predominate the NER's exports it is quite perplexing as to why the export performance of Assam, having a relatively stronger industrial base among all the seven states of the region, and Tripura. being more handicapped than Meghalaya in terms of access to national market, is so poor. Although a detail investigation can only reveal the causes of the poor performance, an analysis of the commodity structure of NER's exports and the import structure of Bangladesh may provide partial explanation.

The export from NER mainly consists of mineral and horticultural products. Mineral products contribute 89.41 per cent of the total export value. They consist of only two minerals, viz., coal and limestone. Both are mined in the southern belt of Meghalaya and directly exported to Bangladesh through the custom check posts along Meghalaya- Bangladesh border as well as Karimganj (Assam) - Bangladesh border - without any value addition. Horticultural products like ginger, oranges, citrus fruits, garlic, pears etc., contribute 5.83 per cent of total NER's export. These are produced mainly in Meghalaya and N.C. Hills of Assam. Although the commodity basket of agricultural production in the plains of NER and in eastern region of Bangladesh has much similarity, the same between the hills of NER and the plains of Bangladesh is dissimilar. The complementarity between the resource base of the hills of NER and the plains of Bangladesh provides a firm basis for trade between them. Meghalaya, with an estimated reserves of 563 million tonnes of coal. 4147 million tonnes of limestone, 4.44 million tonnes of kaolin, 80.97 million tonnes of clay and 2.54 million tonnes of glass sand[7] coupled with congenial climatic condition for large-scale horticultural production, and traditional trade linkage with the production and consumption centres across the border, is a treasure house for Bangladesh. The Chhatak cement company, at Chhatak in Bangladesh, the only major public sector cement manufacturer, completely depends upon Meghalaya for limestone. Besides this cement company the tea gardens, jute mills and brick manufacturing units in Bangladesh largely depend on the Meghalaya coal. In fact, the demand for mineral products in Bangladesh is far more than the supply from Meghalaya.

TABLE E

Exports from NER to Bangladesh: 1996-97

Commodity Group	*Value (Rs. in Lakh)*
Mineral Products	9269.58(89.41)
Horticultural Products Produced in NER	603.98 (5.83)
Agro-Horticultural products produced outside NER	493.52 (4.76)
Total	10367.08 (100)

However, as far as the exports of coal and limestone are concerned, neither Tripura nor Mizoram has got any reserves of these two minerals so far. Although Assam has got reserves of both, but there is hardly any marketable surplus. Thus the poor performance of Assam and Tripura in mineral product oriented exports from NER to Bangladesh is explained to a large extent.

However, imports of mineral products constitute only a small percentage to total imports of Bangladesh. The country, having a weak industrial base, imports different manufacturing products that constitute mire than 50 per cent of the total import.

TABLE F

Commodity Structure of Imports of Bangladesh: 1991

Commodity Groups	*Percentage Share to Total Import*
All Food Items	29.90
Agricultural Raw Materials	3.30
Fuels	13.70
Ores and Metals	2.50
Manufactured Goods	50.20
Unallocated	0.40
Total	100.00

Source: The Least Developed Countries 1995 Reports, UNCTAD, UN.

The commodity structure of imports of Bangladesh shown in Table-F also represents the contemporary demand structure of that country. Indian exports to Bangladesh roughly constitute 6-7 per cent of total import demand of that country, an analysis of the commodity structure of Indian exports reveals that the contribution of the manufactured goods to total exports was 78.13 per cent during 1991-92 and 76.52 per cent during 1997-98.

TABLE G

Commodity Structure of Indian Exports to Bangladesh

Commodity Groups	*Percentage Share to Total Exports*			
	1991-92	*1994-95*	*1996-97*	*1997-98*
Agricultural and Allied Products	17.39	8.49	11.58	16.07
Ores and Minerals	3.38	5.82	5.03	4.66
Manufactured Goods	78.13	81.86	80.92	76.52
Other Commodities	1.25	3.82	2.48	2.75

Source: CMIE, Foreign Trade, August, 1998

The principal items in manufactured goods that India exports to Bangladesh consist of cotton yarn fabrics, glass/glassware/ceramics, primary and semifinished Iron and steel, drugs and pharmaceuticals, electronic goods, dyes and intermediates. paperl wood products, ›lastic & linoleum products and chemicals.

Except paper and wood products, the NER itself has to bring these items from the national market. As a result, the production structure, whatever weak it may be, of the manufacturing sector of the region, as of now. is not complementary to the demand structure of manufactured goods in Bangladesh. However, the region has potential resources to produce a few of these items. In fact, the long run gains from trade with Bangladesh depends on the regions capacity to value addition instead of marketing its raw materials.

Commodity Structure of Exports from NER and of Imports of Myanmar: Is There Any Basis for Trade

It has already been pointed out in the previous section that unlike Indo-Bangladesh trade, where goods flow almost unilaterally from India to Bangladesh, the Indo-Myanmar trade exhibits just a reverse trend, that is goods are mainly flowing in India. Since 1991-92, the average volume of Indo-Myanmar trade has roughly been estimated at Rs. 400 crores. Of which the share of Indian export is 25% whereas the share of Indian imports is 75%.[8] Myanmar, one of the least developed countries in the world with very weak industrial base, mainly exports agro-forest based products and imports manufacturing goods.

The principal items of Indian exports consist of cement, glass and glassware, cycles, drugs and pharmaceuticals, auto parts and accessories, iron and steel bars, primary and semi finished iron and steel, and cotton yarn. In return India mainly imports pulses, wood and wood products and fruits and nuts.

TABLE H

Commodity Structure of Imports of Myanmar: 1991

Commodity Group	*Percentage Share to Total imports*
All Food Items	1.2
Agricultural Raw Materials	0.3
Fuels	0.9
Manufactured Goods	97.0
Unallocated	0.5

Source: UN UNCTAD, The Least Developed Countries 1995 Report.

The same commodity structure of exports is also observed for the exports from NER. The official trade between NER and Myanmar flows through Moreh custom checkpost in Manipur. Although Nagaland. Mizoram and Arunachal Pradesh do have land borders with Myanmar, and both Mizoram and Arunachal Pradesh have LCS, one each, along their borders, none of them has been opened for official trade. As a result, NER -Myanmar official trade essentially reduces to Manipur-Myanmar trade.

During 1996-97, the volume of exports from NER to Myanmar amounts to about Rs. 30 crores where the contribution of manufacturing sector is about 80% and that of agro-horticultural products 20% (Table 3.8). Most of the items, particularly the manufacturing goods that are exported through Moreh are procured from outside the region. Similarly. excepting agro products. goods which are imported in the region originate outside Myanmar. Moreh-Tamu sector is essentially the transit route for products originating outside both NER and Myanmar. Consequently the organic link between trade and growth of the real sector of the local economy is very weak.

As the commodity production structure of NER in general and Manipur in particular is. by and large, similar to that of

Myanmar. both producing primary products and importing manufactured goods, the economies of these two areas are basically competitive rather than complementary. As a result the basis for trade between NER and Myanmar is very weak.

III

UNPROTECTED BORDERS AND UNRECORDED TRADE

It is well known that land borders between India and NC are drawn neither on the basis of human ecology nor physiography, the political expediency of the raj had been the prime consideration which had made a mockery of natural justice to many human groups denying them to live together what they had been doing, hitherto, for centuries. The partition of the country and consequent redrawn political boundary have made the border management a stupendous task before both the local as well as national government. The large part of 1500 kms border between NER and Bangladesh as well as 1450 kms border with Myanmar have remained unprotected, unmanned and, in many places, ill demarcated. In both cases, different 'people' living across the border, at different stretches, have age old socio-economic ties based on linguistic, cultural and ethnic affinities. Hard physiography, impenetrable hills and forest along Myanmar border and circuitous riverine routes along Bangladesh border coupled with unifying social environment have made the borders ripe sanctuaries for illegal trade (smuggling).

Unofficial Trade Between NER and Bangladesh

Although it is difficult to arrive at any precise estimation of the volume of unofficial trade, the direction and composition of such trade can be delineated to some reliable extent. A study on 'cross border trade between India and Bangladesh,[9] by NCAER has revealed many aspects of the unofficial trade between NER and Bangladesh. It has covered most smuggling prone bordering districts of West Bengal (9). Assam (3) and Tripura (3). Of the three border districts in Assam, four centres of unofficial trade viz., Sutarkandi and Steamerghat (Karimganj Ferryghat) in Karimganj having trade link with Sutarkandi and Latu of Sylhet districts of Bangladesh respectively, Katigorah in Silchar having link with Jakiganj in Sylhet and Golakganj in Dhubri connected with Bhurungahari in Rongpur. have been surveyed. Similarly in Tripura one trade centre each for three border districts, viz., Billonia in South Tripura having link with Sabram in Nowakhali district of Bangladesh. Agartala in West Tripura having link with Akhaura in Brahmanberia, and Kailashar in North Tripura connected with Hicklia in Moulavibazar, have been surveyed. Based on the sample survey of selected trading centres and information collected from other non-surveyed centres and districts, the study has made state level generalisation of volume, direction and composition of unofficial trade along Assam, Tripura and West Bengal borders with Bangladesh.

Principal commodities smuggled into Bangladesh through Assam and Tripura include: food/edible goods, live animals, wood/timber, cotton, printed saris, bicycle/ bicycle parts, cosmetics, biddies, babyfood, cement, coal and kerosene. The total volume of unofficial exports to Bangladesh through this three border states is estimated at Rs. 1165 crores annually. Of which West Bengal accounts for as much as 96% (Rs. 1121 crores). Assam 3% (35.5 crores) and tripura 1% (8.1 crores). Although much of the unofficial trade runs through the border districts of West Bengal, unofficial exports through Tripura is as much as 50 times higher than official exports and for Assam it is double the volume of official exports (compare Table 3.7).

Unofficial exports of sugar, the study identified, take first rank in smuggled-out commodities in Karimganj followed by cotton printed saris. In all the districts of Tripura and Dhubri in Assam wood and timber constitutes the single most important smuggled-out item which accounts for 49 to 64% of the smuggled volume in each district.

TABLE I

Commodity Groupwise Percentage Distribution of Total Volume of Unofficial Exports to Bangladesh

Commodity Group	*Assam*	*Tripura*
Food and Live Animals	40.1	22.3
Forest Products	24.8	52.5
Textile manufactures	25.8	2.8
Other Industrial Manufactures	1.8	1.6
Industrial Raw Materials	0.4	—
Other Consumer Goods	7.1	20.8
All commodities	100.0	100.0

Source: Chaudhari, 1995, Cross Border Trade Between India and Bangladesh, NCAER, New Delhi.

The study did not cover border districts and trade centres of Meghalaya and Mizoram. While unofficial trade through Mizoram border is believed to be negligible, it is substantial along the Meghalaya-Bangladesh border. Although no formal study has been made to gauge the extent of smuggling through Meghalaya border, it is learnt that the volume of illegal exports of coal, limestone and agro-forest based products will be 4 to 5 times higher than the volume of official exports from Meghalaya to Bangladesh. The findings of the paper on 'Coal trade between Meghalaya and Bangladesh: A case study of Borsora trade route', presented in this seminar also corroborates what is gathered from informal discussions with the exporters and officials of enforcement agencies.

However, the unofficial imports into NER are, by and large, confined to only two major items of mass consumption, viz., synthetic fabrics and hilsa fish. Besides these two, some amount of electronic goods, third country origin, like calculators, rechargeable emergency lights, torchlights, toys as well as VCPs and VCRS are also smuggled-in in the region. The study has estimated the volume of unofficial imports in Assam and Tripura at Rs. 1.8 crores each.

Thus both the official and unofficial trade between NER and Bangladesh flow in the same direction, that is, unidirectional exports to Bangladesh. The exports of mineral products predominate the composition of official exports from the region followed by agro-horticultural products, while consumer goods and forest products contribute a significant share to the total volume of unofficial exports. Faced with the problem of persistent deficit in her BoP current account, the economy of Bangladesh appears not to be in a position to import them officially. However, the unofficial exports indicate that there is a hidden demand for these items. Since the regions unofficial exports, on a conservative estimates, are 4 times higher than its volume of official exports, this indicate the potential to which the legal exports can be raised.

Unofficial Trade Between NER and Myanmar

Trade between NER and Myanmar mainly flows through unofficial channels. Big operators from Aizawl, Imphal, Kohima, Silchar, Guwahati and Shillong work through the local agents at the different trade centres like Moreh, Champhai, Vaphai, Khazwal, Lungwa, etc., along the Myanmar borders of the region. In the bordering states of Manipur, Mizoram and Nagaland a large section of population, particularly of border district towns and state capitals, including people in public life and administration, educated unemployed youths, common man, women and children are involved in unofficial trade. As the bordering states largely depend on Myanmar supply for a number of consumer items which come from China, Japan, Thailand, and other South East Asian countries, and the commodities also fetch handsome profit margin when sold to other parts of the country, the import trade is, indeed, lucrative. Discussions with officials of various agencies reveal that entanglement of politicians, bureaucrats, security person and people in the enforcement agencies in unofficial trade has virtually blurred the domain of legal and illegal trade along the NER-Myanmar border.

Except a 'Study on Promotion of Border Trade between India and Myanmar"[10] prepared by Indian Institute of Foreign Trade (IIFF) in 1995, no serious attempt has been made from any quarters to assess the various aspects of this trade. Even the IIFT study is largely impressionistic rather than analytical. Although one may question the reliability of IIFT estimates on volume of trade as these are estimated on the basis of very simplistic assumptions, the study helps in understanding the composition of trade. However, the study is not meticulous enough to analyse the direction of trade.

As we have noted earlier in the previous section that unlike NER-Bangladesh trade, NER-Myanmar trade is primarily a transit trade. Through all the trade centres in the border districts of NER, consumer durable goods of third country origin are smuggled-in at large scale. These include electronic goods like TV sets, washing machines, dish washers, high frequency transistor radios, etc., which mainly come from Japan. Besides Japanese electronics, Chinese textiles like blankets, bedsheets, ready-made garments are also brought-in in large quantities. Apart from these consumer items, iron scrap and brass scrap are also smuggled-in from third countries. In addition to these third country origin goods, products of Myanmar like teak and agar woods, pulses. ground nuts, betel nuts, gems and stones also enter into Indian side. Above all, there exists a brisk trading in narcotics like heroine, brown sugar, raw opium, charas etc., and high value low weight contrabands like gold, silver, rubies, jade, etc., which are smuggled-in all along the Myanmar border. Of course, trade in narcotics and high value metals has not been included in normal commodity trade here, a special mention of this trade is made here because it has much bearing in structuring the normal commodity trade flows between NER and Myanmar.

Coming on to the unofficial exports from NER, precursor chemicals, used in the manufacturing of narcotics in Myanmar, are the most important product group besides essential consumer items like babyfood, tea leaves, cotton yarn, kerosene, cycle, diesel etc. It may be noted that the smuggled in commodity basket is much 'wider and high value oriented than smuggled out basket that leads us to make a conjecture that the unofficial trade flows are also almost unidirectional, that is, from Myanmar to NER/India, as good as official trade.

The IIFT study has estimated the annual volume of trade that takes place at Moreh, Champhai and Lungwa at around Rs 2200 crores. Of which Moreh contributes the larger share of Rs. 1600 crores followed by Champhai Rs. 500 crores, and Lungwa contributes around Rs. 100 crores. If this figure is to believe, then the extent of unofficial trade stand more than 44 times compared to official trade[11] and the volume of trade through NER-Myanmar border is atleast five times higher than the NER-Bangladesh trade.

IV

NER-NC TRADE: IMPLICATIONS FOR DEVELOPMENT AND POLICY FORMULATION

Having studied the structure of NER-NC trade, both official and unofficial, the major observations and their implications need to be highlighted.

1. NER is having a significant trade with two of the four NC, that is, Bangladesh and Myanmar.
2. While the NER. Bangladesh trade has a firm basis in their differences in natural endowments, the NER. Myanmar trade is basically a transit trade

having a very weak link with their resource base and commodity structure of production.

3. Whereas much of the NER-Bangladesh trade flows through legal/official channels, it is just reverse in case of NER-Myanmar trade.
4 While the NER-Bangladesh trade is characterised by unidirectional flow of goods from NER to Bangladesh. the direction is reverse in case of NER-Myanmar trade.
5. While the NER-Bangladesh trade basically involves flow of mineral products/raw material from NER to Bangladesh, much of the NER-Myanmar trade involves exchange of consumer goods mostly originated outside both the areas.
6. The total volume of NER-Myanmar trade is likely to be four times more than that of the NER-Bangladesh trade.
7. While the NER-Bangladesh trade is acting as a 'vent' for region's surplus, facilitating the extraction and use of minerals, and consequently generating income and employment and thereby gradually unfolding the future scope for trade, commerce and industry, this growth effect is negligible in case of NER-Myanmar trade. The later, being mingled with drug trafficking and, in some cases, controlled by the various extremist groups, is largely responsible for the fast degeneration of social environment along the NER-Myanmar border.

As a result, any future trade policy for the region should involve a twin strategy, one each for these two frontiers. Firstly, expansion of NER-Bangladesh trade through elimination of state incompetency manifested in utterly inadequate supply of institutional and infrastructural inputs, for which the remedial measures have already been suggested by IIFT[12] a decade back and also by Shukla Commission[13] recently. Secondly, consolidation of the NER-Myanmar trade through providing an effective regulatory framework which will divert the flow of goods from unofficial to official channels.

Although transit trade has its own importance, the gains from trade is likely to go to the distant operators leaving only a marginal sum for the local agents in the form of commission. The growth generating effect of such trade may not be felt in the transit area. As a result, planned efforts are necessary in order to link up the trade with the production sector of the local economy.

All these years borders have been viewed as liabilities by the state in our country. In this era of globalisation, these are, in fact, our assets, particularly in the context of the NER. The sooner the state plans, NEC plan and central plan are synchronised to create a trade friendly environment, the better will be the prospect of border trade in the region.

NOTES & REFERENCES

1. Directorate of Revenue Intelligence, *Annual Report*. 1997-98
2. Relates to 1998.
3. Relates to 1993.
4. Relates to 1991-92.
5. Government of India. Ministry of Finance, Department of Revenue, Notification No. 63/94-Customs(NT)
6. Government of India, Ministry of Commerce and Indian Institute of Foreign Trade (IIFT), *Industrial Development and Export Potential of the North Eastern Region.*
7. Figures for Estimated Mineral Reserves are as Supplied by the Directorate of Mineral Resources, Government of Meghalaya. Shillong
8. GOI, Ministry of Commerce and IIFT, *op. cit.*
9. Sudhakar K. Chaudhari, 1995, *Cross Border Trade Between India and Bangladesh*, Working Paper No. 58, NCAER. New Delhi
10. IIFT, 1995, *Study on Promotion of Border Trade Between India and Myanmar*, New Delhi
11. It is learnt from the Custom Officials that, on an average, the annual volume of exports through Moreh amounts to around

Rs. 30 crores while the same for imports is around Rs. 25 crores.

12. IIFT, 1987, *Export Potential Survey of North Eastern Region*, New Delhi.
13. GOI. Planning Commission. 1997, *Transforming the North East*, High Level Commission Report to the Prime Minister.

TABLE 3.1

Detail of the Length of the Land Border Between the North Eastern States and Neighbouring Countries

				Total
1.	NER-Myanmar Border			
		With Mizoram	368 kms	
		With Manipur	352 kms	
		With Nagaland	280 kms	
		With Arunachal Pradesh	450 kms	1450 kms
2.	NER-China Border			
		With Arunachal Pradesh	1000 kms	1000 kms
3.	NER-Bhutan Border			
		With Arunachal Pradesh	200 kms	
		With Assam	450 kms	650 kms
4.	NER-Bangladesh Border	With Assam	350 kms	
		With Meghalaya	400 kms	
		With Tripura	400 kms	
		With Mizoram	350 kms	1500 kms
	Grand Total			4600 kms

Source: DRI, Shillong

TABLE 3.2

India's Trade with China

(Rs in Lakh)

Year	*Export*	*Import*	*Trade Balance*
1991-92	11877	5142	6735
1992-93	40918	33699	7219
1993-94	87533	94697	(–) 7164
1994-95	79824	238890	(–) 159066
1995-96	111288	271606	(–) 160318
1996-97	218254	268703	950449
1997-98	253089	430438	(–) 177349

Source: CMIE, Foreign Trade, August 1998

TABLE 3.3

Percentage Share of India's Total Export to and Imports from China

Year	*Percentage Share of Total Export*	*Percentage Share of Total Imports*
1991-92	0.27	0.11
1992-93	0.76	0.53
1993-94	1.25	1.30
1994-95	0.97	2.66
1995-96	1.05	2.21
1996-97	1.84	1.93
1997-98	2.00	2.84

Source: CMIE, Foreign Trade, August, 1998.

TABLE 3.4

India's Trade with Bangladesh

(Rs in Lakh)

Year	*Export*	*Import*	*Trade Balance*
1991-92	79849	1406	78443
1992-93	102902	3523	99379
1993-94	134929	5607	129322
1994-95	202413	11985	190428
1995-96	350909	28722	322187
1996-97	308480	22091	286389
1997-98	283939	19005	264934

Source: CMIE, Foreign Trade, August 1998.

TABLE 3.5

Percentage Share of India's Total Export to and Imports from Bangladesh

Year	*Percentage Share of Total Export*	*Percentage Share of Total Imports*
1991-92	1.81	0.03
1992-93	1.92	0.06
1993-94	1.93	0.08
1994-95	2.45	0.13
1995-96	3.30	0.23
1996-97	2.60	0.16
1997-98	2.25	0.13

Source: CMIE, Foreign Trade, August, 1998.

TABLE 3.6

India's Trade with Myanmar

(Rs in Lakh)

Year	*Export*	*Import*	*Trade Balance*
1989-90	129	8813	(–)8684
1990-91	334	15346	(–)15012
1991-92	946	12562	(–)11616
1992-93	2045	32224	(–)30179
1993-94	6525	37824	(–)31299

Source : IIFT, Study on Promotion, *op. cit.*

TABLE 3.7

Export to Bangladesh Through LCS in NER: 1996-97

(Qnt in 1000 MT/Value Rs in Lakh)

Commodity	*Assam*		*Meghalaya*		*Tripura*		*NER*	
	Qnt	*Value*	*Qnt*	*Value*	*Qnt*	*Value*	*Qnt.*	*Value*
Coal	45.22	728.76	488.71	7949.80	—	—	533.93	8678.56
Lime Stone	—	—	304.44	583.57	—	—	304.44	583.57
Onions	0.81	42.09	0.10	6.98	0.05	2.06	0.96	51.13
Ginger	12.38	338.86	5.95	33.21	0.05	0.20	18.38	372.27
Oranges	0.10	6.82	0.30	20.27	0.12	8.19	0.52	35.28
Rice	5079.94	434.98	17.81	1.56	20.00	1.82	5117.75	438.36
Citrus Fruits	244.18	20.52	72.71	4.11	0.18	0.11	317.07	24.74
Dry Chilly	4.47	166.44	—	—	—	—	4.47	166.44
Garlic	0.02	2.42	0.18	1.56	0.01	0.57	0.21	4.55
Pears	0.01	0.39	0.01	0.32	—	—	0.02	0.71
Stone Boulder	0.02	0.13	1.14	7.32	—	—	1.16	7.45
Apples	0.04	0.81	—	—	0.21	3.21	0.25	4.02
Total		1742.22		8608.70		16.16		10367.08

Source Office of the Commissioner of Customs. Note: Average Price of Oranges per MT exported through Assam and Tripura LCS has been adjusted at per with export price at Dawki LCS. Export Price of thy chilly through Sutarkandi LCS has been adjusted at per with the export price at Karimganj Ferryghat LCS. Stone Boulders are valued at Rs. 640 per MT.

TABLE 3.8

Export Through Indo-Myanmar Border for the Year 1996-97 Through Moreh L.C.S.

Commodity	*Quantity*	*Value (in Rs.)*
Wheat Flour	26955.00 M.T.	215210561/-
P.V.C. Leather Cloth	3000.00 MTRs.	152229/-
Dry Chilly	648.13 M.T.	20519540/-
Anise Seed	365.27 M.T.	5588411/-
Suman Rose	43.38 M.T.	6428070/-
Cumin Seeds	121.59 M.T.	3264563/-
Garlic	2476.32 M.T.	22345635/—
Coriander Seeds	77.00 M.T.	152300/-
Bush Essence	11.40 M.T.	3184602/-
Rock Salt	33.88 M.T.	229563/-
Bleaching Powder	178.70 M.T	3792479/-
Agarbati	0.09 M.T.	6004/-
Soya Nuggets	77.56 M.T.	2011560/-
Bicycle Parts	682 CASES	5809879/-
Night Lamp	3.00 M.T.	339398/-
Steel Balls	150,000 PCs	321721/-
Hosiery	3580 DOZ.	261669/-
Ammonium Chloride	45.00 M.T.	408600/-
Onion	38.46 M.T	1192300/-
Stainless Steel	9.33 M.T.	839222/-
Jute Rope	42.50 M.T.	750000/-
Ballpen	2.61 M.T.	504877/-
Steel Plate	20.00 M.T.	190000/-
Table Cover	1.59 M.T.	172505/-
Chewing Tobacco	105 CRTN	154980/-
Ajawain	5.10 M.T.	71324/-
Maltova	4.56 M.T.	555940/-
Water Filter	24253 PCs	1821490/-
Fenugreek Seeds	29.25 M.T.	468000/-
Khajur	1.25 M.T.	10000/-
PT Saw	3000 PCs	555000/-
Total		297312421

Source: Office of the Commissioner of Customs, Shillong.

4

Certain Observations on Informal Border Trade with Neighbouring Countries and Economic Prospects of the North Eastern Region*

—Srinath Baruah

Introduction

The SAARC nations had decided to have regional trade liberalisation to do away with tariff barriers and other restrictions in phase manner to move towards a South Asian Free Trade Area (SAFTA) by the end of the year 2000 A.D. So the country will enter into a new era of economic liberalisation and regional co-operation at the very beginning of the 21st century. This decision of the SAARC nations will definitely have certain positive implications on the economic prospects of India's north-eastern region having about 98% of its border with the neighbouring countries—Bhutan, Bangladesh, Myanmar and China.

There is bilateral trade between India and other SAARC countries as well as with Myanmar. One of the major objectives of sub-regional co-operation like SAFTA and SAPTA would

* This paper is based on the survey on Informal Border Trade in North Eastern Region conducted for UN-ESCAP study on India's Border Trade with Select Neighbouring Countries carried out by Research and Information System for Non-Aligned and Developing Countries, New Delhi, 1996.

be to enhance inter-regional trade among the members with the help of border trade and consequently contribute to the development of the border regions. The share of India's official trade with select neighbouring countries like Bangladesh, Bhutan, Myanmar, Nepal and Pakistan constitute only a small fraction of country's total external trade. In fact, the formal exports to these five select neighbouring countries constituted less than 3% of country's total exports 1990 and 1994 as indicated in Table 4.1 below.

TABLE 4.1

India's Official Trade with Select Neighbouring Countries in 1990 and 1994

(in $ Million)

Country	*1990*		*1994*	
	Export	*Import*	*Export*	*Import*
Nepal	40	14	91	16
Bhutan	—	—	7	
Bangladesh	297	22	509	26
Myanmar	1	44	23	106
Pakistan	43	49	64	46
Total (Group)	381	129	694	194
Exports to rest of the world	17813		24150	
Exports to above five neighbouring countries as % of exports to rest of the world	2.14%		2.87%	

Source: IMF, Direction of Trade Statistics, 1995

It is expected that the fostering of border trade will, inter alia, help in increasing this share to a satisfactory level as a result of which the economic activities of the border states will increase.

There is also significant volume of informal border trade between India and above mentioned select neighbouring countries. However, there are lack of adequate provision of transit and transport systems and other infrastructure hindering the growth of border trade. The countries border trade with three neighbouring countries Bangladesh, Bhutan and Myanmar is mainly operated through the north eastern region as well as through West Bengal with Bangladesh. Although there are formal trade agreements of the government of India with the governments of Bangladesh, Bhutan and Myanmar (see reference section) for operation of official border trade with these countries, the volume and diversification of informal trade with these neighbouring countries operated through the north eastern region is manifold. Keeping in view the above backgrounds we propose to highlight in this paper certain aspects of informal border trade (such as transit system, volume and composition of traded goods, modus operandi etc.) with Bangladesh, Bhutan and Myanmar operated through the north eastern states and to assess the probable impact of SAFTA on the growth of border trade and its consequent effect on their economies, more particularly that Assam in the beginning of the twenty first century.

Transit Points of Informal Border Trade

Trade with Bhutan

Informal trading with Bhutan is carried out primarily through two border points from Assam. These two points (routes) are Gelephu and Samdrupjankar — both are border towns on Bhutan side within one kilometer from Assam-Bhutan border. There is another small place known as Bhairabkunda at the junction of Assam-Bhutan-Arunachal Pradesh border but no such informal trade practically take place at that border point.

Trade with Myanmar

Border trading with Myanmar is done only through

Mizoram and Manipur. Although south-east Arunachal Pradesh and south-eastern part of Nagaland are having border with Myanmar, practically no informal trade takes place through these border areas. As understood, the border vigilance is more strict on those parts because of insurgency and the economic conditions of the people of Myanmar as well as of Indian side on these border areas are reported to be poor for which the local demand for imported goods is very limited on both sides of the border. The informal border trade with Myanmar is mainly carried out through Moreh border point of Manipur. Moreover, Champai of Mizoram is another border trading route through which informal trade with Myanmar is operated.

Trade with Bangladesh

Informal trade with Bangladesh is mainly operated through Assam, Meghalaya Mizoram and Tripura. These routes are Fakiragram, Mankachar and Karimganj in Assam, Lichubari and Dawki in Meghalaya, Tlangbung in Mizoram and Kailashsahar, Agartala, Sonamora, Bilonia and Sabroom in Tripura. Tripura has about more than 800 kilometer border (almost free border) with Bangladesh and thus a happy hunting ground for the informal traders.

Pattern of Informal Border Trade

The Pattern of Exports

Informal exports from India through the various routes across the country's north-eastern border are predominantly of essential consumer goods such a foodgrains and medicines. According to informed sources, there has been a spurt in the volume of informal exports particularly to Bangladesh following the heavy depreciation of the Indian Rupee in 1991. Since then, items like foodgrains have become much cheaper on the Indian side of the border in terms of foreign currencies. There has also been instances of reversal of trade of fish, which is a traditionally imported item from Bangladesh, is now being exported from India to Bangladesh. Although the Hilsa variety of fish is continued to be imported from Bangladesh, the Rohu variety of fish produced in Andhra Pradesh is now exported in substantial quantity across the Tripura-Bangladesh border. The fact that fish produced in Andhra Pradesh is exported through distant Tripura, rather than through the obvious shorter routes, indicates irrational distortions in the regional trading arrangement.

Export of coal produced in Meghalaya to Bangladesh, which is officially allowed to some extent, reportedly exceeds the amount which is officially recorded (reliably reported to be double the amount officially recorded). In other words, informal export of this item continues though it is allowed to be formally exported.

The major items of exports to Bhutan through informal trade are basically consumer goods like rice, sugar, clothes, utensils, kerosene etc. But in case of Myanmar, the items of exports are mainly transport equipments (bicycles), engineering goods and paints.

The Pattern of Imports

In contrast to the composition of informal exports from India, informal imports to India are mostly luxury consumer goods including harmful goods like narcotics. For instance, imports from Bhutan almost entirely comprised of alcoholic beverages. Similarly, the most significant item imported through the Manipur-Myanmar border is narcotics. Most surprisingly, it has been reported that many defence personnel like BSF in the Manipur-Myanmar border were involved in the informal trade in narcotics and drugs,. It was also reported in local dailies of Tripura that the Indian Border Security Forces and Bangladesh Border Security Forces in collusion help traders to carry out informal border trade in certain border points taking certain amount of commission from the traders from both sides of the Tripura-Bangladesh border.

Other items that comes in through this route are clothes (mostly jeans), timber and electronic consumer goods. Informal imports from Bangladesh also consists of various luxury and fancy consumer items like TV sets, VCR/VCP, camera, lamp shades, cosmetics and toiletries. Imports across Mizoram border are also of similar items.

It is interesting to note that all these luxury and fancy consumer goods informally imported through the neighbouring countries are not locally produced in these countries. They are produced in the industrialised countries of South-east Asia and elsewhere like China, Thailand, Hongkong, Singapore, South Korea , Japan etc. Thus if the trade policy of India is further liberalised allowing freer import of consumer goods, the informal imports across the country's north eastern border is likely to decline. Moreover, it will bring substantial revenue to the state exchequer rather than the same being pocketed by the custom and police officials.

Apart from the import of luxury and fancy consumer goods, there is also an inflow of gold and foreign currency. The detailed accounts of informal border trade (both exports and imports separately) with Bangladesh, Bhutan and Myanmar are furnished in Annexes 1 to 8.

Modus Operendi of Informal Border Trade

Traders on either side of the border cross over almost freely for carrying out trading activities. Since the population in the border areas is ethno-culturally more or less homogeneous on either side of the border, it is easy for anyone to carry out trading activities conspicuously on the other side of the border. Moreover, there is practically no physical barrier in the border either in the form of border fencing or the border roads or even strict vigilance by security forces etc. Thus traders from Bangladesh often cross over to India to buy commodities. They usually pay in Indian currency which can be acquired at a small commission from the border agents. These agents also help traders in getting their goods across the border. The goods are transported by road as well as by country boats or even by porters on foot. In the inflow of imports from Bangladesh, a large number of small traders are involved. They acquire the items from the border agents and sell them through retail outlets, which are owned by themselves or by others.

There is also certain form of barter system prevailing in many parts of Indo-Bangladesh border. A sizable number of individuals on either side of the border cross over border to sell their produce in the weekly or daily markets and return home purchasing necessary consumer goods out of their sell proceeds in those markets. These individuals hardly bring back any currency from these markets. Unfortunately, data on the quantum of these type of barter trade are not reliably available. These bartered items mostly belong to agricultural and livestock products and common consumer goods like cloths, sandals etc. For instance, if an individual wants to get a pair of hawai sandal or a piece of cloth or a few litres of kerosene, he crosses over the border either with a pair of duck or a chicken or with a bag of vegetables; sells them in the daily or weekly market and purchases the hawai sandal or the cloth or kerosene and returns back practically without bringing any currency.

There is also informal trade of daily labourers. In most of the border points of Tripura-Bangladesh and Assam-Bangladesh border, the labourers from Bangladesh cross over India in the morning to work as daily labour and return in the evening purchasing consumer goods mainly food items from Indian markets at the border points. Bangladeshi labourers are preferred on Indian side as their rates are cheaper. It is roughly estimated that about four to five thousand such labourers cross over to India daily.

There is also informal trade in form of service. Many Bangladeshi national cross over to the border towns on Assam and Tripura bordering with Bangladesh to see movies in the Cinema halls. Of course, the data on the number of such persons are not available,.

Concluding Observation

It is quite certain that the operation of the SAARC agreement on SAFTA at the very beginning of the 21st century will give a big boost to the border trade with Bhutan, Bangladesh and Myanmar through the north eastern region. It is also expected that the new arrangement of border trade will bring more revenue to the border states of this region, particularly Assam, Manipur, Meghalaya, Tripura and Mizoram.

At present neither the state governments nor the central government earn any revenue on account of the informal border trade. The existing restrictions have merely enabled the border agents to act as middlemen and earn commission. Relaxation of trade restrictions along with the imposition of small tariff on both exports and imports, will help border trade to flourish and yield good amount of revenue to the government. High tariff rates, on the other hand, may be counter productive as these will induce evasion and help sustain smuggling.

It may be noted that many of the wholesale traders operating particularly in Tripura-Bangladesh border welcome the proposal for free trade zone with the neighbouring countries and they are prepared to pay some tariffs to the' government officially for operation of trade as they are already paying a substantial amount to the police and custom officials as well as to the border security forces as bribe for illegal operation of trade. Moreover, they feel that under the free trade zone system, they can operate their trade in an open atmosphere without any anxiety and the level of trade is likely to boost up. Of course, we also agree with the apprehension of these traders that there will be some loss of jobs of middlemen and commission agents connected with these informal border trade.

There will be high rate of growth of tertiary sector activities particularly trade and commerce, banking and insurance services, transport and communication, warehousing services etc. in the whole region after the removal of legal' restriction on border trade and this will accelerate the general economic activities of this region because of inter-sectoral linkages. However, all the constituent units of the entire north eastern region will not be benefited on the same footing. Arunachal Pradesh and Nagaland may not get much of the advantages of the new regime of border trade. Assam, Meghalaya, Manipur, Mizoram and Tripura through which the informal border trade is currently operated are expected to be immensely benefited not only in terms of increase in the activities of the tertiary sector but also increase in the activities of the secondary sector. Increase in border trade as a result of operation of SAFTA might encourage the Indian producers to have production units of their export oriented industries in these border states to have the benefit of avoiding escalating transport costs of finished products now produced elsewhere in the country.

It is reasonable to expect that Assam will be most benefited state in the region from the new trade regime because of her strategic location and relatively better infrastructural facilities compared to other states of the N.E. region. Being the gateway to the N.E. region and having direct rail and road links with the rest of the country as well as with the rest of the N.E. region, Assam has a definite locational advantage which will offer relatively better prospects of economic activities and their linkages.

In order to take advantage of the new liberalised trade regime in the SAARC region, all the border trading states of the north eastern region 'must take adequate steps to improve the provision of infrastructural facilities like transport and communication system, banking and insurance, warehousing and better hotel facilities at the transit points etc. But the most important infrastructure required for healthy growth of border trade and its consequent effect on the economic activities of the states of the N.E. region is the social peace which calls for immediate solution to the insurgency problem of the region.

REFERENCES

1. Research and Information System (1996), *India's Border Trade with Select Neighbouring Countries,* New Delhi, 1996.
2. International Monetary Fund (1995), *Direction of Trade Statistics,* 1995
3. Govt of India and Govt. of Bangladesh, *Trade Agreement Between India and Bangladesh,* signed at Dhaka on 4th October, 1980.
4. Govt. of India and the Govt. of Myanmar, *Agreement Between the Government of the Republic of India and the Government of the Union of Myanmar on Border Trade,* signed in New Delhi on 21st January, 1995.
5. The Govt. of India and the Govt. of Bhutan, *Agreement on Trade and Commerce Between the Government of Republic of India and the Government of the Kingdom of Bhutan,* signed at Thimpu on 28th February, 1995.

ANNEXURE-1

Exports to Bangladesh (via Mizoram)

Name of item	Unit	Volume	Value (Rs. lakh)
1. Pepper	quintals	1570	62.80
2. Sesamum	quintals	4587	68.80
3. Raw-Cotton	quintals	8700	258.28
4. Orange			357.76
5. Lemon			183.60

Imports From Bangladesh (via Mizoram)

Name of item	Unit	Volume	Value (Rs. lakh)
1. Alcoholic product (Scot Emulsion)	bottles	4400	15.40
2. Clothes	—	—	72.60
3. Electronic goods	—	—	14.40
4. Typewriter .	pieces	82	3.68
5. Cosmetics	—	—	2.70
6. Animal Products	—	—	5.40

N.B. There are individuals who directly import from Bangladesh some of the basic food items like edible oil, sugar, pulses, clothes, utensils etc. for their family consumption as well as for small trading in the border villages. Since the number of such individuals are not known, these items could not be included in the import figures. Two samples of such individual importers indicate that on an average each such individual imports annually edible oil of Rs. 1275, Pulses of Rs. 4800, sugar of Rs. 2250 clothes of Rs. 3500 and utensils of Rs. 300.

ANNEXURE—2

Commodity-wise Annual Data of Exports and Imports Between India and Bangladesh (Via Tripura)

EXPORT FROM INDIA TO BANGLADESH

Name of Item	Unit	Quantity	Value (Rs. lakh)
1	2	3	4
1. Corex Cough Syrup	bottles	168000	38.40
2. B.G. Phose	pieces	72000	28.80
3. Injection	pieces	96000	9.60
4. Tablet	pieces	144000	2.16
5. Avil Expectorant	bottles	4800	0.86
6. Cotton Print sari	pieces	1206000	1179.60
7. Bed Sheet	pieces	6000	4.80
8. Shawl	pieces	6000	10.20
9. Pant (suiting)	pieces	3600	7.20
10. Oranges	thousand nos	192	2.88
11. Mangoes	Qtls.	1200	12.00
12. Jack Fruits	thousand nos.	480	24.00
13. Dry Fish	Qtls.	120	2.64
14. Fish	Qtls.	23450	1055.25
15. Rice	Qtls.	92840	584.64
16. Ajanta Wall Clock	pieces	12000	16.20
17. Prestige Table Clock	pieces	5760	10.94
18. Hero Cycle	pieces	14400	189.36
19. Hercules (MTB)	pieces	3600	61.20
20. Hero Ranger	pieces	1920	30.72
21 Atlas cycles	pieces	3600	54.00
22. Cycle parts	—	—	93.60
23. Tyre	pieces	2400	1.44
24. Sugar	qtls	134160	2158.32
25. Pulses (Mashur)	qtls	18000	432.00

1		2	3	4
26.	Bidi	thousand nos.	3600	3.49
27.	Paper	rim	53760	53.76
28.	Tooth-paste	cages	2400	4.80
29.	Audio Cassette (Film)	pieces	24000	6.72.
30.	Video Cassette (Film)	pieces	14400	54.00
31.	Bamboo	thousand pieces	1380	24.86
32.	Cane & Bamboo (goods)	—	—	1.92
33.	Zarda	Kg	2400	31.20
34.	Turmeric	Qtls.	537	16.11
33.	Cumin	Otls.	42360	2515.20
34.	Chilli	Qtls.	43872	1603.44
35.	Matches	box of 100	145512	72.75
36.	Salt	Qtls.	75600	282.00
37.	Onion	Qtls.	39600	28.32
38.	Garlic	Qtls,	1920	57.60
39.	Flour	Otls.	14640	96.72
40.	Costly Sari	pieces	144000	210.00
41.	Silk Sari	pieces	96000	211.20
42.	Dhuti	pieces	36000	21.60
43.	Lungi	pieces	576000	428.40
44.	Cotton Silk Sari	pieces	120000	252.00
45.	Khair (for pan)	kg	2400	7.20
46.	Glass	doz.	235200	99.74
47.	Fencidol (medicine)	—	—	1547.90
48.	Cosmetics	doz.	52800	177.46
49.	Grapes	cases	76800	125.76
50.	Milk Powder	Otls.	13440	1678.80
51.	Hashish (Ganja)	Qtls.	336	230.40
52.	Foreign Liquor	cases	3366	284.80

1	2	3	4
53. Vitamin Tablets	pkts.	72000	12.24
54. Vitamin vile	bottles	24000	9.60
55. Hamoglobil (medicine)	bottles	168000	84.00
56. Mritosanjibani (Ayurvedic medicine)	bottles	96000	52.80
57. Waterberry's compound	bottles	48000	31.20
58. Other medicine	—	—	132.00
59. Mineral water	bottles	50000	9.00
60. Timber (koroi)	cft	36000	54.00
61. Timber (Teak)	cft	24000	48.00
62. Timber (Sal)	cft	36000	72.00
63. Timber (Gamari)	cft	146400	220.80
64. Timber (Salpost)	pieces	24000	24.00
65. Timber (Mangoes)	cft	24000	31.20
66. Timber (Jack Fruit)	cft	24000	31.20
67. Electric Fan	Nos	24000	240.00
68. Pressure Cooker	Nos	2400	14.40
69. Stainless steel utensils	Qtls.	240	33.60
70. Kerosine	litters	192000	23.04
71. Cow	litters	26400	186.00
72. Bull	Nos.	4800	144.00
73. Dal (Linthal)	qtls	12000	300.00
74. Chilli (Red)	Qtls.	240	9.60
75. Rubber (Smoked)	Qtls.	360	1.26
76. Tea	Qtls.	2400	129.00
77. Fruits	Qtls.	2400	96.00

Import to India from Bangladesh (Via Tripura)

	Name of commodity	*Unit*	*Volume*	*Value (Rs. lakh)*
	1	2	3	4
1.	Polythene Bag (Big)	thousand pkt.	1356	474.60
2.	Palm Oil	thousand its	1236	469.68
3.	Egg	thousand Nos	9120	143.16
4.	Resins	qtls	1152	9.17
5.	Cardamon	qtls	1020	306.36
6.	Plastic Shoe	thousand pairs	1200	207.12
7.	Polythene Bag (Small)	thousand pkt	360	14.40
8.	Gold	10 grams	7200	345.60
9.	Synthetic Silk Cloth	mts	96000	24.00
10.	Pant Piece	piece	19200	19.20
11.	Pant Piece	thousand mts	120	57.60
12.	V.C.P.	pieces	4960	298.40
13.	V.C.R.	pieces	4880	392.00
14.	T.V. Small (B/W)	Nos	80	2.40
15.	T.V. Small (Colour)	Nos.	80	6:40
16.	Radio	Nos	3000	6.00
17.	Tape recorder	Nos	2000	2.40
18.	Blank Cassette (Video)	pieces	48000	85.20
19.	(VCP + VCR) Parts	—	—	24.00
20.	Fish (Seasonal)	qtls	240	8.40
21.	Blue Film Cassette	pieces	2400	6.72
22.	Blank Cassette (Audio)	pieces	48000	7.68
23.	Sidol (Dry Fish)	qtls	144	12.96
24.	Shrimp (Dry Fish)	qtls	24	1.01
25.	Other Dry Fish	qtls	48	3.60
26.	Perfume	doz	120	1.20
27.	Wrist Watch	pieces	2000	1.20
28.	Ball Pen	doz	2400	0.72
29.	Ink per	doz.	400	0.48
30.	Soap	doz	2400	1.44

1	2	3	4
31. Emergency Lamp	Nos	200	1.00
32. Whisky	bottles	2000	7.00
33. Old Garments	1.30		
34. Blankets	pieces	500	3.00
35. Camera	pieces	120	3.00
36. Photo Film	doz	480	4.80
37. After Shave Lotion	doz	120	1.15
38. Video Games	Nos	400	1.00
39. Cordless Telephone	Nos	280	12.00
40. Gas lighter	doz	200	1.92
41. Cosmetics	sets	400	2.40
42. Torch Light (Small)	doz	300	0.44
43. Torch Light (Big)	doz	240	1.15
44. Cigarettes	thousand pkts.	20	6.00
45. Umbrella	nos.	720	0.43

ANNEXURE—3

Commodity-wise Annual Data on Imports between India and Bangladesh via Western Meghalaya (Baghmara and Chibbari routes)

Name of Commodity	*Unit*	*Volume*	*Value (Rs. lakh)*
1. Clothes	—	—	0.84
2. Mosquito Net (cotton)	—	—	0.90
3. Shirt Pieces	—	—	0.90
4. Pant Pieces	—	—	1.08
5. T-shirts	—	—	0.12
6. Vegetables	—	—	2..64
7. Eggs	thousand nos.	120	1.68
8. Poultry Products	—	—	1.74
9. Goat	—	—	7.68
10. Soap (Small)	—	—	0.31
11. Soap (Large)	—	—	0.48
12. Dry-Fish	—	—	13.20
13. Petro-Max	—	—	0.08
14. Sandals (Ladies)	—	—	0.84
15. Sandals (Gents)	—	—	0.84
16. Shoes (ladies)	—	—	0.24
17. Shoes (gents)	—	—	0.24
18. Torch-Light	—	—	0.12
19. Gold	k. gram	4.5	21.30
20. Tape Recorder	Nos	60	0.45
21. Radio	Nos	100	0.36
22. V.C.R.	Nos	5	0.90
23. V.C.P.	Nos	7	0.84
24. Video Cassette	—	—	0.13
25. Camera	Nos	20	0.34
26. Wrist Watch	Nos	100	0.30
27. Torch-Bulb	—	—	0.04
28. Calculator	Nos	100	0.24
29. Audio Cassette	—	—	0.36
30. Other electronic goods	—	—	2.40

Export from India to Bangladesh (via West Meghalaya)

Name of Commodity	*Unit*	*Volume*	*Value (Rs. lakh)*
1. Sugar	qtls	10950	175.16
2. Salt	qtls	4170	16.68
3. Rice (fine)	bags	5760	54.72
4. Rice (coarse)	bags	8100	63.18
5. Potato	qtls	175	1.05
6. Onion	qtls	60	0.48
7. Pulses (Masur Dal)	qtls	160	3.87
8. Pulses (Mug dal)	—	—	0.42
9. Tea	kg	600	0.36
10. M. Oil	tins		4.22
11. Atta (flour prod.)	qtls	220	1.54
12. Vanaspati ghee	tins	96	0.67
13. Kerosine	liters	10800	0.43
14. Salted Mixture (Snacks)	kg	720	0.36
15. Plastic Bucket	—	—	2.56
16. Plastic Jug	—	—	0.12
17. Plastic Mug	- -	- -	0.07
18. Plastic Rope	—	—	0.07
19. Aluminium Goods	—	—	2.14
20. Steel Goods	—	—	3.22
21. Iron Tools	—	—	1.43
22. Cloth	—	—	2.52
23. Mosquito Net	—	—	0.15
24. Soap	—	—	0.63
25. Cup-Plate	—	—	0.07
26. Drinking Glass	—	—	0.24
27. Orange	—	—	0.18
28. Air Bag	—	—	0.42
29. Skin Tight Garment	—	—	0.24
30. Wool	—	—	0.60
31. Cattle	Nos	400	16.00

Note: In the south-western Meghalaya, the border trade with Bangladesh is carried out mainly through two border points, namely, Baghmara and Chibbari. But the volume of trade is not very significant. The number of trading dealers are also very limited. This may be due to moderately better border vigilance by the security forces for restricting militants' movement to and from Bangladesh. There is only one trader dealing with electronic goods. Most of the traders could not give the volume of all traded goods. In most of the cases, they could, however, give the item-wise value of exports and imports.

ANNEXURE—4

Commodity-wise Imports and Exports Between India and Bangladesh via East and South Meghalaya Border

ESTIMATED QUANTITY AND VALUE OF INFORMAL IMPORTS TO INDIA FROM BANGLADESH (APRIL 1995 TO MARCH 1996)

	Items	*Quantity*	*Rate*	*Value (Rs. lakh)*
1.	Fish	44,700 kg.	@Rs. 62.50/kg.	Rs. 27.94
2.	Poultry eggs	136 cases	@Rs. 275/case	Rs. 0.37
3.	Pulses	Assorted	Different rate	Rs. 0.10
4.	Poultry Birds	600 nos.	@Rs. 150/bird	Rs. 0.30
5.	Synthetic fabric	Assorted	@Rs. 150- Rs. 1600 per metre	Rs. 31.53
6.	Ready-made garments	Assorted	@Rs. 70-Rs. 500 per piece	Rs. 33.61
7.	Old garments	Assorted	Different rates	Rs. 12.05
8.	Electronic goods	Assorted	@Rs. 200- Rs. 20,000 per item	Rs. 28.50
9.	Watches	Assorted	@Rs. 35- Rs. 1,600 per watch	Rs. 2.35
10.	Gold	4364 gins	@Rs. 5,500 per 10 gms	Rs. 24.00
11.	Silver	2 kgs	@Rs. 7000/kg.	Rs. 0.14
12.	Copper	N.A.	N.A.	Rs. 0.01
13.	Ornaments (gold/silver)	N.A.	N.A.	Rs. 2.51
14.	Medicines	N.A.	N.A.	Rs. 1.00
15.	Motor vehicle parts (foreign)	Assorted	Different rates	Rs. 7.48
16.	Misc. items (toys, cosmetics, balms etc.)	Assorted	Different rates	Rs. 146.51

ESTIMATED. QUANTITY AND VALUE OF INFORMAL EXPORTS FROM INDIA TO BANGLADESH (APRIL 1995 TO MARCH 1996)

Items	*Quantity*	*Rate*	*Value (Rs. lakh)*
1. Biri	250 bundles	@Rs. 40/bundle	Rs. 0.10
2. Salt	1645 quintals	@Rs. 270/q.	Rs. 4.44
3. Sugar	6340 quintals	@Rs. 1000/q.	Rs. 63.40
4. Cows & buffaloes	782 heads	@Rs. 2900/-head	Rs.22.00
5. Other livestock	Assorted	Different rates	Rs.21.00
6. Cotton yarn	Assorted	Different rates	Rs. 15.00
7. Cotton textiles	Assorted	@Rs.80-400 per metre	Rs.66.00
8. Spices	Assorted	Different rates	Rs. 0.10
9. Kerosene	12,000 litres	Rs.4/litre	Rs. 0.48
10. Medicines	Assorted	Different rates	Rs.44.48
11. Motorised vehicle parts	Assorted	Different rates	Rs.45.97
12. Cycle parts	Assorted	Different rates	Rs. 0.80
13. Other machinery parts	Assorted	Different rates	Rs. 0.10
14. Electronic	Assorted	Different rates	Rs. 0.10
15. Gold	1000 gins	@Rs.5,500 per 10 gms	Rs. 5.50
16. Wooden logs	9309 cft. (Assorted species)	@Rs.95/cft. (average)	Rs. 8.84
17. Ganja	5880 kgs	@Rs.540/kg.	Rs.31.75

ANNEXURE—5

Commodity-wise Annual Data on Exports and Imports Between India and Bangladesh via Assam (Mankachar and Karimganj Routes)

Exports to Bangladesh (via Assam)

Name of Commodity	*Unit*	*Volume*	*Value (Rs. lakh)*
1	2	3	4
1. Cattle	number	13956	339.64
2. Wood	cft	87412	415.88
3. Kerosene	thousand lts	1523	69.86
4. Salt	qtls	20332	61.52
5. Bicycle	Nos	5562	83.72
6. Sugar	qtls	2794	54.63
7. Garlic	Qtls	4368	88.92
8. Battery (for emergency light)	pieces	1404	4.37
9. Leather	pieces	16640	48.36
10. Fish (Andhra)	qtls.	624	24.96
11. Chilli	kg	4376	2.95
12. Bidi	pkt.	13200	7.22
13. Automobile Parts	—	—	0.83
14. Rice	qtls	390	3.51
15. Incidal Tab.	Thousand Nos.	152	0.72
16. Polybion Injection	Nos.	4000	0.12
17. Bacadax Tab.	Thousand Nos.	668	1.34
18. Baralgan Tab.	Thousand Nos.	14	0.10
19. Cinkara	Bottle	10400	2.84
20. Dexorange	Bottle	2040	0.76
21. Infidon Injection	Thousand	9100	0.36
22. Neurobion Inj.	Ample	4680	0.22
23. Basphapen Tab.	Thousand Nos.	12	0.12
24. Hawai Sandal	pairs	7200	2.52

1	2	3	4
25. Shoes (Plastic)	pairs	3600	3.42
26. Plastic Sandal	pains	7200	2.16
27. Dry Fish	kg	5400	5.40
28. Timber	cft.	2250	6.76
29. Bangla Pati (pan)	pkt.	15750	6.3
30. Khasia Pati (pan)	pkt.	31500	8.19
31. Pulses	Qtls.	1000	25.00
32. Clothes	—	—	12.00

N.B.: Items nos. 15 to 23 are medicines.

Import From Bangladesh to India (via Assam)

Name of Commodity	*Unit*	*Volume*	*Value (Rs. lakh)*
1	2	3	4
1. Gold	kg.	238	1189.30
2. V.C.P	pieces	1262	127.06
3. V.C.R	pieces	1280	151.79
4. Cloths	pieces	136240	33.80
5. Tape Recorder	pieces	16536	105.3
6. Coconut Oil	lts	436280	264.83
7. Clock	pieces	4784	15.08
8. Goat	Nos	10036	63.96
9. Jute	qtls	17028	992.16
10. Poultry Products	kg	22469	13.78
11. Egg	Nos	36400	0.63
12. Tea Sets	set	2600	13.00
13. Camera	pieces	1171	11.18
14. Mosquito Net	pieces	1664	11.34
15. Tin	bundle	1456	37.44
16. Silver	—	—	26.52
17. Audio Cassette	pieces	4564	1.54
18. Fish	kg	7680	4.45
19. Umbrella cloth	Metre	6880	2.75

1	2	3	4
20. Electric lamp	pieces	120	0.45
21. Wrist Watch	pieces	3073	6.59
22. Calculator	pieces	1310	2.08
23. Decorative Table lamp	pieces	42	0.34
24. Decorative Table lamp with clock	pieces	56	0.53
25. Medicine	—	—	0.14
26. Synthetic Fabrics	mts	13600	4.08
27. Anchor Milk	pkts	320	0.70
28. Melamine Dishes	sets	10	0.18
29. Premier Lamp	pieces	50	0.35
30. Pen	—	—	1.50
31. Torch light	nos	2500	0.80
32. Perfumes	bottles	1200	0.96
33. Used clothes	—	—	2.00
34. Toys	—	—	1.20
35. Hair dryer	Nos.	250	1.10
36. Radio	Nos.	600	1.44

ANNEXURE—6

Commodity-wise Exports to Bhutan (via Assam)

Name of Commodity	*Unit*	*Volume*	*Value (Rs. lakh)*
1	2	3	4
1. Clothes	—	—	644.66
2. Rice (fine quality)	bags	7400	78.16
3. Rice (medium)	bags	216600	1513.30
4. Atta (flour prod.)	bags	112784	668.90
5. Maida (flour prod.)	bags	6660	40.26
6. Suzi (flour prod.)	bags	7960	55.53
7. Pulses (Machur Dal)	quintls	900	18.45
8. Sugar	bags	76240	924.42
9. Tea-leaves	kg	270120	141.83
10. Mustard Oil	tins	7716	41.90
11. Dry peas	gags	10820	93.51
12. Milk	packets	120	1.56
13. Salted mixture	kg	2400	1.01
14. Jute rope	kg	32530	8.15
15. Plastic Rope	kg	1080	0.65
16. Plastic Tripal	—	—	16.76
17. Lux Beauty Soap	boxes	720	2.02
18. Potatoes	—	—	18.18
19. Onion	—	—	4.84
20. Eggs	curtons	6000	12.60
21. Colgate toothpaste	boxes	960	3.84
22. Jeans Pant (Full)	pieces	15000	31.20
23. Jeans Pant (Half)	pieces	3120	7.44
24. Cotton (Simul)	quintals	24	1.44
25. Cotton (Raw)	quintals	354	2.44
26. Plastic mat	pieces	1320	1.39
27. T-Shirt	pieces	42300	36.12
28. Ladies Coat	pieces	13500	19.32

1	2	3	4
29. Mosquito net	rolls	120	1.44
30. Cosmetics (make up item)	—	—	8.40
31. Cabbage	quintals	3840	8.52
32. Couli Flower	quintals	2980	8.15
33. Chili	quintals	724	5.67
34. Brinjal	quintals	60	0.32
35. Tomatoes	quintals	1320	3.96
36. Plastic Bucket	pieces	85040	36.25
37. Plastic Jug	—	—	33.48
38. Plastic Mug	pieces	840	0.05
39. Cocoanut rope	quintals	7236	184.00
40. Steel Goods	—	—	4.11
41. Alluminium Goods	kg	722790	867.35
42. Air Bags (Small)	pieces	15420	30.36
43. Air Bags (Large)	pieces	4470	3.66
44. Toys (Plastic)	boxes	180	0.55
45. Plastic Ball	boxes	210	0.88
46. Chappal	pairs	1200	0.54
47. Shoes	pairs	1320	5.08
48. Shirt Pieces	rolls	120	1.32
49. Pant Pieces	rolls	144	2.30
50. Bhutia Shawl	pieces	1200	1.44
51. Underwears (ladies)	boxes	1200	4.32
52. Underwears (gents)	boxes	1200	4.56
53. Cotton Belt	pieces	2400	0.60
54. Socks	pairs	1200	0.38
55. Cattle	—	—	68.00
56. Chik and ducks and ducks	quintals	730	36.50
57. Dry-Fish	quintals	1017	11.97
58. Fish	kg	1625	0.49

1	2	3	4
59. Pig	—	—	73.47
60. Goat	quintals	365	25.55
61. Wool	quintals	100	20.00
62. Half pant (Boys)	pieces	31500	7.88
63. Blouse	dozens	405	1.22
64. Cap	dozens	270	0.32
65. Sweater (Woolen) Full	pieces	5500	9.71
66. Sweater (Woolen) Half	pieces	5500	8.25
67. Maggi (Single)	curtons	10500	42.00
68. Maggi (Double)	curtons	24000	168.00
69. Yarn	quintals	7500	3000.00
70. Sando Gangi	dozens	675	1.69
71. Full Gangi	dozens	675	2.19
72. Gur (Molases)	quintals	173	1.99
73. Pulses (Mug Dal)	bags	1800	18.90
74. Banaspati (Dalda)	tins	6480	41.68
75. Edible Oil	tins	10800	59.40
76. Parboil Rice	bags	36000	288.00
77. Battary	cases	10800	11.02
78. Drinking Glass	cases	20520	7.90
79. Lantern Chimni	cases	4000	2.00
80. Table Chimni	cases	4000	2.00
81. Tea Cup	cases	17600	27.57
82. Tea Plate	dozens	1643	1.86
83. Bulb	boxes	936	7.24
84. Tube light Equipment	boxes	1440	126.00
85. Wire (Flexible)	quales	26400	10.56
86. Wire (General)	quales	144000	144.00
87. Switch	boxes	672	13.41
88. Switch Board	boxes	5440	26.29
89. Electric Fan	pieces	2160	12.96
90. Electric Holder	boxes	2400	7.20

1	2	3	4
91. P.V.C. Pipe	bundles	5000	5.00
92. D .V. Box	boxes	264	1.85
93. Bulb Sade	boxes	160	0.80
94. Battery Box	pieces	1040	2.86
95. Battery Plate	pieces	9100	0.91
96. Battery Separator	pieces	10400	0.10
97. Battery Clip	packets	182	0.18
98. Battery Acid	bottles	1170	0.06
99. Main switch	boxes	22	0.18
100. Beans (vegetable)	quintals	900	5.40
101. Pan (betel)	gaddies	468	0.94

Imports from Bhutan
(via Assam Through Gelephu + Samdrupjankhar)

	Names of Items	Units	Volume	Value (Rs. lakh)
1.	Spacial Courier (Drinks)	boxes	3120	50.54
2.	Royal Supreme Whisky	boxes	4200	38.81
3.	Dragon Rum (H)	boxes	4080	31.33
4.	Dragon Rum (F)	boxes	3960	28.51
5.	Black Mountain (F)	boxes	2640	15.84
6.	Black Mountain (H)	boxes	3840	25.81
7.	Chngta Whishy (F)	boxes	3360	15.62
8.	Pacham Gin (F)	boxes	4080	13.47
9.	Juchung Brandy (F)	boxes	3960	18.85
10.	Juchung Brandy (H)	boxes	4200	18.00
11.	Soney Liquor (F)	boxes	3360	14.11
12.	Changta Whisky (H)	boxes	2760	14.57
13.	Soney Liquor (H)	boxes	4440	21.13
14.	Orange Liquor (F)	boxes	2400	12.00
15.	Orange Liquor (H)	boxes	2460	11.71
16.	Calculator	pieces	2400	4.44
17.	Electronic Watch	pieces	2800	7.68
18.	Electronic Videogame	pieces	600	1.80
19.	Camera	pieces	1020	3.00
20.	Emergency Light	pieces	900	2.88
21.	Foreign Lighter	pieces	4800	0.39
22.	Foreign Shoes	pairs	3600	10.80
23.	Foreign Chappal	pairs	3600	4.68
24.	Orange	bags	720	8.64
25.	Kerosene Oil	litters	346750	10.92

ANNEXURE—7

Commodity-wise Volume and Value of Informal Trade with Myanmar Through Mizoram Border

EXPORT FROM INDIA TO MYANMAR

	Name of Commodity	*Unit*	*Volume*	*Value (Rs. lakh)*
1.	Medicines	—	—	544.40
2.	Tools (General)	—	—	5.50
3.	Maltova	—	—	11.73
4.	Nescafe	—	—	8.24
5.	Clothes	metre	19600	11.76
6.	Bubble gum	—	—	4.86
7.	Paint	—	—	232.64
8.	Cosmetics (Rose powder)	cases	120	0.96
9.	Nestum	cases	180	1.23
10.	Rice Milling Machine	Pieces	200	100.00
11.	Bicycle	Pieces	940	11.28
12.	Pressure Cooker	Pieces	2300	6.90
13.	C.I. Sheet	Bundle	10400	15.60
14.	Horlicks	Pieces	3600	1.98
15.	Sewing Machine	Pieces	140	2.80
16.	Ox's Parts (parts of Ox meat)	quintals	12	1.20
17.	Raw-Cotton	bales	120	1.80
18.	Urea (Fertilizer)	bags	6600	26.40
19.	Diamonds			540.00
20.	Agni. tools (I & S)	pieces	2000	4.50
21.	Lungi (cotton garment)	pieces	1200	0.60

Imports from Myanmar to India (via Mizoram)

Name of item	Unit	Volume	Value (Rs. lakh)
1. Clothes	metres	153200	69.08
2. Dry Battery (small)	—	—	0.30
3. Blankets	pieces	4040	56.94
4. Vitamins (A+D)	packets	1500	3.75
5. Cosmetics	—	—	17.18
6. White-Onions	quintals	30	1.05
7. Cigarette	—	—	220.26
8. Toys	—	—	2.10
9. Dry-Fish	packets	2400	0.96
10. Spices	—	—	1.51
11. Carpet	—	—	142.04
12. Cotton Shawl	pieces	300	1.38
13. Dinner Plate	sets	240	4.32
14. T-Shirts	pieces	3300	6.66
15. Make-Up (Cosmetics)	—	—	20.86
16. Umbrella	—	—	2.64
17. Air-Bags	pieces	7900	10.84
18. Bath Soaps	—	—	7.44
19. Polythene Bags	kg	1960	3.96
20. Readymade Garments	pieces	1200	3.60
21. Dinner Sets	sets	90	1.71
22. Bed-Cover	pieces	600	1.50
23. Television	pieces	720	104.14
24. Tape Recorder	pieces	100	54.00
25. Video	pieces	150	36.00
26. Shoe	paris	7000	3.16
27. Soft Drinks	—	—	13.60
28. Lace (Nylon)	—	—	9.99
29. Beef product	tins	4000	0.72
30. Mosquito Net	metre	4000	2.00
31. Jean-Pants	pieces	1600	4.48
32. Electronic goods	—	—	2.20

1	*2*	*3*	*4*
33. Slipper (chappals)	pairs	2400	0.72
34. Alcohol Products (Scot Emulson)	bottles	360000	1260.00
35. Tea-cups	cases	80	1.18
36. Petromax lamp	pieces	120	2.40
37. Dry-Battery	pieces	720	0.36
38. Tools	—	—	0.10
39. Gas Lighter	—	—	0.72
40. Stationery goods	—	—	2.40
41. Cattle	Nos	2960	157.60
42. Pigs	Nos	2080	65.80
43. Skin-tight pant (big)	pieces	4000	2.60
44. Skin-tight pants (small)	pieces	4000	1.60
45. Brassiere (ladies cloth)	pieces	480	0.34
46. China silk	metre	4000	2.00
47. Pettycoat (ladies coat)	pieces	4000	1.20
48. Jackets	pieces	1200	4.20
49. Sweater	pieces	400	2.10
50. Tyres (MRF)	pieces	1200	66.00
51. Kuhva (nuts)	quintals	960	52.80
52. Stones and Pearl	—	—	180.00
53. Gold	—	—	225.00
54. Utensils	—	—	12.48

ANNEXURE-8

Commodity-wise Annual Data on Exports and Imports of Informal Border Trade with Myanmar via Manipur
Import to India from Myanmar (via Manipur)

Name of item	*Unit*	*Volume*	*Value (Rs. lakh)*
1. Jeans trousers	nos.	127750	383.25
2. Gents' T-shirts	nos.	109500	273.75
3. Ladies coat	nos.	109500	328.50
4. Ladies T-shirts	nos.	91250	228.12
5. Lip sticks	nos.	127750	63.87
6. Perfumes	nos.	73000	87.60
7. Telephone instruments	nos.	18000	270.00
8. Shoes	pairs	91250	136.88
9. Toilet Soaps	dozens	9125	7.30
10. Wrist-Watch	pieces	73000	146.00
11. Camera	pieces	3650	54.75
12. Emergency Lamp	pieces	3650	43.80
13. Blankets	pieces	18250	182.50
14. Video-Cassettee	pieces	36500	43.80
15. Supari (Betelnut)	kgs.	27300	438.00
16. Fishing Net	pieces	48000	72.00
17. Heroin (narcotics)	kg.	480	576.00
18. Precious Stone (Gems)	—	—	3600.00
19. Teak Wood	truck loads	1825	912.50
20. T.V.	nos.	400	56.00
21. V.C.R	nos.	150	33.00
22. V.C.P.	nos.	250	22.50
23. Gas Lighter	nos.	400	0.60
24. Tape recorder	nos.	1000	8.00
25. Stereo System	nos.	200	16.00
26. Radio	nos.	500	2.50

The following goods are also imported from Myanmar to the tune of about Rs. 5 to 6 crores a year. Their item-wise detailed quantity could not be provided as they are purchased by the traders from across the border as assorted goods. These items are:

1. Pencil Eraser
2. House Knife
3. Super Glue
4. Folding Scissors
5. Myanmadi Ball Pen
6. Arrow Ball Pen
7. Reynolds Ball Pen
8. Ceramic Pen
9. Wingsung Fountain Pen
10. Hero Fountain Pen
11. Table Tennis Ball
12. Table Tennis Bat
13. Badminton Racket
14. Badminton Shuttle
15. Staple Machine
16. Staple Pin
17. Cutting Knife
18. Cutting Knife (folding)
19. Penci!
20. Benain Pencil
21. Measuring Tape
22. Scale
23. Gum
24. Calculators
25. Colour Envelope
26. Map Chart etc.
27. Pencil Box
28. Umbrella

N.B. It has been reported that a sizable amount of weapons is also imported through this border point (Morah) illegally, but their quantum and value could not be ascertained from the traders because of the sensitivity of the item.

Exports from India to Myanmar

Name of item	*Unit*	*Volume*	*Value (Rs. lakh)*
1. Bicycle	varies between Rs. 5500.00 and 6000.00 lakh		
2. Iron nails	———		10.00
3. Engineering goods (Machinery)	———		450.00
4. Paints	———		120.00
5. Medicine	———		40.00
6. Tea			
7. Coffee			258.00
8. Horlicks and other confectionary items			

N.B.: The value of items nos. 6,7,8 are combined as separate trade data are not available.

5

Liberalisation of Border Trade: Prospects and Impediments

—M. P. Bezbaruah

Since India's North-Eastern Region shares most of its boundary with foreign countries, it is only natural that several border points of the region should emerge as active centres of trans-border international trade. While trading along the Indo-China border in Arunachal Pradesh might have remained less active due to the difficult terrain as well as the unresolved border dispute between the two countries, towns such as Moreh, Champain, Tlangbung, Kailashsahar, Agartala, Sonamora, Bilonia., Sabroom, Karimganj, Dawki, Baghmara, Lichubari, Mankachar, Fakiragram, Gelephu, and Samdrupjankar dotted along the international boundary of Manipur, Mizoram, Tripura, Meghalaya and Assam, have been important centres for trading activities with Myanmar, Bangladesh and Bhutan. A part of this trading activity takes place under multilateral agreements and India's bilateral trade arrangements with the neighboring countries. However, the volume of trading activities that take place outside such formal arrangements reportedly far exceeds the volume of formal trade. There are several arguments in favour of liberalisation of border trade to give a boost to trading activities in general and to formalise, at least in parts, the existing informal trade.

1. First of all, legalisation of these trading activities will encourage the involvement of such people in

border trade who may be currently dissuaded from it because of its illegal status.

2. Legalisation will also enable governments to earn revenue through imposition of duties on imports and exports. Currently this potential government earning is being pocketed by agents and corrupt officials in return for facilitating the illegal informal trade.
3. One major constraint on economic development of the North-Eastern Region arising from its geographical isolation from the rest of the country has been the lack of easy access to markets outside the region. Further opening up of border trade can remove this constraint considerably by providing the region market outlet in and through the neighboring countries.
4. Moreover expansion of trading activities along the border is bound to have spin off for related sectors of transport, storage, communication, hotels and restaurants, banking and insurance, etc. which in turn will also serve the cause of overall economic development of the region.

However, an examination of the existing pattern of informal border trade, as revealed by a survey[1] carried out in 1996 with which the author was also associated, indicates that liberalisation of border trade may have some negative implications too. For example, it has been found that the informal exports from India through the North Eastern Region consist mostly of such essential commodities as foodgrains and medicines. Since the region itself is deficient in production of foodgrains, freer export of this essential item of consumption may lead to its shortage and price hike in the region. Hence, to safeguard itself from such adverse consequence of liberalisation of export trade in such commodities, the North Eastern Region has to attain self sufficiency in production of foodgrains and to benefit significantly from the liberalised trade the region should be able to generate exportable surplus.

The composition of informal imports of India through the north eastern border also indicates that liberalisation of border trade is not going to be without impediments.

Harmful goods like alcoholic beverage and narcotic drug weight heavily in the bag of informal imports from some neighboring countries into the region. For instance, informal imports from Bhutan almost entirely consist of alcoholic beverage. Similarly, the major item imported from Myanmar across Manipur border is narcotics. It is difficult to see border trade being liberalised to the extent of legalising the import of such items.

The other major group of informal imports consists of luxury and fancy consumer items such as apparels, electrical and electronic consumer durables, cosmetics etc. These items are smuggled mostly from Bangladesh and to some extent also from Myanmar. These goods are however produced not in our neighboring countries but mostly in the industrialised countries of East and South-east Asia. Most of these commodities are currently in the negative list of imports of the Government of India. Liberalisation of border trade of this group of items would require transferring these items to the Open General License list or some alternative formal arrangement. But if the import of these goods is liberalised, they are more likely to be imported from the country in which they are produced, and as a result their import through the neighboring countries is likely to fall.

Moreover, liberalisation of border trade will be possible only if countries on both sides of the border see benefits in doing so. For instance Bangladesh, which runs a deficit in the balance of both formal and informal trade with India, may not agree to further opening up of trade if the process is perceived as beneficial to India only. Hence liberalisation of border trade should not be viewed merely as an instrument for enhancing market access for the North Eastern Region. The process can be successfully pursued only with a spirit of give and take with the neighboring countries. While looking for opportunities of exporting to these countries we should also be ready to accept more imports from them.

Indeed, consumers in the region can actually benefit greatly from enhanced imports from across the border. It will however be necessary to explore new items for import For instance the world class Bangladeshi textile, which is exported to many developed countries, can easily find a market in this region too. There is however some multilateral trade agreement related problem to be sorted out before import of such items can be made formal. Moreover such a prospect is likely to be resisted by the domestic textile lobby in India, as it stands to lose from such imports. Import of timber, which now goes on informally from and through Myanmar, if formalised and increased can benefit the region greatly as this forest product is becoming increasingly scarce and the forests themselves are getting depleted on Indian side of the border. But export of this product may not be sustainable in the long run without creating major environmental problem for the exporting country.

Thus, some economic and legal adjustments have to take place on both sides of the border for healthy and mutually beneficial border trade to grow. However border trade is more likely to flourish if it is backed up by wider economic co-operation between countries of the region. Active trade, backed up by broader economic co-operation, can greatly benefit the peoples on both sides of the border from the matching of the complementarities in their resource bases. For illustration, let us consider the following. It is widely believed that states like Meghalaya and Tripura have good natural conditions for horticulture. One of the constraints in exploiting these conditions has been the inadequacy of processing and marketing facilities for the output of horticultural crops. Now Bangladesh, which possesses cheap and hard working labour in relative abundance, can be a base for processing horticultural output from these states in a cost-effective manner. The processed product can then be marketed in Bangladesh or India or any other country at a competitive price. Such a process will not only generate income and employment for farm households in this region but also help the Bangladesh economy to develop its processing industry and diversify its export

REFERENCE

1. The survey on 'Informal Border Trade in the North Eastern Region' was carried out for a UN-ESCAP sponsored study by Research and Information System for Non-Aligned and Developing Countries, New Delhi on 'India's Border Trade with Select Neighboring Countries' (1996).

6

Border Trade in North East India: An Overview

—B.K. Sarma & S.N. Goswami

The north eastern region (NER) of India comprising seven states viz., Arunachal Pradesh, Assam, Manipur, Meghalaya, Mizoram, Nagaland and Tripura has the longest international land border with China, Bhutan, Bangladesh and Myanmar. Arunachal Pradesh is surrounded on three sides by the international border with Bhutan to the west, China to the north and Myanmar to the east. Geographically Assam is a shadow of its formerself. Assam shares international boundary with Bangladesh and Bhutan. Manipur is bounded by Upper Myanmar in the east. The international border of Meghalaya is with Bangladesh whereas Mizoram is bounded on the east and south by Chin Hills and Arakan of Myanmar and on the west by Chittagong Hill Tracts of Bangladesh. On the east Nagaland shares India's international boundary with Myanmar. Tripura is surrounded by Bangladesh on all sides, except for a narrow neck in the north-east.

Border trade is referred to as exchange of goods and services among different countries in border points. Border trade is intimately linked with socio-economic development of a region. However, social pollution, environmental and socio-cultural degradation are some of the off shoots of border trade which are evident in every border point of the NER. On the other hand with long borders between NER and neighbouring countries and with the globalisation of economy along with emphasis on regional cooperation among the SAARC countries under South Asian Free Trade Association (SAFTA), the prospect of economic development of the NER has, of late, emerged. The proposed SAFTA by 2001 has brightened the potential to give further boost the export oriented economic growth of NER. In addition to traditional and primary export products, there has been prospect of exporting bamboo based products, handloom and handicrafts, phytochemical products etc., under Export Promotion Capital Goods Scheme (EPCGS).

Indo-Bangladesh Border

Indo-Bangladesh border is 1500 kms long and travels along the states of Assam, Meghalaya, Mizoram and Tripura. The Bangladesh area adjacent to the Indian border are mostly plains with small stretches of hill-tracts along the border falling in Tripura only. These plain areas have a fairly well established infrastructure of roads and rail communication network which facilitates the transportation, storage and distribution of contraband goods. The principal commodities smuggled through Indo-Bangladesh border are:

Import

Gold, synthetic fabrics, photo films, edible items like fish, eggs, vegetables, electronic goods, narcotic drugs etc.

Export

Cotton yams, cotton fabrics (inferior quality), bidis and bidi leaves, spices, rice, sugar, chilies, fresh fruits, livestock, coal, limestone, ganja, fish, tea, plywood, handloom and handicraft products.

Trade with Bangladesh takes place from the following border points Meghalaya : Bhagmara, Dalu, Ghasuapara, Mahendraganj of West Garo Hills, Bholaganj, Balat, Shella Bazar, Ryngu of East Khasi Hills ; Barsora of West Khasi

Hills and Dawki of Jaintia Hills. Assam: Karimganj, Stemeghat and Suturkandi; Tripura: Manu. Agartala and Srimantapur

Indo-Myanmar Border

The Indo-Myanmar border is 1640 kms long. This border is especially sensitive to the smuggling of narcotic drugs due to its proximity to the Golden Triangle. Since the resumption of Indo-Myanmar trade under barter mechanism, smuggling has reduced considerably. The facility for free entry/exit of local people under permits for a distance of 40 kms on either side of the border is now allowed. Since 1960, there has been rampant illegal cross border trading with Myanmar. However, from April 12, 1995, Indo-Myanmar border was formally opened by the Commerce Ministry of both the countries. The cross border trade between the two countries takes place in Moreh of Indian side and Tamu in Myanmar side. Trade also takes place through Champhai in Mizoram and Border points in Nagaland. The major commodities smuggled through Indo-Myanmar border are:

Import

Teak logs, narcotic drugs, silver, gold, precious stones, electronic goods, synthetic fabrics, spices (cloves, cardamom, poppy seeds), betelnut, rapeseed mustard, pulses and beans, garlic, onion, chilies, spices, tobacco, resin, coriander seeds, soybean, roasted sunflower seeds etc.

Export

Cotton yarns and fabrics, bicycle and parts, old motor vehicle parts, sewing machines etc., medicines etc., engineering goods, paints etc.

Indo-China Border

Indo-China border is 1175 kms long and demarcates the states of Arunachal Pradesh and China's Tibet. The border is inaccessible being covered by dense forests and mountains. There are small markets in towns adjoining the border like

Tawang and Bomdilla where small quantities of cheap Chinese goods are sold.

Indo-Bhutan Border

Indo-Bhutan border which is 800 kms long demarcates states of Assam and Arunachal Pradesh with that of Bhutan. Small quantities of third country's goods occasionally find their way across this border. The 'chief items exported to Bhutan include rice, sugar, clothes etc. and imported items are alcohol, canned products. Indo-Bhutan border trade at Udalguri in Darrang district of Assam is a point from where substantial trade is going on between Assam and Bhutan.

Border Trade in NE India

Border trade between India and Myanmar was formalised through signing of India-Myanmar Border Trade Agreement (BTA) on January 21, 1994 and operationalised on April 12, 1995 through Moreh border (Manipur). The second designated Border Trade Point at Champhai (Mizoram) is yet to be operationalised. India has no formal BTA with Bangladesh so far, yet considerable amount of border trade is taking place between Bangladesh and three NE states of Meghalaya, Assam and Tripura. Although official trade statistics do not reflect the volume of border trade between India and the neighbouring countries, it is believed that a substantial volume of trade takes place along the borders of NE states, Bangladesh and Myanmar. A study conducted by the Indian Institute of Foreign Trade estimated that unofficial trade between Tripura and Bangladesh exceeds Rs. 100 crores, with which the state has a border of about 839 kms. The official or legal trade and unofficial or illegal trade between these countries and India go side by side. The official trade includes both official export-import trade and official border trade. On the other hand, the unofficial or informal trade is known as smuggling. The annual volume of border trade, both illegal and legal, is shown in Table 6.1 and 6.2.

TABLE 6.1

Annual Volume of Illegal Border Trade (Estimated)

Sector	*Turnout (Rs. in millions)*
Moreh-Tamu (Manipur)	16,000
Champai (Mizoram)	5,000
Lungwa (Nagaland)	1,000
Total	22,000

TABLE 6.2

Export/import Figures of Official Trade

(Rs. in Millions)

	1994-95	*1995-96*	*1996-97*	*1997-98 (upto Oct.)*
Export	698.2	1699.0	1292.8	594.3
Import	nil	78.6	265.6	341.1
Total	698.2	1777.6	1558.4	935.4

, It is observed that volume of informal border trade exceeds several times the official volume of import-export trade. The total trade during 1993-94 was estimated at Rs. 22,000 million as against Rs. 4435 millions of the official trade (Lahkar, 1998). The situation in Indo-Bangladesh border is also not different from that of Indo-Myanmar trade. The volume of illegal export to Bangladesh through the borders of West Bengal, Assam and Tripura was estimated at Rs. 11,650 millions which again exceeds the volume of official export to that country of Rs. 10,500 millions in 1992-93. This indicates the enormous potential for Indian exports to Myanmar and Bangladesh and therefore, an introspection with regard to border trade policies with neighbouring countries is of paramount importance. Further, the role and importance of border trade for the growth of NER's economy has intrinsic and instrumental value. Side by side the demand structure of the neighbouring countries and production and resource structure of NE states have to be studied in order to find out whether the trade is complementary or competitive. Other important issues to be studied include volume of official export-import trade, nature of trade flows, commodity structure and trade agreements.

Illegal Border Trade

An international border of 5211 kms are stretched across the seven NE states. Of this 1 596 kms are shared with Bangladesh, 1640 kms with Myanmar, 800 kms with Bhutan and 1175 kms with Tibet (China). Inaccessible terrain, stiff cliffs and thick jungles are the basic characteristics of most parts of the international borders under NER. In such inhospitable topogeographic conditions, combating smuggling is most hazardous. It is not easy to stop smuggling altogether along the borderline. A two-pronged strategy is required to curb this menace: i) anti-smuggling units of the custom equipped with anti-smuggling machinery to be located at strategic points along the border line; and ii) second line anti-smuggling units to be located in the hinterland equipped with information bank — the real nerve centre in this regard. Optimum use of Custom resources and combating the drug menace should be given priority. Due to the proximity of the region to the Golden Triangle in Myanmar and Thailand, drugs have assumed an alarming proportion in the region. Massive Anti-Drug Operations should be regularly undertaken by the Customs for the seizure of drugs and also for destruction of illicit cultivation of opium poppy and cannabis. The narcotics seizure by Customs is shown in Table 6.3.

TABLE 6.3

Narcotics Seizure by Customs

	1995-96	*1996-97*	*1997-98 (upto Oct.)*
Ganja (kg)	7514	3093	8081
Heroin (g)	3458	223	1735
Others (lit)	—	—	2160 (Codeine phosphate solution

The letter and spirit of the legalized border trade between India and Myanmar had been reduced to a farce because of the powerful businessmen- politicians nexus. The case of onion is a case in point. Despite the fact that Myanmar nationals are selling onion at Moreh as cheap as Rs. 5 a kg , the shops of Manipur have been selling onion at Rs. 28 a kg. So also the tasty Manipur rice is sold at Rs. 12.50 a kg in Manipur whereas rice of such grade is sold at Rs. 9 a kg at Moreh - 109 km away from Imphal. The rice could be imported in terms of truckloads to stabilise price and ensure uninterrupted supply in the market. However, the proposal is not okayed for the large scale import of rice under legalized trade. In other words, the rice business is monopolised by a handful of traders.

TABLE 6.4

State-wise Trade on Export and Import for the Year 1997-98 (in Crores)

Meghalaya	*Assarn*	*Tripura*	*Manipur*	*Total*
Export				
80.77	**43.70**	**97.00**	**25.16**	**150.62**
Import				
37.55	**4.65**	**5.39**	**37.16**	**47.59**

Source: Commissionnerate Customs, Shillong.

Apart from rice, lentils and various kinds of beans and dried fish are available at Moreh at very cheap price. Government does not do anything for allowing the private traders. The legalized border trade has neither benefited the Government nor the people of Manipur in the real sense of the term. Besides, the state exchequer is not benefited much since most of the approved items for export- import have little demand. The items which have demand from Indian side are drugs, illegal weapons, gold, precious stones and electronic gadgets. But these items are not in the approved list and therefore, cannot be taxed. The official circles are keeping the revenue figures as closely guarded secrets since the tax collection does not satisfy the legalized border trade. These stark realities are, however, overlooked and illegal border trade is going on. The state-wise daily trade of export and import for the year 1997-98 is presented in Table 6.4.

Liberalisation of Border Trade

The decision of the SAARC nations to have regional trade liberalization by South Asian Free Trade Area (SAFTA) by the year 2001 will have positive implication in the economic prospects of NER of India (Barua, 1998). Under SAFTA by 2001, there has been significant rise of import from the neighbouring countries to India. (Table 6.2). With the liberalisation of the border trade, the activities like trade and commerce, banking and insurance services, transport and communication, warehousing facilities etc. will be increased in NER which in turn will accelerate the economic activities of the region.

However, in order to take the advantage of the liberalisation of border trade, the NE states have to take steps to improve the infrastructure facilities like transport and communication systems, banking and insurance sector, better warehousing service and even hotel facilities in the transit points. Further, for healthy growth of border trade social peace and immediate solution to the problem of insurgency is a must. The informal trade should be reduced through proper legalized trade policy.

Interestingly most of the consumer and electronic goods imported to the country are not produced in the countries from where these are imported. These are produced mainly in the industrialised countries like China, Japan, Singapore, South Korea etc. If the trade policy of India is liberalized to allow free import of consumer goods, the informal imports from the neighbouring countries will decline and this in turn will bring revenue for the country. Trade between India and Myanmar during 1997-98 was 255 million US dollars which was 19% more than the previous year. There is immense scope to diversify and broadbase cooperation in trade between the two countries. Myanmar is already seeking cooperation with India in the field of industry. So also new vistas are opened up in Indo-Bhutan cooperation which may be exploited to boost the economy of NER. Informal trade of all sorts including daily labours in most of the points of Indo-Bangladesh border should he stopped forthwith.

According to an estimate, NE states are loosing 1000 crores of rupees due to on going illegal trade along Indo-China and Indo.-Myanmar borders. In this context, the reopening of Still Well road which has a total length of 1 079 miles connecting two neighbouring countries - China and Myanmar will help to boost trade and to contain illegal trade along the borders of China and Myanmar. Since resumption of trade under barter mechanism, one acute problem relating to balance of payment has cropped up. It happens due to the policy of import first and export later. The imbalance trend of export and import upto December 1996 stand at Rs. 28,42,62,02/-= and Rs. 11,37,58,627/- respectively. This has to be properly looked into. After liberalisation of the economic policies, considerable impetus is received in this front. But trade is tremendously hampered for bottleneck of infrastructures.

Problems and Prospects

Infrastructure in terms of good road communication remains the major problem of trade from NE region to Bangladesh, Myanmar, Bhutan and China. All the roads leading to different Land Custom Stations are in deplorable conditions. Other infrastructural constraints are lack of weigh bridges, good dumping ground, truck parking place, drinking water facilities, electricity, medical and telecommunication facilities etc. in most of the Land Custom Station (LCS). Absence of warehouses and cold storage facilities pose serious problems for export of perishable commodities. Lack of coordination among various agencies relating to exports is another bottleneck. High cost of transportation, frequent disruption of communication due to natural calamities, law and order situation, insurgency etc. create numerous problems of border trade. Lack of awareness of export formalities, information and marketing strategies as well as banking facilities are also the major drawbacks for export from this region.

The roads from Karimganj to Sutarkandi LCS in Assam, Jowai-Dawki road in Meghalaya, Raghna Bazar in Tripura, Imphal to Moreh and Silchar in Manipur and Assam, Mon to Lungwa and Kohima to Ponkhungri and Molei in Nagaland, Habung in Lunglei district and Marpara in Aizawl districts of Mizoram and Zemithang in Tawang district of Arunachal Pradesh to the border of China and Bhutan need to be improved by widening and double laning (NH 39) to enable operationalisation of border trade with Myanmar, Bangladesh, China and Bhutan. A number of resource based products of NE region viz., mineral resources (coal, limestone, sillimanite, gypsum, china clay, oil and natural gas), agricultural resources (rice , pulses, oilseeds, maize, jute, potato, mesta), horticultural products (pineapple, banana, orange, papaya, lemon, arecanut, pears, plum, passionfruit, ginger, turmeric, chilies, cardamom, bayleaf, tomato, squash), forest resources (wood, cane, bamboo, medicinal herbs and plants), sericulture (eri, muga and mulberry silk), floriculture (orchids and other flowers), plantation products (tea. rubber) may be exported provided infrastructural facilities are created. Further, there has been enough scope to develop export oriented projects / industries such as coal and limestone based, petrochemical based, agro based, forest based, medicinal plants based, sericulture based, jute based, floriculture based horticulture based; and handloom and handicraft based. To encourage export, the Government of India has liberalized Export and Import Policy and simplified procedures. The Govt. has given the Export House status to AIDC (Assam) MIDC (Meghalaya). Export Promotion

Industrial Park is envisaged for even' state with 100% funding upto 15 crores by Central Govt. subject to 25% export commitment. To promote export of spices from NE region Spices Board in Guwahati has undertaken different schemes like developing drying yards for improving quality of spices, warehouse and cold storage facilities and training spices particularly of production of organic pepper and Bird Eye chilly.

Ministry of Commerce has also set up Agricultural Processing Export Development Authority (APEDA) office in Guwahati for providing market information, financial assistance for development of infrastructure such as cold storage and fright subsidy for export of agricultural and processed food products. An Inter-Ministerial Task Force (IMTF) under Ministry of Commerce has been set up to examine the trade opportunities and manufacturing potential for export in the region. As a part of the master plan for development of Guwahati airport, the Airport Authority of India (AAI) has planned a cargo terminal with all associated facilities. Studies have also-been taken up for transport optimization as well as transit and transshipment arrangement with Bangladesh, Bhutan and Myanmar. Economic and Social Commission for Asia and Pacific (ESCAP) has set up an expert working group to study the connectivity of NE states with Myanmar and Bangladesh. The development of an effective inland water transport system in the entire Brahmaputra river will facilitate the movement of export goods from Guwahati to Bangladesh at a lesser cost. The vast resources of NE region offer enormous opportunities of trade between the region and the neighbouring countries.

REFERENCES

Barua, S.N. (1998). Assam Tribune, Nov. 24

Lahkar, B.B. (1998). Shillong Times, Nov. 4

7

Border Trade and Associated Problems in North-East India

—N.N. Bhattacharyya

The region lying along the edge of a country is called borderland or frontier. It provides defence and permits exchange to occur. Every border consists of three zones, two of which are the periphery of the adjoining states and the third a central zone, known as borderland where there is mingling of the two countries. Generally the strong and wise countries show close ties between the border zones and the core areas. India's land border is about 17,700 km and of this length North-East India shares approximately 5200 km with China, Bhutan, Myanmar and Bangladesh. This Northeastern region of India is connected with the mainland by a narrow corridor of foot hill land of 32 km width through the northern part of West Bengal. Such terrestrial location of the region converts it into an isolated pocket and this is one of the important causes of the alienation of its population While the rest of India has direct access to the seas and the capital city of New Delhi for contact and trade, India's North-East is virtually sandwiched and land locked by Bhutan, China, Myanmar and Bangladesh.

The present Sino-Indian border is the product of Manchu Policy, Chinese Republican policy and British policy. This border in the eastern sector is 1,140 km long and it includes Bhutan foot hills, Arunachal Pradesh, major parts of Darrang and Sonitpur district of Assam. In 1962 China invaded this border area and claimed 5200 sq. km of border territory south of the McMohan Line. Forests provide main source of income and agriculture is limited in river valleys with rice as staple food. Now attempt has been made to harness the immense water potential for hydel generation. The cottage industries of Arunachal Pradesh include a number of exquisite items like carpets with Mahayana Buddhist motifs, handloom textiles, silver-smithy, scroll painting, intricate cane, bead and bamboo work, bell metal manufacture, wood carving, copper utensils etc. From time immemorial trade between the people of Arunachal Pradesh and Tibetan region, Bhutan and Assam was carried on through mountain passes or *duars*.

The border area of Nagaland, Manipur and Mizoram with Myanmar is peaceful and non-controversial. In this border the boundary line passes through deeply forested hilly areas, with Mizo hills, Manipur and Naga hills on the Indian sides and the Chin hills, Naga hills and Kachin state on the Myanmar side. This line was drawn by the British under the treaty of Yandaboo in 1826. Agriculture is practised on the shifting basis with rice as the main crop. With the development of hydropower, forest industries can be developed in this border region. Generally the trade with Myanmar takes place at Moreh (Manipur), Champhai (Mizoram) and Lungwa (Nagaland). A road connecting Imphal to Mandalay passes through Tamu, a town located on this border.

The border area of Meghalaya, Assam, Tripura and Mizoram is hilly. The length of the border is about 1500 km and covered with forests. Some hill slopes are used for tea and rice cultivation. Cotton, jute, sugarcane and potato are also grown. The region is rich in minerals like coal and limestone and horticultural products. Trade with Bangladesh generally takes place through the border points like Dawki, Bholaganj (Meghalaya), Karimganj, Steamarghat, and Sutarkandi (Assam) Manu, Agartala and Srimantapur (Tripura) etc.

The entire borderlands of India's Northeast is under developed and needs urgent attention of the government. The border lands of the region are very poorly served by railways and roads and the population density of the border areas is also low. Influx of illegal foreigners and smuggling across the border has been a common feature in many areas along the international border between Bangladesh and Assam and Meghalaya and between Myanmar and Manipur border. The trade between the states of North-East India and the above neighbouring countries runs into two broad channels, namely legal (Official export-import trade and official border trade) and illegal (unofficial or smuggling). Major items of export from India to Myanmar are cotton yarn, bicycles, horticultural products, drugs and pharmaceuticals and kerosene etc. and main items of import from Myanmar are blankets, electronic goods, gold, silver, precious stones, teak, food products. The main items of illegal trade are gold, synthetic fabrics electronic goods, narcotics, drugs etc. which are high in value and low weight. At present regular trade between The North Eastern States and the neighbouring countries flows with heavy restrictions. Recently the Commerce Ministry admitted that international border trade between the states of North East India and the neighbouring countries has declined (The Assam Tribune, December 1, 1998). The Myanmar Government took a decision to transact all border trade in US dollars with their exports, besides clamping restrictions on trade of certain commodities. It is confirmed by the Ministry that international border trade through Moreh in Manipur and Tamu in Myanmar had declined during the first half of the current financial year (1998-99), disclosing that export during the period was to the tune of Rs. 172.97 lakhs while import was in the order of Rs. 197.44 lakh. It is reported that the total export through Moreh-Tamu border was 2,531.25 lakh and import for Rs. 3,535.34 lakh in the financial year 1997-98. Now all the marketing centres located on the Manipur border in the township of Moreh have been shifted to the Myanmarese trading Centres in Tamu and

NORTH-EAST INDIA
(Showing Border Regions)

Figure 7.1. North-East-India (Showing Border Regions)

Namphleng. On the Volume of trade with Bangladesh through Jowai-Alarem-Dawki has increased and it was revealed that the total exports were of the order of Rs. 1992.48 lakh, While imports (official) were nil in 1997-98. The trader through this road, specially the coal exporters to Bangladesh face the problem of infrastructural bottlenecks due to bad condition of the road.

In order to boost trade with neighbouring countries and to certain illegal trade along the border, Government should provide necessary infrastructural facility at different trade routes, establishment of railway linkages, free flow of road traffic, improvement of telecommunication links and most importantly free border trade in local produce. The international borders in Northeastern region have been viewed as liabilities and as such many old border roads like Stillwell Road had been closed. This road has a total length of 1726 km and connects China and Myanmar. It ran from Ledo to Pangsau Pass (Myanmar) 60 km, Pangsau pass to Wanling at Mongyu 690 km and Wanling to Kumming 976 km (China). The decision on this project was taken in October 1942 during Second World War and construction work started on December 10,1942 with active co-operation of four persons namely General War Covell and Major General Lewis A. Pick. The road was completed on Feb. 11, 1945. A comprehensive effort may be taken to open the Stillwell road. Once the road is opened, then entire trade of the region would take a new shape and relations with the neighbouring countries would improve. Some flourishing tourist shops, hotels and restaurants would be developed near the crossing points of the two neighbouring states. But such interactions are possible only along an international boundary that marks the line of sovereignty between two friendly countries.

The most important geopolitical premise about North East India is its location and its entire economy is a closed one. The isolated location of the region appears to be standing on the way of industrialisation and hence the Government of

India must offer additional incentives for starting industries in all the states of North East India by formulating a separate industrial policy for the region. Since prospects of large and medium industries appearing remote under the prevailing conditions, the focus has to shift to the promotion of cottage and various tiny industries along with other avenues like fostering of border trade and commence with the neighbouring countries of Bhutan, China, Myanmar and Bangladesh. The recent development of Guwahati airport, establishment of customs clearance, export-import banking and other infrastructural facilities would definitely go a long way in economic development of the region and its neighbouring countries.

8

Infrastructure Improvement for Enhancement of Border Trade in the North-East India: Policy Perspective and Issues

—Dulal Bhuyan

North Eastern Region of India (NER) comprised of seven states of Assam, Meghalaya, Arunachal Pradesh, Manipur, Tripura, Nagaland and Mizoram. As per 1991 census, the NER had a total population of 31.147 million in a land area of 255.5 lakh hectres. At the time of Independence except Manipur and Tripura, the other five states were a single state of Assam.

The N.E. India is surrounded by foreign countries in the four sides, China and Bhutan in the north, Burma in the east and Bangladesh in the south and in the west. The NER is connected to the mainland of India with a narrow strip of land in the west through Bengal.

Physiographically, the area may be grouped into two natural divisions—Hills and Mountains—cover about one fourth of the area and rest is plains and alluvium deposits. The area is extensively dissected by two main river systems, the Brahmaputra and the Surma. The entire regions experience heavy seasonal rainfall, rich in forest and forest based resources and favourable for cultivation of varieties of crops, throughout the year.

Different types of crops — paddy, jute, mastard sugarcane, tea, rubber, fruits like apple, banana, orange etc. are cultivated based on local conditions. Because of the undulating topography, and heavy rainfall and ice capped mountain in the north, the NER has a high potential for hydel power development. As per assessment of the Central water and Power commission, the NER has a hydel power development potential of 14 million Kwt; of which about 1.00 per cent is exploited so far. Some of the mineral resources found in the NER-are coal in Meghalaya, Assam, Arunachal, Tripura, and Nagaland; Limestone in Assam, Meghalaya, Arunachal Pradesh, Nagaland, Manipur; Chilimunarite in Meghalaya.

Other potential biotic/abiotic resources are fish and fisheries in the rivers and marshy land, live stock, and sericulture.

The NER is one of the least developed regions of the country; of the total population, in 1991 census, only 16.13 per cent were living in 195 urban settlements and rest were in 37,788 villages, scattered in the plains and hills.

Primary sector still dominates the economy, about, 3/4th of the work force are engaged in the agriculture. In 1983-84, at current prices, sectoral distribution of Net state Domestic Product in the NER were primary sector — 60.9 per cent (against Indian average 38.4%); secondary sector 12.3 per cent (22.6%) and teritiary sector 26.8 per cent (39.0%). Over the years tertiary sector has been playing important role to the regional economy.

Although, lion's share of the work force are engaged in agriculture, still the region is not self-sufficient in agricultural production. Industrially this is one of the most backward regions of the country. Only limited number of heavy and medium scale industries have come up mostly in Assam (80%) Nagaland (10.4%) and in Arunachal. The type of industries are tea, plywood, oil refinery, jute, petrochemical, paper industry and fertilizer. Some agro-based and Forest based small sector industry have come up and scattered in different states, about half in Assam, followed by Tripura, and Manipur.

Mainly, trading items produced in surplus in the NER are tea, coal, forest products, and betal nuts. Although the region has a long heritage on sericulture and horticulture that has not been developed with modern input, to the full potential. The NER is still far below the all India Index on Basic Infrastructure mainly, road, transport and communication, and power.*

With this back ground, let us discuss the border trades the NER with the neighbouring countries.

Throughout the history, the economy of the NER, is based on agriculture and allied activities. In pre-British days, the ideal village economy in Assam was one of (so also the NER) self-sufficiency. Every family provided for itself by agriculture and craft all the requirements of daily life (Borpujari, H.K. 1993, quoted from, Mills, "Observation"). Trade is mainly confined to agriculture and animal produce following barter system, exchanged for foreign salt. Some luxury items mainly for higher classes mostly in upper Assam were also included in the list of items. However after the British occupation trade in modern line has been opened up. "Hats" have been arranged adjacent to the Sadar stations, where in neighbouring villagers participated. The items were, Assamese cloths, cotton and muga thread, coarse rice, pulse, turmeric, ginger, chillies, mustard oil, tobacos, and opium. This was the secnario in 1880's and mainly concerned with internal trades. These hats were subsequently extended to different parts adjacent to the tea gardens also. With the development of tea gardens, urban centres were emerged as a result of seat of administration.

By the close of the nineteenth century, shops have come up in the convenient transport heads — "streams and roads" and 'hats' in the interiors formed the local centres for the collection of exports and distribution of imports.

Since the process of economic diversification had been set in to, along with the British occupation; mainly due to tea cultivation, jute cultivation, exploitation of forest and mineral resources — coal and oil and construction of road, railways, and improvement of steamer services. By the close of the 19th Century, trading of commodities have been integral part in the production, imposed on the self sufficient ideal village economy. Principal items of imports to Assam (greater) included: coal, cotton twist and yarn, piece goods (European), gram and pulse, rice (husked) liquor, brass, copper and other metals, iron, salt, sugar, opium, tobacco, woolen-goods. Major articles of exports were — tea, oilseeds, cotton (raw), jute (raw), silk (manufactured), timber, bamboos, coal and coke, lime, betal-nut, oranges. By and large these items were remain same till the time of independence.

Merchants from Dhaka collected the local produced in exchange of foreign articles, food staff, and business. In the Brahmaputra valley, people from Rajasthan controlled the trade while in Khasi Hills, by the Khasis, in Naga Hills by the Angamis; changsil, was the trading place between the Mizos of Mizoram and Silchar.

Bhutias and their neighbours, during winter, came down to plains, through the duars, or the 'pass' to sale the items like rock salt, gold dust, musk, woollen, yak tails, Chinese silk, and purchase clothes, raw silk thread, rice , dried fish, etc. The Mishimis, perceed as middle man between Kochin and China, bartered salt, woollens, ivory, copper, gold, amber, honey and mishmi-teeta. Major centres were Sadiya and Beesa. The Bhutias came by the routes-Bijni, Sidli, Ripu and Goma leading to Goalpara, Darrang passes to Kamrup. The trade and fair centres were Udalguri, Ghagrapara, Daimara, Daranga, Subankhata in Kamrup.

The Kaupos or the Khampas carried out trades to the Tibet, across Bhutan and Tawang through two passes, Dhaini and Udalguri.

Assam Manipur, trade was carried by two routes through Cachar and Kohima, Cattlers were imported from Burma via Manipur. Trade out lets from Assam was also through Surma valley—items expected were tea, jute, mastard; from the Chittagong hill kerosene was imported to the Surma Valley.

Almost the entire trade of Assam was with Bengal — from Calcutta; Export markets were at Dacca, Narayanganj, Mymensing. In early days of British occupation trade is mainly carried by steamers and boats and later by the Railways. After opening of Assam Bengal Railways and hill section, Chittagong port has been major exporting centre. Increase in trade and commerce in Bengal led to emergence of the wealthy middle class, of the tests and Basaks, the people in the vallyes of Assam lived and died as an agricultural community. The process of drainage of vast resource of the province thus began, continued, without any break, till our own time. (Barpujari, P. 128, 1993).

Till the time of Independence of the country, the trades etc. continued in this line; only the plains of the N.E., the mineral resources, the forest resources have been the focus of attention of the British. Especially the tea, and jute have been the major producing items. The NER has been producing raw materials like jute, cotton, mustard, crude oil and coal and timber; to support the production and transportation as desired by the colonial power, rail road, motor road and navigation ways have been developed in a coordinated manner. Calcutta has been developed as an major Industrial and trading centre, Dhaka and Chittagaon were the major ports connected by road and rail and navigation. Hill areas by and large relatively isolated, except Shillong, which was remained developed by the British; otherwise other Hill settlements remained undisturbed.

However, after the independence, the NER lost its importance due to lack of strong policy initiatives; the Border trades virtually officially closed with Bangladesh, and Burma. However illegal trades continued; of late, in the nineties, the area was come to the focus again.

The NER has vast potential for border trades with Bhutan and China, Myanmar and Bangladesh, and some of the ASEAN countries like Thailand, Combodia etc., if special facilities are created. The NER has the following scope.

1. The NER may act as transit zone between trades with Indian mainland and with neighbouring countries,
2. The NER may produce items those have demand in the neighbouring countries. This may be in two sectors — manufacturing sector and farming sector. Export oriented-Industrial zone may be developed in the selected urban centres-; Action in this line is already initiated at Guwahati, may be taken up in Agartala, Imphal, Aizawl, Tinsukia, Dimapur, Silchar.

Items produced traditionally — in the textiles sector like silk cloth, woolen and warm clothes and other industrial products — like brass metal, etc. should be upgraded with modern input like technology, design and management.

In the farming sector too the NER has vast potential to produce in abundance food items, spices, fruits, vegetables, in hills and plains and may be exported; tea, coffee, jute, rubber, and other cash crops may be cultivated in new areas.

The major border routes and centres may be developed:

(1) With Bhutan and China through Assam are (a) Sarbhang-Seralapara, (b) Deosri Gelekphu (c) Guwahati-Rangia-Darranga-Derthang (d) Udalguri.

(2) With China through Assam-Arunachal Pradesh-a) Tezpur-Bomdila-Tawang (b) N. Lakhimpur-Daparijo-Nasa (c) Jonai-Pashighat-Shimong Ninggning (d) Sadiya-Mekha Avini-Bruini, (e) Sadiya-Mekha Malunil-Tajobum (f) Sadiya-Tezu-Chirangla-Kahao.

(3) With Burma through Assam and Arunahcal (a) Tinsukia-Winstong- Mogoung (b) Khonsa-Wakha.

(4) With Burma through Assam and Nagaland-(a) Nazira-Mon-Clieu (b) Jorhat-Mokokchug-Terçusang-Poveyn (c) Dimapur-Kohima-Jessami-Laruri.

(5) With Burma through Manipur—a) Imphal-Ukhrul-Saipaw, b) Imphal-Ukhrul-Kamjong-Moluailup-Homalino, c) Imphal-Kampang-Mintha, d) Imphal-Moreh-Tamu-Paung.

(6) With Burma through-Mizoram and Assam—a) Silchar-Aizawl-Champhai-Tiddim.

(7) Trade with Bangladesh through Mizoram—a) Lungle-Demagiri-Rangamatti-Chittagong.

(8) Trad with Bangladesh-through Tripura-a) Agartala-Comilla-Laksham-Noakhali, b) Udaipur-Sabrum-Ramgargh-Chittagong, c) Kamalpur-Kammalganj.

(9) Trade with Bangladesh through Meghalay on-a) Shillong-Dawki-Sylhet-Commilla-Dhalua b) Tura -Burengapara-Baghmara-Durgapur-Nasirabad-Dhaka.

(10) Trade with Bangladesh-through Assam and Meghalaya-a) Guwahati-Mankachar-Bengunbari-Dhaka b) Karimganj-Syllet-c) Karimganj-Silua-Kamalgonj-Comilla-Chittagong-Cox's Bazar.

These routes may be developed in a planned manner. Priority should be given to the route already having better facilities and needs minimum improvement and have highest potential. Some of these routes are—(1) Chittagong-Dhaka-Mankachar-Guwahati (2) Guwahati-Ranjya-Darranga-Dewanagiri-Tashingang Dzong-Byakar Dzong (3) Tezpur-Bomdila-Tawang (4) Tinsukia-Sadiya-Mekha-Bruini (5) Tinsukia-Lisok-Mogang (6) Jorhat-Mokokchung-Twnsang-Koklak-Ponyn (7) Nagaon-Dimapur-Kohima-Imphal-Moreh-Tamu-Paungbyin (8) Silchar-Aizawl-Champhai-Tiddin (9) Aizawal-Lungle-Dewuagiri-Rangamati-Chittagong (10) Silchar-Karimganj-Comilla, 11) Guwahati-Shillong-Dawki-Jayamitiapur-Sylhet-Comilla (12) Tura-Burlugapara-Nashirabad.

Infrastructure to be created in the trading centres: trade information centre, exhibition hall for trade items , customs clearance centre, transport and communication, warehouse, hotels, insurance provision, currency exchange centre in selected towns etc.

However, to improve the regional economy and to sustain it, the infrastructure may be improved the traditional sector of farming and manufacturing in the NER, where the local people are directly involved may be upgraded. The NER is poorly developed in all aspect of infrastructure in comparison to the all India average. Now the changing sc-enario of liberalisation of Indian economy, regional trade liberalisation among SAARC countries, land locked nature of the foreign countries proximity to NER-all have added advantage to flourish border trade through the NER.

Govt. of India should formulate an integrated boarder trades improvement policy-specially for the NER including man power development (entrepreneurship), developing trade information centre in specific urban centres, having trade information on domestic and foreign countries, Improvement of single window facilities for government rules regulations and clearance.

Planning commission, state planning board of the States of the NER, NEC should evolve combined policy and create fund for promotion of border trades. Border Trade Promotion

Council may be set up within NEC under joint initiative of Central Govt. and State Govts. of the NER.

Considering the specific natural advantage and traditional production, export oriented production complex may be developed in manufacturing and farming and allied sectors within the NER, otherwise with all potential to flourish its economy, the NER will remain economically a backward area having rich natural and mineral resource.

REFERENCES

1. *Assam Tribune,* Vol. 60. No. 319, Nov. 24, 1998 "A Report in Liberalisation of border trade to boost NE Economy".
2. Barpujari, H.K., *The Comprehensive History of Assam,* Volume, V, Publication Board Assam, 1993.
3. *Basic Statistics of North Eastern Region,* 1995; North Eastern Council, Shillong, 1995.
4. Jhingan, M.L., *The Economics of Development and Planning,* Konark Publishers Pvt. Ltd. Delhi, 1990.
5. North-Eastern States-(Map), A MAP's Publication, Madras, 1984.

9

Exports from North-Eastern Region: Potential and Problems

—M.K. Mero

Introduction

The legacy of partition of the erstwhile Indian sub-continent and the emergence of national boundaries has placed the seven N.E. States in a geographically isolated, land-locked region without having the natural harbour or sea ports. This locational disadvantage coupled with poor infrastructural facilities within the N.E. Region as a whole has led to a situation where each one of the seven states is looking more to the neighbouring countries than to mainland India for economic relations. On the other hand, lack of infrastructural facilities and the slow pace of industrialisation have constrained the scope for promoting exports to neighbouring countries from the region to any significant extent. However, with the globalisation of economic as well as the emphasis on regional cooperation among the SAARC countries under SAPTA agreement, a ray of hope have emerged for the people of the region. The proposed move towards the establishment of South Asian Free Trade Association by the year 2001 has the potential to give a tremendous boost to the export oriented growth of the N.E. Region. Border Trade is expected to get impetus.

Present Seenario of Exports

Present export from the region by and large consists of

traditional and primary products like tea, spices, fresh fruits, minerals, agricultural products, plywood, cement and other chemical and allied products, petrochemical products and a few engineering items. Besides these, some firms have set up bamboo processing units for export of bamboo products under Export Promotion Capital Goods Scheme.

(1) *Tea:* Tea remains India's single largest traditional item and most of the export is from Assam. It account for estimated amount of Rs. 6920 crore during 1996-97.

(2) *Spices:* Species like ginger, dry chillies form a major component of export products from North Eastern Region. In the absence of any established processing units for the species, only the unprocessed spices are exported by road mostly to Bangladesh.

(3) *Plywood:* Another traditional item of export is plywood mainly from Arunachal Pradesh. However, due to the recent checks on deforestation and movement of timber by Supreme Court Order, the North Eastern Region has lost the edge in the export of commercial plywood.

(4) *Minerals:* Coal and limestone have become the major component of export particularly from the state of Meghalaya and Assam since 1992 after coal has been decanalised and decontrolled. It is exported mostly to Bangladesh and Nepal.

(5) *Fresh Fruits:* Fresh fruits like oranges, citrus, pears, grapes and apples are being exported mostly to Bangladesh through various Land Custom Stations. Though there are few fruit processing units set up by various states and organisation like NERAMAC, the export of processed fruits in different forms remains by and large negligible.

(6) *Handicraft and Handloom:* The North Eastern Region possessed variety of handicraft and handloom products. However, this sector remain unorganised apart from various State Co-operative Societies, cane furniture, handloom shawls,

brasswares, decorative items made of wood and bamboo are some of the items which are being exported but through Export House located at Calcutta and Delhi. This is mainly because of lack of facilities and infrastructure coupled with total ignorance or export formalities by the local populace.

The state-wise export and import data for the year 1997-98 is shown in the Annexure-I.

Present Scenerio of Border Trade: Border Trade between India and Myanmar was formalised through signing of India-Myanmar Border Trade Agreement on January, 21, 1994 and operationalised on April 12, 1995 through Moreh Border (Manipur). The second designated Border Trade Point at Champhai (Mizoram) is yet to operationalise as there is no positive response from Myanmar side. India has no formal Border trade Agreement with Bangladesh so far. However, considerable amount of Border Trade is taking place between Bangladesh and 3 N.E. States of Meghalaya, Assam and Tripura either through authorised Custom Check Post or on an informal basis.

Border Trade in Moreh is regulated through 2 gates. Gate-1 is for the movement of goods as per the Export Import Policy of the Government. Trade is allowed to be conducted in freely convertible currencies or in currencies mutually agreed upon by the two countries including counter trade. Grade-2 is primarily meant for Barter Trade and is regulated by D.G.F.T. Notification (No. 289 (PN)/92-97 dated 10.4.95) and R.B.I. (A.D. Circular No. 8 dated 17.5.97) as well as the Custom Notification which allows exchange of locally produced goods for personal consumption exclusively by residents staying within 40 KM either side of the Border. Currently 22 Items are permitted for exchange. These are (1) Mustard/Rape Seed (2) Pulses and Beans (3) Fresh Vegetables (4) Fruits (5) Garlic (6) Onion (7) Chillies (8) Species (9) Bamboo (10) Minor Forest products excluding Teak (11) Betel Nuts and Leaves (12) Food items for local consumption (13)

Tobacco (14) Tomato (15) Reed Broom (16) Sesame (17) Resin (18) Corriander Seeds (19) Soyabean (20) Roaster Sunflower Seeds (21) Katha (22) Ginger (23) Any other commodities as may be mutually agreed upon between the two sides.

Resource Based Products of North Eastern Region

(i) *Mineral Resources:* Coal, Limestone, Granite, Sillimanite, Gypsum, China Clay, Oil & Natural Gas etc.

(ii) *Agricultural Products:* Rice, Pulses, Oilseeds, Maize, Jute, Potato, Tomato, Mesta, Betelnuts, Squash etc.

(iii) *Species:* Ginger, Turmeric, Chillies, Garlic, Black Pepper, Coriander, Cardamom, Cumin, Tezpat.

(iv) *Horticulture Products:* Pineapple, Banana, Orange, Papaya, Lemon, Aricanut, Pears, Plum, Passion Fruit, Guava etc.

(v) *Forest Resources:* Wood, Cane, Bamboo and variety of aromatic, medicinal herbs and plants.

(vi) *Sericulture:* Eri, Muga and Mulberry Silk.

(vii) *Floriculture:* The region has variety of Orchids and other flowers.

(viii) Water Resources for Hydro Power Generation.

(ix) Tea and Rubber Plantation.

(x) Fishery.

Projects Which can be Developed for Export Purpose

(i) Coal and limestone based industries.

(ii) Natural Gas based projects.

(iii) Petrochemical based projects.

(iv) Granite based projects.

(v) Agro based projects.

(vi) Forest based projects.

(vii) Medicinal Plant and Herbal based projects.

(viii) Silk based projects.
(ix) Jute based projects.
(x) Floricultural projects.
(xi) Food particularly Organic food products.
(xii) Pisciculture and Acquaculture.
(xiii) Horticulture based projects.
(xiv) Rubber based project.
(xiv) Pharmaceutical and Engineering Products.
(xv) Handloom and Handicraft Products.
(xvi) Hydro Projects.
(xvii) Ancilliary and Cottage Industries.

Present Export Promotion Measures

(i) Apart from the liberalisation of Export and Import Policy and simplification of procedure, the present Exim Policy with a view to promote export from North East has introduced double weightage for calculation of FOB/NFE for the purpose of recognition of Export House, Trading House etc. for export of goods manufactured in N.E. States. Besides, 1% additional special Import Licence shall be granted for the export of products manufactured and exported from N.E. States provided the export of these products is more than 10%.

(ii) With a view to encourage export, the Govt. has given the Export House Status to the designated State Corporation like AIDC (Assam), MIDC (Meghalaya), without any export performance which entitles them Special Import licence for export made by them.

(iii) To encourage the industries for setting up of manufactured export products, Export Promotion Industrial Park is envisaged for every states with 100% funding upto 15 crores by Central Govt. Subject to 25% export commitment. Export Promotion Industrial Park is already underway in the states of Assam and Meghalaya. Industrial Growth Centre is being set up in each state which will provide integrated infrastructure to the Industrial units located in the centre.

(iv) In order to develop and promote export of spices from North Eastern Region, Spices Board in Guwahati has been carrying out various schemes like developing Drying Yards for improving the quality of spices, warehouse and cold storage facility, scheme for production of organic pepper, varietal improvement of Bird Eye Chilly as well as various training programme.

(v) Ministry of Commerce has also set up Agricultural Processing Export Development Authority Office in Guwahati this year in order to provide market information, financial assistance for development of infrastructure like cold storage and freight subsidy for export of agricultural and processed food products.

(vi) An Inter-Ministerial Task Force under Ministry of Commerce has been set up to examine the trade opportunities and manufacturing potential for export in the Region. In addition, Airport Authority of India has planed a Cargo Terminal with all associated facilities as a part of the master plan for development of Guwahati Airport. To conduct a transport optimisation, a study is also underway, with a view to examining international linkages as well as transit and transshipment arrangement between countries like Bangladesh, Bhutan, and Myanmar. Besides, Economic and Social Commission for Asia and the Pacific (ESCAP) has set up an expert working group to study the connectivity of North Eastern Region with Myanmar and Bangladesh.

Export Potential From North Eastern Region

A recent study conducted by Indian Institute of Foreign Trade *(IIFT) shows very high volume of informal trade or illegal trade with neighbouring countries. It has estimated at around Rs. 600 crore value per annum in terms of export from assam, Meghalaya and Tripura to Bangladesh* and with Myanmar through Moreh

(Manipur) and Champhai (Mizoram) and Lungwa in Nagaland is estimated at Rs. 2000 per annum. This large volume of informal or illegal trade is a matter of concern. At the same time, it also shows the export potential of the North Eastern Region.

Problems of Export from North Eastern Region

1. *Infrastructure:* Lack of infrastructure, particularly good road communication remains the main problem for export from North Eastern Region to Bangladesh and Myanmar. All the export facilitating roads leading to various Land Custom Stations are in deplorable condition. Lack of weigh bridges, dumping ground, truck parking space in the various Land Custom Stations is another problem. In addition to this, most of the Land Custom Stations located in the border area are without facilities like drinking water, electricity, medial and tele-communication facilities. Absence of warehouses and cold storage facilities remain the problem for the exporters of perishable items.

2. Due to the slow pace of industrial develpment in North Eastern Region, the export of manufacture items remains by and large negligible.

3. Absence of coordinated efforts of various agencies and departments relating to exports is another factor.

4. Lack of awareness of export formalities, information and marketing strategy are also the major drawbacks for export from the region.

5. Export from this region through the main land faces numerous problems like high cost of transportation frequent disruption of communication arising out of natural calamities, law and order situation etc.

Suggestions for Promotion of Border Trade

(i) All the 7 North Eastern States having a long border

with neighbouring countries particularly Bangladesh and Myanmar are natural market for the region. Therefore, it is important to emphasize the development of border villages and towns into trade centres. Road communication, drinking water, electricity, medical, telecommunication facilities, restaurant, motels, tourist lodges has to be developed so as to facilitate export oriented industries to come up for marketing in the neighbouring countries.

The state-wise export facilitating roads which require to be developed on priority basis:

(a) *Assam:* The road from Karimganj to Sutarkandi Land Custom Station should be improved and widen so as to facilitate export of goods smoothly.

(b) *Meghalaya:* (A) The 52 km. stretch Jowai-Amlarem-Dawki road as well as the link road Jowai-Amlarem-Dawki (B) road and bridges from Nangal-bibra to Gasuapara LCS (C) Widening of the present border road in Borsora (LCS) area for commercial use.

(c) *Tripura:* Integrated development of infrastructure in Akhaura (LCS) in Agartala including widening of road, dumping and truck parking facility space near the check post. 24 km. road improvement in Old Raghna Bazaar LCS.

(d) *Manipur:* Improvement and double laning of the NH 39 which connects Imphal to Moreh and Silchar.

(e) *Nagaland:* Widening of road from Mon of Lungwa (proposed trade centre), and 143 km. road from Kohima to Ponkhungri and Molei to enable operationalisation of border trade with Myanmar.

(f) *Mizoram:* Champhai in Mizoram corresponding to Rih in Myanmar as the second route in border trade agreement is yet to be operationalised. Road improvement is almost complete. To facilitate arrangements relating to border trade with Myanmar, the Ministry of Commerce has sanctioned a sum of Rs. two crores for construction of a composite building in Zhakawthar a new border township. Habung (Demagiri) in Lunglei District and Marpara in Aizawl District are required to be developed as border trade route with Bangladesh.

(g) *Arunachal Pradesh:* Road from Zemithang (Tawang Dist.) to the border of China and Bhutan need to be developed for border trade.

All the above roads are commercially viable and these roads should be designated as exports corridor and be accorded the highest priority by the planners in matters of funding.

(ii) Besides the development of an effective Inland Water Transport for passenger as well as cargo traffic in the entire Brahmaputra riverine routes is essential. This will facilitate the movement of goods from Guwahati via Dhubri to Calcutta Port as well as to Bangladesh at a lesser cost.

(iii) It is also important for the government to pursue vigorously with neighbouring countries to accord transhipment and transit facilities for the exporters of the region of an early date.

(iv) There is also need for Nodal Agency by setting up of Trade Development Authority for N.E. Region as well as a permanent Trade Exhibition Centre in Guwahati for marketing of North Eastern products.

(v) As suggested in the study conducted by IIFT Export Development Wing may also be created under the aegis of NEC headed by Trade Advisor for organising Export Entrepreneurship developing programme, commissioning of market studies in the neighbouring countries and for overall development of export infrastructure.

(vi) It is also suggested for a more policy incentives in the export-import policy for the exporters of the region (majority of which are small exporter) so as to induce the exporters to route their exports through banking channel or regular trade.

(vii) The State Govt. should formulate the policy for export promotion. It is suggested that a Board of Trade may be constituted as an advisory institution for export promotion in each state. In addition a post of Export Commissioner or Director of Export Promotion should be created to coordinate the export related activities in the state.

(viii) A special package of incentives may also be provided to promote export oriented industries in the region such as transport subsidies, exemption from levy of sale tax and octroi on indigenous raw materials for industries manufacturing export products by the State Govts.

(ix) In addition, to achieve export-led rapid industrialisation, the Govt. of India may give serious consideration of declaring the N.E. Region as an Export Promotion Zone by extending all incentives and facilities to attract investment in the region as suggested in the study of on industrial development and export potential of the N.E. Region conducted by IIFT.

(x) For enhancing in the Indo-Myanmar Border Trade it is necessary to increase the basket of exchangeable goods and further liberalisation of bilateral trade. Early steps may be taken to open Border Trade through Mizoram and Nagaland routes. Further it is suggested for revival of Haat system as existed between Meghalaya and Bangladesh before the partition to elevate the socio-economic problem faced by the people in the border areas with Bangladesh.

ANNEXURE—I

State-Wise Trade on Export and Import for the Year 1997-98

	Meghalaya	*Assam*	*Tripura*	*Manipur*	*Total*
	Value (Rs.)	*Value (Rs.)*	*Value (Rs.)*	*Value (Rs.)*	*Value (Rs.)*
	1	2	3	4	5
Export	80,77,38,560.23	43,70,64,537.00	97,00,747.04	25,16,67,199.00	150,62,51,043.27
Import	37,55,443 01	4,65,96,608	5,39,38,731.90	37,16,39,991.00	47,59,30,773.91

Source: Customs House, Shillong.

10

The Nature of Border and Border Trade of Northeast India

—Zahid Husain

Introduction

Trade is a natural economic activity, it is transaction of goods/products or exchange of things for the purpose of earning and meeting needs. Trade is a flow of commodities from producers to consumers. The commodities can flow between persons, human groups and countries. The exchange of things can take place in kind and cash. If such exchange of goods is done on the international boundary line or in the vicinity of it by the people living there it is known as 'border trade'.

Border is a peripheral land of a country, adjacent to the international boundary. It can also be called a frontier. In fact, border is a relative term. Relative to the point from where it is looked at. For example, the entire Northeast is a border land in terms of India as a whole. But within the Northeast, the peripheral areas along the international boundary are considered as border. On the other side of the international boundary, contiguous to our border, lies the border zone of the neighbouring country. Therefore border is never a singular entity. It is always in context of the neighbour's border. It means borders of two neighbouring countries exist together.

The borders have their own natural environment, human

endowment, history, strategic importance and problems. Trade is bound to occur between people of two borders, for both the borders lie on the periphery of the respective country, far from the mainland or production centres. Therefore, the trade activity between people of adjacent borders helps them to get things of their requirement from each other. Owing to spatial proximity and socio-cultural relations, the economic linkages develop automatically for the mutual benefit of the people of the borders. Trade is a result of law of comparative advantage and exchange of relationships and goods between people having different modes of production. Such trade activities have been traditionally going on in most of the border areas of the world. However, various physical and human environmental conditions of the borders govern the intensity and nature of the traditional border trade practised there. And this is the main theme of the present paper. The paper is based on fieldwork, study of maps and information collected from books. In this connection the works of Allen et.al., (1979), Dalton (1960), Elwin (1959), Fisher (1978), Mackenzie (1979), Mukherjee (1992), Rutomji (1981) and others can be mentioned here.

In the strict sense, naturally occurring trade between the people of the borders is called border trade. Traditionally, this has been in operation in the North-eastern part of the Indian sub-continent from centuries at different levels and dimensions. A number of hats (market/fair centres) have emerged here in due course of time to carry-out border trade at higher levels and dimensions. Generally these hats have come up in the plains, especially in the Brahmaputra valley in front of the mountain passes, e.g., Udalguri. The indigenous border trade has been going on from centuries in the Northeast India. Of course, it has been influenced by the social, cultural, economic and political situation prevailing in the region. This trade can be called informal trade or done by the people themselves naturally. Whereas there is another type of trade, known as official trade, in which the enlisted commodities are exported and imported through the permitted gates, e.g., Moreh, Dawki, Karimganj etc. The central government is interested to open some more gates in Northeast India for such trade.

Types and Levels of Border Trade

Theoretically, the border trade can be of different types and it can take place at various levels and dimensions. The first and most important is the transaction of surplus goods, especially agricultural and horticultural products, between the people of two adjacent borders. This is done daily or at regular intervals at the suitable places on international boundary. In such cases, the boundary becomes 'a place of meeting' instead of 'a line of separation'. The people trade in the products produced by themselves with the people across the boundary line. They are permitted to sell and purchase goods by the guards on the boundary. The distance of the place of trade is usually within one day's march. This is real and basic border trade where barter is common. Such border trade occurs in the border areas of Assam, Meghalaya, and Tripura with Bangladesh. It is but natural, for people trade with the people living in close proximity to each other. This happens everywhere — in the mainland and on border of a country. The only difference is of an international boundary in the latter, and that makes it a border trade. Otherwise, this is almost similar to trade among people having different modes of production or living in different habitats (ecosystem).

The second level of border trade exists among the people of villages on both sides of the boundary line at more than one day's march. They also trade in goods produced by themselves in their respective habitats. Generally it takes place daily, but in weekly markets on borders as well. This is slightly higher level of border trade but with lesser frequency, and found almost in all border areas of the Northeast region.

The third level of border trade includes the sell and

purchase of those commodities, which are not only produced by the border people in their habitats but also at production centres in the mainland of their respective country. It means goods produced beyond the border area are also brought for sale. The place of transaction may lie beyond the border and trade is done once or twice a year at hat. Such trade used to take place at Udalguri, Sadiya, etc., which can be called transmountain flow of commodities. At smaller scale such goods can be sold in the second level of border trade mentioned above. In the third level of border trade even, people not living in border area may take part. Thus, the level and dimension of border trade goes higher but frequency is further reduced. Sometimes it may happen that the products and people involved in such trade are from far away places than the border. In such a situation the role of border dwellers become secondary. However, the level and amount of transaction is very high in this level of border trade, which is allowed by government to take place through the main trade routes. Various examples of such trade can be cited, but for lack of space. However, the above-cited books can be consulted for details. So these are the types and levels of border trade. In the strict sense, the author does not include the trade of commodities, which takes place through the border, in which people and goods are not from the border area. Hence, here border trade means trade of goods produced in the borders and sold by the people of the borders. It is simply inter-border trade. Even the intra-border trade is not part of it.

In contrast to the above the flow of goods across the border on a few routes is actually a case of 'international trade' in which goods produced far away from the border and even in foreign countries are involved. The border people are not main operators in it. This international trade can be of two types. In the first, the products of two neighbouring countries are traded. Whereas in the second the products of foreign countries are traded through the borders, e.g. Moreh, Champhai, Dawki, etc. The latter type of foreign trade does not help in the development of agricultural and industrial economy of the two neighbouring nations in general, and of the border areas in particular. A third party is actually benefited financially and industrially from such trade, e.g. Japan, South Korea etc. This trade is usually done unofficially, called smuggling. While in the first case a list of permitted items of export and import can be announced by the governments after mutual agreement, which definitely helps in the development of these countries.

The above-mentioned types of border trade and 'international trade' have been going on from centuries in the Northeast part of India. However, this paper discusses the nature of real border trade practised by the border people of the Northeast, and also the influence of the nature of border on the trade.

The Nature of Border

The nature of border is divided into physical and human. The physical nature includes the topography and location of the border. The discussion on nature of our border will remain inconclusive, if the nature of border of adjacent country is not taken into consideration. Understanding about nature of border is significant because it influences the nature, magnitude, extent and degree of border trade.

To understand the nature of border, it is necessary to start with formation of external boundaries of this region, which led to ultimate creation of borders. Frankly speaking, formation of North-eastern border of India is a geographical, historical and cultural legacy. Geographical in the sense of its location and topography. Location wise this region happens to be on the periphery of the Indian sub-continent itself where the orientation and extent of mountain ranges and river valleys have helped in making it a geographical region. From historical point of view formation of its external boundaries is the result of different historical events. Whereas the racial, ethnic and cultural traits of the people make it a separate region. These are result of assemblage and miscegenation of racial and cultural elements in the crucible of Northeast India under the influence of various human migrations through this corridor. All these have given rise to a unique region having well integrated but diverse physiographic units, number of ethnic groups, varied cultures and typical economies.

The North-eastern part of India became a 'land locked' or 'blocked land', in course of time, due to formation of historical Indo-Bhutan boundary, Indo-Burma boundary in 1826, Indo-Tibet in 1914 and Indo-Pak boundary in 1947 (subsequently turned into Indo-Bangladesh border in 1972). The 'land locked' situation can be understood by the fact that 98% of its boundary is international, touching neighbouring countries, viz., Bhutan, Tibet, Myanmar and Bangladesh. Only a narrow belt of land connects the region with the rest of India. This piece of land can be called 'umbilical cord' (though popularly known as Siliguri neck) because the role it plays in the joining the Northeast region with rest of India. The 'umbilical cord' has only 2% of the total boundary of the Northeast. In the beginning it is about 65 km wide on the Assam-Bengal boundary. This 'umbilical cord' narrows down and passes through the Siliguri neck, which is 23 km broad between the international boundaries of Nepal and Bangladesh. On the other side, one of the southern points of the Northeast region is hardly 25 km away from the Bay of Bengal. The lack of infrastructural facilities has enhanced the isolation. All these put the region in a very sensitive, strategic and economic situation. Due to it, the people of the Northeast in general and of its border in particular are directly or indirectly compelled to maintain the traditional trade relations across the boundary for their subsistence and survival

About 29.44% of boundary of India run on land. About one third of which lies in Northeast region. Interestingly, the total length of international boundary of the Northeast region is 5211 km, i.e., 98 % of total boundary. Out of about 1596 km long boundary is with Bangladesh (touching Assam, Meghalaya, Mizoram and Tripura), 1640 km is with Myanmar (along boundaries of Arunachal Pradesh, Manipur, Mizoram and Nagaland), 800 km is with Bhutan (meeting Assam and Arunachal Pradesh) and 1175 km is with Tibet Autonomous Region of China (touching Arunachal Pradesh). A 65 km long boundary, i.e., 2 % only, running along the state boundary between Assam and West Bengal joins the region with the rest of India. The Siliguri neck lies further west because of international jigjawsaw boundaries of Bangladesh. Otherwise, the Brahmaputra Valley is 100 km wide in the west where it merges in the vast plains of the Ganga River. Therefore, a transit route through the Bangladesh is a necessity of the Northeast. A recent news item (The Hindustan Times, 30.7.99) indicates that the government of Bangladesh has permitted a road transit to India. This transit will connect the western side of the region for easy transport of goods from one part of India to another. It is suggested that India should also request Bangladesh to agree to a road transit to Bay of Bengal either from Tripura or Mizoram which are hardly at 50 km distance from the sea, especially the Chittagong port. If this transit comes into existence, the land-locked condition of the Northeast region will be removed to some extent.

Now we come to discussion on physiographic nature of borders. Here, it is noted with a sense of dismay and surprise that accurate data on length of international boundaries of 'Seven Sisters' is not available. Therefore, here only nature of border is discussed. The Assam-Bangladesh borders are in plains allowing easy movement of people and goods from both Brahmaputra valley and Barak valley. Important border settlements on our side of border are Golakganj, Dhubri, Mankahar, (in the Brahmaputra plains), Karimganj and Kalkali Ghat (in the Barak valley). The latter two are connected with Sylhet of Bangladesh.

The hilly border areas of Meghalaya and Mizoram meet the plain border areas of Bangladesh, except some western ranges of the Mizo Hills touching the Chittagong Hills as borders. Tripura has mixed border, i.e., both hills and valleys merging with the border of Bangladesh. Assam border with Bhutan is the only border where the plains meet the hills. Whereas the rest of the border of the Northeast is hilly country, including the higher Himalayas and Indo-Burma ranges, which meets the hilly border of Bhutan, Tibet and Myanmar. Some exceptions are found in the eastern Manipur border where hills meet the plain border of Myanmar.

In terms of topography and ecosystem the nature of the Northeast region can he clearly understood with the help of the following Chart 10.1. It shows nature of two borders.

It is easily discernible from the Chart 10.1 that broadly four types of physiographic situations occur when our border meets with border of neighbouring countries. These are: i) Hills to Hills, ii) Hills to Plains, iii) Plains to Hills, and iv)Plains to Plains. The border trade is expected to be more where two types of borders are found. It is because people are able to get products from each other's ecosystem or habitat. That's why hill and plain people do better trade than only the peoples from plains do or hills do.

Nature of Human Environment on Borders

Border trade is also governed by the kinds of human groups living in border areas. By this we mean the ethnic composition on both sides of the international boundary. If similar human groups are settled in borders or when spatial distribution of an ethnic group transcends the international boundary, the trade is bound to be intimate and stronger.

Some communities of Northeast India are distributed on both sides of the international boundary. These groups are the Garos, Khasis, Tangsas, Nagas, Kukis etc. In this category the Buddhist communities of Arunachal Pradesh, especially

CHART 10.1

Nature of border of the North-east India

Sl. No.	*Area*	*Nature of Borders*
1.	Assam and Bhutan	Brahmaputra plains to Himalaya Mountains
2.	Assam and Bangladesh	Plains to plains (part of the Brahmaputra plains)
3.	Meghalaya and Bangladesh	Hills to plains (Meghalaya Plateau with the Surma Plains)
4.	Mizoram and Bangladesh	Hills to Hills and Hills to Plains both
5.	Mizoram and Myanmar	Hills to Hills
6.	Manipur and Myanmar	Hills to Hills and Hills to Plains both
7.	Nagaland and Myanmar	Hills to Hills
8.	Arunachal Pradesh and Bhutan, Tibet and Myanmar	Hills to Hills
9.	Tripura and Bangladesh	Hills and Plains to Plains.

of the western part (Tawang and Kameng), can also be included, who have more or less akin Buddhist groups across the international line in Bhutan and Tibet. The social, cultural, religious and the ethnic similarities among human groups encourage stronger economic ties in the form of border trade. The history is full of such relations, which are still continued despite formation of 'impermeable' boundaries.

Border trade can be between more or less similar people or dissimilar groups. Border trade practised by the Monpa, Na, Memba, Khamba, Tangsa, Naga, Kuki, Garo, Khasi and Jaintia is generally between more or less similar groups living across the boundary. Whereas, border transactions done by the Bodo, Aka, Miji, Nishi and Mishmi people are with different groups of people across the boundary.

The nature of human groups has profound influence on border trade and economy of the people living in the border zone. Border trade is more strong and necessary where borders lie in different ecosystems (i.e., hills and plains). This is because different kinds of things are produced in the two distinct ecosystem. That leads to exchange of surplus goods of one ecosystem with another. Both the ecosystems offer something to each other. For example, border people of the Northeast take their agriculture, horticulture, forest, animal husbandry and handicraft products to plains to sell there. These include maize, millet, chilli, clothes, forest products, etc. Coal is exported from Meghalaya to Bangladesh. On the other hand they procure items produced in the plains, such as rice, fish (dry and fresh), utensils, cotton cloths, etc. Tourist centres of the hills do attract plain dwellers. The Balphakram National Park of the Garo hills has special interest of the people of Surma Plains. While the fish, especially Hilsa is very much in demand among the hill-dwellers. This type of border trade is seen in along the border of Meghalaya, and also in the western border of Mizoram and Tripura where the hills meet the plain areas of Bangladesh.

Undoubtedly, economic linkages are smooth, strong and natural between more or less similar people settled in both side of the borders. These economic ties are further strengthened when the similar groups are living in different physiographic borders, e.g., hills and plains. The Garo, Khasi and Jaintia have such advantageous border trade relations.

The Northeast India has a few communities who are not living near the boundary; even then they have developed border trade relations with people across the boundary. Arunachal Himalaya can boost of such human groups who brought/bought goods from Tibet and then sold it to their hill and plain neighbours. In this case name of Miji, Sherdukpen, Bokars, Bori, Nishi, Ramos, Pailibos, Adis, etc., can be mentioned, who had trade relations with the Tibetans and also with their countrymen. The flow of commodities was two ways. Rock salt, silver and bead ornaments, utensils, woollen clothes, swords, etc. were main items brought from Tibet. While the items carried there were chillies, hides, raw wool, plant dyes, maize, millet, etc.

On the other hand, the Tibetans used to bring their goods from Tibet to Assam plains to sell them in yearly fairs and hats. The items included were rock salt, iron implement, hand woven cloths, swords, musk, ornaments, etc. Now some hindrances are felt in pursuing such traditional border trade due to maintenance of impermeable international boundary.

Conclusions

Border is a peripheral land lying along the international boundary and in context of border of the neighbouring country. The two borders are complimentary to each other. The Northeast India is a landlocked region. About 98% of its boundary are international and the 'umbilical cord', which connects this region with the rest of India, has only 2% of its boundary. Though isolated in one sense, but the region has never been devoid of socio-cultural and economic relations with its neighbours. A flourishing border trade did exist here. There is a need to revive and strengthen it in the changed situations for the benefit of the border people.

The borders have their own natural and human environment, which influence the trade, taking place between them. Economic linkages develop naturally between people of two borders, for both have spatial proximity and both are far away from the mainland or production centres of their respective country. Therefore, surplus products are bartered or purchased by each other to maintain their survival. Such a trade is most strong and necessary where borders are in different topographic units or ecosystem, e.g., hills and plains, and also in the borders occupied by more or less similar people. Border of Northeast India has several examples of such strong trade relations with neighbouring border people. Though the traditional border trade has been affected by formation of old and new international boundaries, even the trade goes on as a necessity of the border people. Plans should be made to further encourage and strengthen the border trade, so that the economy of the border people gets a boost. This will definitely bring development and prosperity among the border people. Mutually beneficial border trade helps in having a better bilateral relation between two neighbours, which is one of the agenda of SAARC also. A prosperous, peaceful and developed border can be pride of a country. But all these cannot be done at the cost of security and integrity of our country. Hence, a strong vigilance has to be maintained against illegal trade, unlawful activities, and infiltration in the border without jeopardising the interests of the border people.

The border trade and economy are beneficial to each other. Hence all efforts should be made to develop both. Establishment of ' fair' border trade is necessary for the development of economy of the people because most of the border areas have difficult terrain, isolation and lack of infrastructure. The border people face insurmountable problems in selling their products, especially the perishable agro-horticultural products. Therefore, the planners, politicians, administrators and academicians have to pay attention towards the development of trade and economy of the border people. So that peace, tranquillity, and prosperity can usher in the border to strengthen the country as a whole. Definitely, a strong and prosperous border means a strong and happy nation.

REFERENCES

Allen, B.C., Gait, E.A., Allen C.G.H. and Howard, H.F. 1979, (Reprint). *Gazetteer of Bengal and Northeast India.* Mittal Publications, Delhi (First published in 1884).

Dalton, E.T. 1960, (Reprint). *Descriptive Ethnology of Bengal.* Firma K.L. Mukhopadhyaya, Calcutta, (First published 1872).

Elwin, Verrier. (ed.), 1959, *India's Northeast Frontier in the Nineteenth Century.* Oxford University Press, London.

Fisher, James, F. 1978, *Himalayan Anthropology—The Indo-Tibetan Interface.* Mouton Publisher, The Hague.

Mackenzie, A., 1979 (Reprint), *The Northeast Frontier of India,* Mittal Publications, Delhi, (First published in 1884).

Mukherjee, B.N., 1992, *External Trade of Early Northeast India.* Har Anand, New Delhi.

Rustomji, N.K., 1981, *Sikkim, Bhutan and India's Borderlands.* In The J.S. Lal (ed.), *Himalayas: Aspect of Change,* Oxford University Press, Delhi, pp. 236-252.

11

Prospects of Border Trade in Power in the North Eastern Region

—Atri Chakraborty

As we all know, the North Eastern states share a boundary of about 5211 km with their neighbouring countries, viz., Bangladesh, Myanmar, China and Bhutan. Thus, it is but inevitable that a substantial amount of border trade will take place along the borders, which is both official and unofficial, legal and illegal. For the economic development of the region, it is time to officially recognize this cross border trade, legitimize it, and channelise it along the best possible avenues.

Host states of this region are indeed waking up to this fact and have already started taking steps along this direction. For example, recently, Tripura signed a ten year contract with Bangladesh to export fruits. And with the state's orange production poised to receive a massive boost, the Tripura Govt. owned Tripura Small Industries and Bangladesh's Shyama Associates have signed an agreement for ten years to supply fruits and fruit products. Again, in Nagaland, for revival of the international border trade centres with Myanmar at Pongsha in Tuensang and Longwa in Mon District, the Government has identified some products which have good demand in the centres. According to official sources, the Nagaland Government is proceeding with the building up the necessary infrastructure in and around the identified centres with the Nagaland Industries Development Corporation, side by side, envisaging active role in promotion of such units producing and marketing export potential products.

Taking into consideration resources and potentials available in the North Eastern Region, in relation to feasibility, viability and exportability of goods which have demand, an indicative list of goods can be prepared.

But though this cross border trade in different types of goods ranging from processed fruits and vegetables, wood and bamboo products to cattle and livestock have been recognised and of late, tentative steps are also being taken to give it official sanction, there is one area which is largely over looked. And that is the huge untapped area of power. In the field of power, the whole north-eastern region is in an advantageous position, which can be best exploited for this region's benefit, through trade.

A vast field of untapped potential lies in the field of power. Even on the other side of the country, talks have been initiated on the feasibility of power exports to Pakistan. Talks are also on, on the issue of exports and imports of power among the SAARC countries. The Union Government has decided to purchase 2000 MW of power from Pakistan. A high level committee has been set up to work out the modalities. The power is expected to be evacuated through the SAARC grid to be set up by Power Grid. This proposed Rs. 1,000 - 15,000 crores project for creation of a transmission link between India and Pakistan to facilitate the electricity import from Pakistan to India is expected to be funded by the Asian Development Bank (ADB). The same process can be initiated in the North Eastern region also, and all to this region's advantage.

According to Mr. Kumaramangalam, Union Power Minister, the Government is in fact trying to facilitate free flow of power with neighbouring countries like Nepal, Bhutan and Bangladesh (apart from Pakistan on the western side). According to power Ministry sources, a SAARC grid will become operational within a year. Officials from SAARC countries recently met in Dhaka to prepare a blue print for formation of the grid. A vast field of untapped potential lies in the field of power in the entire north eastern region. This region with its huge potential of hydro-electric power and abundance of natural gas (in Tripura) is in an advantageous position vis-a-vis trade (in power) with the neighbouring countries.

The North Eastern Regional Power Grid comprises of transmission network of seven states, viz. Arunachal Pradesh, Assam, Manipur, Meghalaya, Mizoram, Nagaland and Tripura. This region has a total installed capacity of 1500 MW, including effective, small, isolated generations in different states. New projects with total capacity of 1116 MW have been identified for commissioning in the Tenth Plan and advance actions are being initiated on the same during the Ninth Plan. Besides, about 52 projects in this region are under various stages of investigation. The Ministry of Non-Conventional Energy Sources has supported 28 projects in this region.

To understand the power scenario in the North Eastern Region, let us look at the different constituents.

I. A. States

1. Assam State Electricity Board
2. Meghalaya State Electricity Board
3. Electricity Department, Government of Nagaland
4. Power and Electricity Dept. Government of Mizoram
5. Power and Electric Dept. Govt. Arunachal Pradesh
6. Electricity Department, Government of Tripura
7. Electricity Department, Government of Manipur

B. Central Sector

1. North Eastern Electric Power Corporation (NEEPCO)
2. National Hydro Electric Power Corporation (NHPC)
3. Power Grid Corporation of India Limited.

II. NER Power Scenario

1. Total Installed Capacity = 1500 MW
   - (i) Hydro = 555 MW
   - (ii) Thermal = 945 MW
2. Peak Demand = 850 MW

One important factor in this region is that the ratio of peak demand to off peak demand is high. This requires backing down of generation during off-peak hours. If. on the other hand, during off peak demand in this region, power can be off loaded by exporting through an integrated grid system, it will be a viable proposition.

The other positive factor in initiating border trade in power in this region, is the huge reserves of hydro electric power potential. This will be apparent from the following figures:

Hydro Potential in North Eastern Region:

	State	*Potential Assessed at 60% Load Factor (MW)*
1.	Meghalaya	1070.00
2.	Tripura	9.00
3.	Manipur	1176.00
4.	Assam	351.00
5.	Nagaland	1040.00
6.	Arunachal Pradesh	26756.00
7.	Mizoram	1455.00
	Total (NER)	31857.00

There are at present 8 hydro electric projects with a total installed capacity of 664 MW under execution and scheduled to be commissioned in the IX Plan.

Three schemes (Ranganadi: 405 MW, Doyang : 75 MW and Kopili : 25 MW) are being executed under the central sector and the balance, having total capacity of 159 MW under state sectors.

With such huge reserves of hydro-electric power potential in the north-eastern region, blue print can be drawn up for a grid network spanning the neighbouring countries. Moreover, exploiting the hydro-power potential in this region is also cost effective because compared to thermal power hydro power is cheaper. Therefore, going in for hydro power generation with orientation towards exports will give the region a favourable position regarding balance of trade with neighbouring countries. There are also many fring benefits associated with hydro power projects. Fisheries and agriculture flourish in the catchment areas and these will also boost up exports, as after meeting domestic demand, these can be exported.

There is also abundance of natural gas in Tripura, which can be exported from the gas projects there to Bangladesh, if there are transmission systems of gas pipelines.

But so far we have been looking at the power potential in the NER, but in order to harness this potential and be in a position to export power to neighbouring countries we also have to be aware of the specific problems in this region. To mention a few these are

(i) Poor Communication Facilities

The communication system in the region as a whole is not upto the mark. In fact, communication with a number of substations becomes impossible during rough weather conditions and this makes operation of the systems difficult.

(ii) Difficulty in operation and maintenance

Due to the hilly terrains involving substantial forest areas, the operation and maintenance of the lines is quite difficult and considerable time is taken in restoring the lines after faults.

(iii) Problem of insurgency

Insurgency is a matter of great concern in completing different projects on time. Moreover, the manpower posted at various substations are under threat from militant organisations, affecting execution, operation and maintenance of lines and substations.

These problems have to be tackled before this region can effectively realise its power potential and be in a position to export power.

Next, there arises the question of technically nitty grities of power transfers. India now possess the technical know how involved in inter-regional power transmissions through the advanced HVDC (High Voltage Direct Current) system which is both efficient and cheap.

Then, there remains the question of funding the costs involved in setting up of grid systems, spanning neighbouring countries. But with international agencies like OECF and ADB already showing their willingness to invest in power generation in this region, the problem of funding may not be difficult to solve.

What is needed at this stage now is to initiate a blue print from power transfers between the North Eastern Region and its neighbouring countries, keeping in mind the geographical and cultural uniqueness of this region. Any progress alone these lines should not be at the cost of any harm to the environment.

REFERENCE

1. Action Plan for the Development of the Power Sector in the NER, Government of India, Ministry of Power.

PART III

CONTEMPORARY TRADE: NORTH-EASTERN REGION AND MYANMAR

12

Indo-Myanmar Border Trade: An Assessment on the Moreh-Tamu Sector[1]

—C. Joshua Thomas

It has been observed by an earlier study[2] that, Border Trade has significance to the economies of the north-eastern States due to their peculiar geographical location. Indeed it is interesting to note that all the seven States in north-east have a longer border with outside world than with India — a mere 2%, that is, roughly 33 km. of the border is with India, namely, the "chicken-neck" or "narrow corridor" connecting Assam with West Bengal and this narrow stripe is often vulnerable to natural calamities. Meghalaya, Assam and Tripura share a common border with Bangladesh; while Mizoram, Manipur and Nagaland share border with Myanmar and Arunachal Pradesh is bordered by Tibetan region of China and the Himalayan range of mountains. In addition, Assam has border with Bhutan also. Thus, the peculiar geographical location has led to the seven north-eastern States developing stronger links with neighbouring countries than with mainland India.

Earlier works more particularly by E.G. Verghese,[3] the Sukhla Committee,[4] the Indian Institute for Foreign Trade Report[5] submitted to the North Eastern Council (NEC) suggested that opening of border trade will activate the industrialisation process of the north-eastern States. In this paper an attempt has been made to study the Indo-Myanmar

Border Trade, an assessment on the shortfall in trade between India and Myanmar and prospects of expanding bilateral relations with Myanmar.

I

India-Myanmar share a common border of 1640 km covering three Indian States in the north-eastern region, viz., Manipur, Mizoram and Nagaland. Myanmar is the largest country on the mainland south-east Asia, with a land area of 6,76,577 sq. km. It has an international border of 5,858 km with India and Bangladesh in the north-west, China on the north-east, and Laos and Thailand on south-east. The population of Myanmar was 44.5 million as per 1994 estimates with an annual growth of 1.8%. Its per capita GDP was $ 220 and trade deficit $ 514 million in 1993-94.

Myanmar is predominantly an agricultural economy, with agriculture constituting 40% to GDP. Its main crops are rice, wheat, millet, beans, pulses, oilseeds, sugarcane, jute and rubber. It is rich in forest resources; nearly 51% of the land areas is covered by forest. Its reserved forest area in 1994 was 1,00,000 sq. km. About thousand species of plants grow in its forest. Teak, mahagony, rosewood, cane and bamboo are grown in abundance. Infact, Myanmar is the world's largest exporter of teak. It is rich in minerals like tin, zinc, gold, silver, coal, bauxite and dolomite. Precious stones like rubies, saphaire and diamonds add to the national wealth of the Country. Its fresh water and marine resources are also immense; it has a coastline of 3000 km.[6]

On the other hand, north-eastern region of India comprises 7 States, viz., Arunachal Pradesh, Assam, Manipur, Meghalaya, Mizoram, Nagaland and Tripura. Located in the north-east most corner of India, this region has a great strategic importance since it has common borders with five foreign countries, namely, Bangladesh, Bhutan, China, Myanmar and

Nepal.[7] From time immemorial, trade between the people of Meghalaya and Bangladesh, Manipur and Myanmar, western Arunachal Pradesh and Tibetan region of China, Tripura and Bangladesh and Assam and Bhutan has been taking place through traditional trade routes. However, inview of the immense potential that exists between India and Myanmar in the fields of trade and economic cooperation, Government of India and the Government of Myanmar signed an Indo-Myanmar Border Trade Agreement on January 21, 1994 (see Agreement in the Annexure - 1) with the following four objectives:

1. To exchange the locally produced commodities by people living along both sides of the Indo-Myanmar border;
2. To deal with the foreign trade transactions in freely convertible currencies or in currencies mutually agreed upon by the two countries, including local currencies or through counter-trade agreement;
3. To make the product available cheaper by transporting by land route; and
4. To provide schemes for employment generation by creating facilities of manufacturing activities through free trade zones or joint ventures establishments on both sides of the border.

With these main objectives in mind the government of India and the government of Myanmar have agreed to open borders on the following three sectors:

1. Moreh (Manipur) in India and Tamu in Myanmar
2. Champhai (Mizoram) in India and Hri in Myanmar
3. Lungwa (Nagaland) in India and in Myanmar.

It has been observed that official trade statistics of either country do not reflect the substantial border trade that takes place between India and Myanmar every year. As mentioned above the three Indian border areas open to border trade are Champhai in Mizoram, Moreh in Manipur and Lungwa in Nagaland. Of these, only Moreh is officially declared open for border trade.[8] In this paper we will focus exclusively on Moreh sector which we visited during the first week of November, 1998, with the financial assistance from the Indian Council of Social Science Research, North Eastern Regional Centre. Most of the data in this paper are collected during the field visit. We could get some official documents from the Land Customs Station (LCS), Moreh Chamber of Commerce, Industries Department Government of Manipur at Imphal and other details are based on the personal interviews with the traders more particularly with the Tamil traders.

II

In exercise of powers conferred by clauses (b) and (c) of Section 7 of Customs Act 1962 (52 of 1962) , the government of India vide Notification No. 63/94 cus (N.T.) dated November 21, 1994 as amended and No. 43/95 cus (N.T.) dated July 21, 1995 appointed Moreh as Land Customs Station (LCS) for the clearance of all goods or any class of goods imported or exported by land from or to the land frontiers of Myanmar and the Imphal-Pallel-Tamu road as the route by which alone all goods or class of goods may pass by land to the said frontier. In a formal inaugural function, the then Union Minister of State for Commerce P. Chidambaram declared the LCS open on April 12, 1995. This office is situated near the Luckchow Bridge which connects India with Myanmar land.

As mentioned earlier, the border trade between India and Myanmar was going on from time immemorial, however, the Indo-Myanmar Trade Agreement was singed on April 21, 1994 and border trade through LCS, Moreh was officially opened on April 12, 1995. Under this Agreement provisions are available for both normal as well as trade in barter mechanism. The free exchange of 22 items listed in Annexure-II of the Agreement by the people living along both sides of the Indo-Myanmar border is also allowed to continue as per customary practices.

Main Items of Exports

Wheat-flour, Bicycle and its parts, Bleaching powder, Ferugreek seeds, Ani seeds, Cumin seeds, Soyabari, Dry chillies, Agarbati, Suman Rose powder, Tea, Garlic, Stainless steel etc.

Main Items of Imports

Betal nuts, Turmeric, Red Kidney bean (Rajma), Kuth Roots, Gram, Resin, Reed-broom etc.

Exchangeable Items

There are 22 items which have been identified and declared as exchangeable items under the Indo-Myanmar Agreement. These items are: 1. Mustard/Rape seed, 2. Pulses and Beans, 3. Fresh vegetables, 4. Fruits, 5. Garlic, 6. Onion, 7. Chillies, 8. Spices (excluding Nut-Meg, Mace, Cloves and Cassia), 9. Bamboo, 10. Minor Forest produce (excluding Tea), 11. Betel Nuts and Leaves, 12. Food items for local consumption, 13. Tobacco, 14. Tomato, 15. Reed- broom, 16. Seasame, 17. Resin, 18. Coriander seeds, 19. Soyabean, 20. Roasted Sunflower seeds, 21. Katha and 22. Ginger.[9]

Most of the twenty two items listed in the Agreement are found not favourable for exchange by the exporters because of its sufficient non-availability under barter trade. This has resulted in heavy trade imbalance with trade deficit in favour of India. The practical experience has shown that it will be impossible to comply with export- import obligation unless the viable items are increased including in-flow up to Imphal for household consumption.

In order to prevail the border trade with Myanmar in a balanced way of export the Manipur government proposed for inclusion of following items with preferential rate of customs duty, they are: Washing powder and Toilet soaps, Cosmetics, Myanmar origin Blanket and Dress materials, Raw cotton and mats, Bamboo caps and Bamboo based household items, Cashew nuts, Jaintri, Nutmeg and Cinnaman, Coffee and pepper, Cotton Yarn, Cycle and Cycle parts, Medicine, Motor cycle, Mopeds and Motor vehicles, Auto parts and accessaries, Milk powder and condensed milk, Cement, Sanitary goods, Crockery and Toilet items, Timber including Agarwood and specified third country goods.[10]

"The Border Trade Agreement," observes the report submitted by the Indian Institute of Foreign Trade (IIFT) to the North Eastern Council (NEC), "besides attempting to improve India's market share in Myanmar, aims at strengthening the economies of north-eastern States by leading to establishment of export oriented industrial units. The fall out of this is expected to be an acceleration in social and industrial infrastructural facilities in the region."[11]

Under the Indo-Myanmar Border Trade Agreement, the border trade is regulated through two gates; Gate-I at the Luckchow Bridge for movement of goods as per existing EXIM policy of the Government of India, whereas Gate-II (which was the only entry point prior to April 12, 1995), continues to be utilised for exchange of goods by head-loads. During April 1997, the Myanmar government constructed a market complex in Gate-II at the no man's land known as Nonpalang. Though Nonpalang market was burned in a fire accident during November 1997, the Myanmarese government constructed concrete structure market complex which has been now the main Tamu market.

The operationalisation of the border trade through Gate-II has become a controversial issue, as most of the traders from Manipur go straight to Gate-II and buy all the needed items instead of buying the same from Moreh market. As a result, the Moreh market is very desolate eversince the Gate-II has become operationalised. The Commissioner of Customs suggested that Gate-II should continue to be closed whereas the Myanmarese authorities are strongly in favour of opening the same. This is one of the main issues which has affected the trading community at Moreh very badly. During the field visit to Moreh and Tamu we had the opportunity to meet and discuss the various members of the trading community, particularly the Tamils. It was revealed during the discussion that nearly 1000 Tamil trading community[12] families left Moreh to elsewhere as the border trade is in its very low ebb.

III

The Indo Myanmar Border Trade which started with high expectation went on smoothly till December 1997. But the trade has almost come to a grinding halt eversince 1998 which is evident from the table[13] given below:

Year	*Total export (Rs.)*	*Total import (Rs.)*	*Revenue collected (Rs.)*
1996	28,42,62.021.00	11,37,15,263.00	1.15.88.742.00
1997	30,79,98,097.00	44,26,79,910.00	3,81,26,322.00
1998	3,87,60,150.00	8,75,31,171.00	8,72,280.00

The above data show that the border trade between India-Myanmar at the Moreh sector is heading towards a definite imbalance. Some of the reasons for the sudden down fall of the border trade according to the trading community and the customs officials at Moreh are:

1. The sudden change of policy by Myanmarese authorities, unilaterally decided to continue the trade by Letter of Credit (L.C.) system in Dollars.
2. Insurgency problem and frequent bandh and road

blockade have hampered foreign trade in the Indo-Myanmar border.

3. Non-availability of importable items in Myanmar combined with higher prices have made import non-profitable to the traders thereby affecting the import.
4. Unilateral ban imposed on some import items like Onion, Garlic, Ground Nut and Rice by the Myanmar authority has also affected the trade, that is import.
5. The restriction of the EXIM policy 1997-2002 have become a stumbling block in conducting free import/export through Moreh-Tamu border.
6. Exhorbitant rate of import duty on some of the commodities like Resin, Soyabean, Katha etc., has discouraged the traders to import these items.
7. The United Bank of India (UBI) Moreh branch has often refused to accept Government deposits thereby creating lots of problems to the traders and customs officials.
8. The temporary ban on export of Wheat Flour by the Indian side has upset the export as wheat flour forms the 93% of total export and Myanmar has already started importing wheat flour through other routes.
9. The condition of road from Moreh to Pallel is very bad and the check posts nearly 8 of them are an earning departments for the government servants and not for the government, frequently hinders the pace of border trade movement.

The above mentioned factors are only a few but there are many other factors which we need further study and in this regard if the NEC or any other funding organisation come forward for a through study on this it will definitely bring some solid suggestions to the policy makers consideration.

Even, at the Universities in the north-east, particularly the NEHU and the Manipur University, perhaps the department of Economics and Political Science may suggest their students to do doctoral research on border trade pertaining to the neighbouring countries.

IV

In this section it is proposed to discuss on some of the suggestions which we gathered in our field visit at Imphal, Moreh and Tamu among the traders, government officials and the common people and we would like to put forward a few of them as remedial measures:

1. The restrictions in the EXIM Policy 1997-2002 have become a major hurdle in conducting the foreign trade through the Moreh-Tamu sector. Hence, the 22 items as indicated in Annexure-I of the Agreement should be exempted from the restrictions of the EXIM Policy.

2. It has been observed in the past that sometimes both Indian and Myanmar authorities unilaterally and abruptly banned import/export of some items listed in Annexure-I of the Agreement in gross violation of the Agreement. For instance, India stopped import of Onion and export of Wheat Flour temporarily in the past and Myanmar authority has banned export of Onion, Garlic, Groundnut, Rice etc., at present for which traders had to incur heavy financial loss due to breach of contract. It will be worth before such banning the traders on both sides should be informed in advance so that they do not enter into fresh contract.

3. As per Handbook of Procedures Vol. 1 only Meghalaya Exporter's Chamber of Commerce has been authorised to issue certificate of origin in the entire north-east. Federation of all Manipur importer/exporter chamber of commerce and industry, Imphal and Moreh Chamber of Commerce, Moreh, should be authorised to issue certificate of origin, which will definitely speed-up the process.

4. As mentioned earlier that the UBI, Moreh Branch, which is the only Bank in Moreh, has often refused to accept government deposits which has been causing great difficulties to both the traders and customs officials alike. Therefore, some immediate steps should be made to receive government deposits in UBI, Moreh branch. Also, Bank air lifting of the cash from UBI is not regular, which lead to huge accumulation of cash and non-acceptance of customs duty in TR6 challans as well as other government taxes.

5. Traders at Moreh feel that some more items should be included in the list indicated in Annexure-I of Indo-Myanmar Border Trade Agreement. For instance, parafin wax, coconut oil, ground nut seed and oil, cosmetics, Myanmar origin blanket and quilt, dress materials, raw cotton and mats, handicrafts (made of bamboo and wood), cashew nuts, cotton yarn, poppy seeds, semi-precious stones, cycle and cycle parts, auto parts and accessories, milk powder and condensed milk, cement, sanitary goods, crockery and toilet items, wooden furniture, hosiery goods, herbal roots, cut piece cloth, cotton lungi, agarbati, pan masala, stainless steel utensils, chemicals like caustic soda, bleaching powder, ammonium chloride, specified third country goods. Perhaps the local traders on both sides should be consulted while preparing the list of additional items.

6. Most of the goods importable from Myanmar are of agricultural nature and forest produces. Out of 22 items betal nuts amounts approximately 80% of the total import and is the only item which is economically viable for import also. After paying 7% customs duty again 7% forest royalty, sales tax 4% (provided C form) or 10% is being charged which makes the value of betel nuts abnormally high. Traders feel that any import goods of foreign origin after paying the necessary customs duties should not be charged forest royalty or sales taxes. According to the officials at the Moreh Chamber of Commerce, sale taxes should be charged at the last point only. It should be noted that the Moreh Chamber of Commerce

had submitted a representation related to this point to the Parliamentary Standing Committee on Commerce of South East Asian Countries when it visited Moreh as part of their north-east tour on January 31, 1997, but still the problem remained as same.

7. Posting of efficient, honest and sincere customs officials in all check points from Moreh-Imphal-Guwahati, who have good knowledge in export-import policy is very much needed for the reviving of border trade. During the discussion we learned posting at the border area is a lucrative posting for the customs as well as security personnel. As such the officials try to earn as much as possible in their short term of posting for which they pay a good ransome to their higher officials. The traders complained that imported onion and garlic were detained frequently despite of producing all the valid import documents. The traders feel all goods of foreign origin once cleared by customs after payments of all customs dues to Central government which could include duty, fine and penalty, depending on the value of goods and the modes of import should be allowed to move completely free to any part of the Indian Union without any encumbrances.

8. The 22 items listed in Indo-Myanmar Trade Agreement, should be exempted from the restriction of EXIM policy 1997-2002, and more items be included, that is, cotton yarn, medicine, herbal roots, handicrafts, wooden furniture and polythene bags.

9. All import items should not be charged more than 5% duty, for instance, resin is 40% basic + 5% additional duty + 4% special duty, comes to 49% is abnormally high. The third country goods be allowed to import through the land route under normal duty.

10. Telecommunication system is vital for the prosperity of trade in an area like Moreh. Though there are more than 500 telephone consumers in Moreh, yet the telecommunication

net work is in a very bad shape and many lines were cut off from the rest of India for several months.

11. The citizens of border town have been thriving for their economic sustenance by way of mutual shopping and marketing with their Tamu (Myanmar) counterpart across the border for years. But this age old tradition has come to a sudden halt ever since the Myanmar government imposed stiff restrictions upon their citizens from shopping in Moreh town which adversely affected the business community in Moreh. This has caused considerable disappointment among the people of Moreh. The members of Tamil Sangam revealed that nearly 350 retail shops have been closed and about 1000 Tamil trading community left Moreh.

12. At present Meghalaya Exports Chamber of Commerce is the only competent authority to issue certificate of origin. Whereas the Moreh Chamber of Commerce officials feel that Manipur Chambers of Commerce, Imphal and Moreh Chambers of Commerce should be authorised to issue certificate of origin which will definitely reduce unnecessary delay in procedural formalities.

13. Further it was reported both at Moreh and Imphal that there are frequent kidnapping of traders and highway robberies between Imphal and Moreh on the National Highway-39. Inspite of repeated demands from the trading community to the State government for providing proper security on the National Highway-39, the problem remain unresolved. If this problem persists then definitely it will hamper border trade very badly in the long run.

V

What has been mentioned in the above paragraphs are all related to the official and legal border trade between India and Myanmar. It should be noted that "two-way trade between India and Myanmar, which amounted to Rs. 37

million in 1966-67 reached Rs. 4435 million in 1993-94. Nearly 85% of it is accounted for by India's imports from Myanmar and the remaining 15% by India's export's to that country. This, however, does not reflect the volume of border trade between the two countries, which is estimated at Rs. 20,000 million per annum."[14] In a nutshell, India's share in Myanmar's imports is rather "insiginificant", it being less than 3%.

It was reported in a discussion in Moreh with the Parliamentary Standing Committee on Home Affairs, that India, Bangladesh, Pakistan and China illegal trade amounts Rs. 15,000 crore but official figure records it as 1000 crore! In the similar way, the illegal trade which operates in Tamu-Moreh amounts as 2000 crore but official record says only 69 crore! The Customs Preventive Force, Moreh, informed us that the seizure effected during the year 1997-98 was Rs. 41,40,000.00 and during the year 1998-99 (upto October 1998) was Rs. 1,56,40,000.00. Major items seized at Moreh gate includes: Nylon fishing net, electronic goods, misc. clothing items, synthetic blanket, cosmetics, toilet items, precious/ semi precious stones, silver, currency, plastic items, cigarettes, medicine, ephedrine hydrocloride etc. The officials were not in a position to give the correct figures. Moreover the officials are very silent about the illegal entry of the dreaded Number-4 etc. Our research at Moreh reveals that the official level legal border trade at the inception yielded a great boost to the revenue but now it is not so and on the contrary it is at its lowest level but the illegal trade is flourishing leaps and bounds. There are 3 main items which are illegally entering into Moreh via Tamu in unspecified quantity, they are: drugs, precious and semi-precious stones and counterfeit currency. It appears there are competition among the officials and non-officials in carrying these items from Moreh to other destination. In an earlier study on insurgency in Manipur, Tarapot Panjam records that nearly 6 kilos of purified heroin is smuggled out of Myanmar into Moreh on every day basis. We have a paper clipping record that about 4 years back when a petrol container returned back from Moreh it carried 2 parts of the container full of ganja and the other part of the container full of heroin. These two record shows that a thorough independent and impartial study is needed on the illegal trade in the Moreh-Tamu sector. There are many areas which need further study and also firm decisive determination from the government and non-governm ent organisations for the promotion of border trade particularly in this Moreh-Tamu sector. There are many porus borders which need dedicated security personnel to guard.

NOTES & REFERENCES

1. This paper was prepared with the financial assistance from the Indian Council of Social Science Research, North Eastern Regional Centre, Shillong for a field trip to collect the relevant primary data at Imphal, Moreh and Tamu. The author acknowledges with thanks for the helps that he received from all colleagues at the Centre. The following persons who assisted him in various ways at Imphal and Moreh deserve special mention includes: Dr. S.V. Job & Mrs. Job, Luminthang Haokip, K. Ahmed (Superintendent, Land Customs Station, Moreh), N. Kumar (Secretary, Moreh Chambers of Commerce & President Tamil Sangam, Moreh), Emmanuel and host of other friends who directly and indirectly assisted in preparation of this paper.
2. Indian Institute of Foreign Trade, *Study of Promotion of Border Trade Between India and Myanmar*, New Delhi, 1995, Prepared for NEC, Shillong.
3. Verghese, B.G., *India's Northeast Resurgent; Ethnicity, Insurgency, Governance, Development* (New Delhi: Konark, 1996).
4. Sukla Committee Report on Transforming Northeast.
5. F.N. No. 3, p. 56.
6. *Ibid.*, pp. 1-2.
7. For a detailed information on the potentiality and the problems of the Northeastern region of India, See, C. Joshua Thomas, "India's North East and Border Trade with Neighbouring Countries: A Case Study on Indo-Bangladesh Relations", in Gurudas Das and R.K. Purkayastha, *Liberalism and India's North East* (New Delhi: Commonwealth Publications, 1998).

8. Indo-Myanmar Border Trade was inaugurated by the then Commerce Minister, P. Chidambaram at Moreh on April 12, 1995.
9. Directorate of Commerce and Industries, Government of Meghalaya, Imphal, How to Start Export and Join Border Trade Business (Pamphlet).
10. Notes for the Visit of Parliamentary Standing Committee on Home Affairs during their visit at Manipur (12-14 October 1998), p. 1.
11. F.N. No. 3, p. 56.
12. For a brief study on the Tamils of Moreh, See, C. Joshua Thomas, "Tamil of Moreh" in *Northeast Daily*, December 6, 1998.
13. Representation submitted by the Moreh Chamber of Commerce addressed to the Chairman, Parliamentary Committee on Home Affairs, October 12, 1998.
14. F.N. No. 3, p. S-2.

13

Indo-Myanmar Border Trade and Its Impact on Industrialisation and Infrastructural Development in Manipur

—G.P. Parasain

Manipur is a land-locked state situated in the extreme corner of North-Eastern India in the border of Myanmar (Burma). This state is rectangular in shape, with mountainous terrain. The highest mountain is 3000 metres above the mean sea level. It lies within the latitude of 23.830 North and 25.680 North and longitude of 93.03° East and 94.74° East The total geographical area of Manipur is 22,327 sq. kms. It has two distinct areas of hills and plains. The areas of plains or valley which is located in the centre of Manipur is only 1,862 sq. kms. There are 9 (nine) districts in Manipur, out of which 4 (four) districts are in the valley and rest 5 (five) districts are situated in the sprawling hills. Manipur occupies 0.68 per cent and 8.75 per cent of the area of the whole country and the entire North Eastern Region respectively.

Manipur is still industrially very backward even in the backward N.E. Region of India with per capita income below the all India average. As many as 45.06% of the people of the state live below the poverty line. There are not enough industries to keep pace wit the rapid growth of population and to deal with the growing problems of unemployment poverty, lack of housing, medical care etc.[1] Add to this, there is the problem of comparative neglect of industrialisation in the state planning. For instance, the 6th plan allocation for the industrial sector in Manipur was 8.33% as against the all India average of 12.28%.[2]

Small Scale Industries

There are hardly any major or medium industrial units in the State worth the name and the few that have already been established are now suffering from varying degrees of industrial sickness. Development of large-scale industries has to follow its own logic and such major industrial units cannot be established anywhere. But that is not so in the case of small-scale and household industries. Given the proper policies and programmes and reasonably adequate infrastructure support, there are many small-scale and household industries whether demand based or resource based, which can be successfully established in Manipur.[3]

By the end of March, 1998 the number of permanently registered Small scale industries both SIDO and NON-SIDO stood at 9090 with an investment in plant and machinery of Rs. 30.05 crores employing 46,390 persons with an annual production of Rs. 134.84 crores. The growth of small industries over the year is shown in the following table.

Growth of Registered PMT, Industrial units showing investment, production and employment:

		At the end of the Year		
Year	*No. of Units*	*Investment (in Rs. crores)*	*Production (in Rs. crores)*	*Employment (Nos.)*
1	2	3	4	5
1979-80	197	0.54	0.15	890
1980-81	381	0.94	0.28	1695
1981-82	552	1.34	0.39	2520
1982-83	705	1.76	4.28	3500

1	*2*	*3*	*4*	*5*
1983-84	975	2.63	7.99	4870
1984-85	1233	3.45	20.14	6150
1985-86	2077	6.15	36.39	10385
1987-88	3996	12.30	67.26	19900
1988-89	5417	16.31	80.26	27000
1989-90	6319	19.20	89.11	31500
1990-91	6788	20.70	94.81	33390
1991-92	7392	22.63	101.45	36910
1992-93	7696	23.61	106.9	38400
1993-94	8096	24.74	116.7	39680
1994-95	8341	26.41	123.16	42613
1995-96	8612	28.23	127.05	43842
1996-97	8918	29.43	132.1	45362
1997-98	9090	30.05	134.89	46390

Source: Directorate of Commerce and Industries, Government of Manipur, Imphal.

The state government has made persistent efforts for rapid industrialisation of the state thereby generating more employment opportunities, alleviation of poverty and removal of economic disparities. Apart from providing a package of incentives and concessions as laid out in its industrial policies and programme in consonance with those of the Government of India the State Government has participated in the industrialistion campaign which began with the incorporation of the Manipur Spinning Mills Corporation Ltd. in 1974 which started its commercial production in 1980. In order to facilitate growth of industries, the Manipur Small Industries Corporation was set up in 1969 and it was further upgraded to Manipur Industrial Development Corporation Ltd. (MANIDCO) in 1987. Manipur Handloom and Handicraft Development Corporation Ltd. was set up in 1976 to directly help production and marketing of handloom and handicrafts products. Subsequently, public sector undertakings like, Manipur

Electronics Development Corporation Ltd. (MANITRON), Khandsari Sugar Factory, Manipur Cements Ltd., Manipur State Drugs and Pharmaceuticals Ltd., Manipur Pulp and Allied Products Ltd. etc. came up in the state. Regional/State branch offices in respect of Small Industries Service Institute, National Small Industries Corporation Ltd., Centre for Electronics Design and Technology and Central Institute of Plastic Engineering and Technology have also come up in the State to invigorate the growth of industries. District Industries Centre in the districts were set up in 1978-79 and decentralisation of industrial growth in the rural areas had begun. Schemes like Seed Margin Money, Self Employment for Educated Unemployed Youths Scheme, and Prime Minister's Rozgar Yojana were instrumental in growth of industrial activities in the State of Manipur.

Indo-Myanmar Border Trade

The Indo-Myanmar Border Trade was inaugurated on 12.4.95 by the then Union Minister of State for Commerce, as a follow-up-measure of the Trade Agreement signed between the two countries on 21st January, 1994 at New Delhi. Later, various Sectoral and inter-Country Delegation Level Talks have been held to gear up the trade on a significant level. Govt. of India vide public Notice No. 239 (PM)92-97 Dt. 10.4.95 has allowed 22 items which are exchangeable by the residents across the border. These 22 items are mustard/rice seed, pulses and beans, fresh vegetables, fruits, garlic, onion, chillies, species, bamboo, minor forest products excluding teak, betel nuts and leaves, food items for local consumption, tobacco, tomato, reed broom, sesame, resin, coriander seeds, soyabean, roasted sunflower seeds, katha,. ginger and any other commodities as may be mutually agreed upon between the two sides.

The total volume of border trade since 12.4.95 upto 25.11.97 was Rs. 120.25 crores of which Rs. 64.60 crores is for export of Indian goods to Myanmar and a corresponding import of

Rs. 55.65 crores from Myanmar, as per record maintained by Land Customs Station, Moreh.

Infrastructure and Industrial Development

To boost up the Indo-Myanmar Border Trade, Government of Manipur initiated the various schemes / project for industrial and infrastructural development of Manipur. These schemes / projects may be described in the following heads:

1. Re-designated of the Industry Department

The Department Industries of the Government of Manipur has been re-designated as "Department of Commerce and Industries" and accordingly separate commerce cell with adequate staff has been provided.

2. General Awareness Programme

The Department of Commerce and Industries, Government of Manipur, so far organised 4 (four) General Awareness Programmes for the benefit of traders, exporters and business communities twice in 1994, once in 1995 at Imphal and from 16th to 18th January, 1997 at Moreh. The programmes were attended by officials from Ministries of Commerce, Home Affairs, External Affairs, Customs, RBI, Export Credit Guarantee Corporation, Federation of Indian Exports Organisation, etc. These programmes have been found quite useful to the participants.

3. Visit Myanmar Year

The Republic of Myanmar celebrated 1996 as visit Myanmar year and many of Indian businessmen, traders from Manipur visited Myanmar on this occasion. The Manipur State Govt. reciprocated by organising a week-long Exhibition at Moreh displaying the local products of Manipur. A good number of visitors from Myanmar also came during the exhibition period. The programmes have been very useful in familiarising the people across the border.

4. Counselling-cum Grievance Redressal Committee for Border Trade

To provide guidance to the traders and to redress their grievances as a single window delivery system, the Manipur, Government has constituted Counselling-cum-Grievance Redressal Committee for Border Trade headed by Commissioner (Commerce and Industries), Govt of Manipur with the following members i.e. (a) Representatives from Ministry of Commerce, Govt of India., (b) The Assistant Commissioner, Customs Govt of India (c) The Joint Secretary (Home), Govt. of Manipur (d) The Principal Chief Conservator of Forest, Manipur (e) The Taxation Commissioner, Manipur (f) The Commandant, B.S.F. Koirengei, Imphal (g) The Commandant, 59, Mountain Brigade, Kakching, Manipur (h) the Superintendent of Police, Chandel District, Manipur (i) The Additional Deputy Commissioner, Moreh. Manipur (j) Representative from Associated Manipur Chamber of Commerce, Imphal (k) Representative from Federation of All Manipur Importer Exports Chamber of Commerce and Industry, Imphal. (l) Representative from Indo-Myanmar Exim. Association, Imphal and (m) Director of Commerce and Industries, Manipur as Member Secretary, The Committee holds meeting from time to time.

5. State Level Export Promotion Committee

A State Level Export Promotion Committee (SLEPC) has been constituted with Chairman and Managing Director, UBI and its 5th meeting was held on 5/3/98 at Imphal and the meeting had discussed various points amongst other (a) holding of Border Trade Awareness Programme at Moreh and Imphal (b) Improvement of Road Communication (c) Warehousing facility at Moreh (d) Availability of uninterrupted power supply at Moreh (e) Availability of telecommunication facilities such as STD and FAX (f) Posting of security guards for currency chest at UBI, Moreh Branch (g) Opening of Currency chest at UBI, Moreh etc.

6. Trade Centres

The importance of setting of trade centres for promoting facilities to the traders and entrepreneurs of Manipur with the new avenue of opening up of regulated border trade between Myanmar and India was considered by the Planning Commission, Govt of India by sanctioning a sum of Rs. 2.00 crores as additional central assistance to the state's Annual Plan, during 1994-95. The site were already finalised. 2 (two) trade centres, one at Imphal and another at Moreh, are under construction.

The centre is to provide infrastuctural facilities such as telecommunication, export-import information cell, show room-cum sales centres, conference hall, boarding and lodging facilities, guest room and restaurants, bank and other relevant Govt extension counters to facilitate the traders/businessmen/entrepreneurs in creating a business like and congenial atmosphere.

7. Export Promotion Industrial Park

The Department of Commerce and Industries, Government of Manipur, proposes for setting up an Export Promotion Industrial Park (EPIP) at Khunuta Chingin near Sora village at Kakching which is about 40 km. from Imphal along N.H. No.39. The scheme launched by the Government of India will enable to provide adequate incentives for building up of infrastructural facilities of high standard to the State of Manipur with a view to create employment opportunities and promote exports. A detailed project report for a total project cost of Rs.15.00 crores is submitted to the Government of India.

8. Export Processing Zone (EPZ)

Under the initiation of North Eastern Council, the Rail India Technical and Economic Services (RITES), New Delhi, had visited Moreh during March, 1996 to assess potential for creating infrastructural facilities and submitted a consultancy proposal to North Eastern Council for establishment of an

EPZ near the hills of Kondeng Lairembi Temple about 3 kms. from Moreh on N.H. 39. The proposed project report will consider facility relating to the power, transport, warehousing/handling, research, development and training institutes, telecommunication, civic facilities, business centres, employment generation, institutional arrangements and linkage and financing agencies. The State Government has approached the North Eastern Council for assistance in setting up one EPZ project. The total cost of EPZ has been estimated at Rs.100.00 crores.

9. Integrated Infrastructure Development (IID)

The Govt of India has sanctioned the IID project at Moreh for a total project cost of Rs.5.75 crones. Land acquisition was under process. Foundation stone has already been laid at the proposed site at Moreh by the Hon'ble Chief Minister of Manipur.

10. The Industrial Policy of Manipur, 1996

The new Industrial Policy of Manipur 1996 has been reoriented to derive maximum benefit by formal opening of border trade. The expert cell in the Directorate of Commerce and Industries is the Nodal Agency which inter-alia educate, train and guide traders/entrepreneurs in international trading, conduct export potential survey, undertake measures to promote trade-motivated industrial activity, optimise use of agriculture/horticulture/forest resources across the border and various export-import activities.

Conclusion

The growth of industry particularly those of small and tiny sectors has been an important feature in the economic development of the State of Manipur since independence. The opening of Indo-Myanmar Border Trade has further boost the economy and industrial development of Manipur. Since Manipur is situated in the border of Myanmar, all the import and export take place through Manipur and therefore, Manipur has to play a major role in the furtherance and promotion of Indo-Myanmar border trade. Govt. of India and the State Govt of Manipur have also realised this importance and initiated various measures for the development and promotion of Indo-Myanmar Border Trade. Important projects for the Industrial and infrastructural development which are already undertaken by the Govt. are construction of 2 (two) trade-centres, setting up of Export Promotion Industrial Park, initiation of Export Processing Zone, sanctioned for the Integrated Infrastuctural Development, constitution of Export Counselling-cum-Grievance Redressal Committee, constitution of State Level Export Promotion Committee and re-orientation of the Industrial Policy of Manipur, 1996, to derive maximum benefit from the border trade. In future also many such industrial and infrastructural projects are to be initiated and sanctioned by the Manipur and Central Government.

REFERENCE

1. Singh, H.N., *Review of Plans, Policies and Incentives of Government and their Impact*, Paper presented in the Seminar on Dynamics of Entrepreneurship Development in Manipur, organised by the Department of Commerce, Manipur University, unpublished, p. 1.
2. Background Note for State Planning Board Meeting Manipur, held on 17.11.89.
3. Singh, H.N., *op. cit.*, p.2.
4. Industrial Policy of Manipur, 1996.
5. Directorate of Commerce and Industries. Govt. of Manipur, Imphal.
6. Status Paper and Agreement on Indo-Myanmar Border Trade.

14

Indo-Myanmar Cross Border Trade: An Overview

—Rajmani Singh

Introduction

With India accepting the membership of World Trade Organisation (WTO) w.e.f. January 1, 1995, pressure has been increasing from the developed and developing countries to open up the Indian market for the entry of foreign goods, services as well as technological know how. There is a high demand from the developed countries to completely abolish the present system of tariffs. Hence time is ready for Indian industries and traders to prepare themselves to face the challenges from foreign goods and services. With this critical juncture to organise seminar on Cross Border Trade has given immense benefit towards the policy makers, industrialists and also traders in general.

Keeping the above point in mind, the present paper is mainly dealt with the problems and prospects of Indo-Myanmar cross border trade with special reference to Manipur. Finally it also covers the suggestive measure to prevent the illegal trade practising in Indo-Myanmar cross border trade.

Manipur, a small state, situated in the easternmost corner of North East India stretching between latitude 23.83°N and 25.68°N and longitude of 93.03°E, and 94.79°E. It has a border of about 854 kms of which 352 kms are international border with Myanmar and remaining 502 kms long border separate from the neighbouring states of Nagaland, Mizoram and Assam in the north, south and west respectively. The National Highway No. 39 is the only lifeline connecting India with Myanmar which is 109 km far from Imphal, the capital of Manipur.

Since 1960s the local traders here are more used to illegal cross border trading with Myanmar (Burma). But it was on 12th April 1995, the Indo-Myanmar cross border trade was formally open by the then Indian Union Minister of Commerce Mr. P. Chidambaram and his Myanmar counterparts, Minister for trade Lt. Gen. Tun Kyi. The cross border trade between the two countries takes place in both side i.e. Moreh in Indian side and Tamu Namphalong in Myanmar side. As per a report presented by Industries Minister of State in the State assembly on 14th July 1998 commodities worth of Rs. 20,65,23,810 were exported to Myanmar through the state and commodities worth of Rs. 33,96,22,340 were imported to India through the state during the year 1997-98 which was far behind the expected annual potential of Rs. 1000-2000 crores.

Problem Area

Though the trade between two countries was formally open four years back, the full swing of trade is yet to take off owing to lack of cross border knowledge among the traders, insufficient infrastructural facilities, non formalisation of currency exchange rate, unable to control the illegal trade and restriction of exchangeable trade items.

Ever since the legal trade between India and Burma was stopped during sixties, businessman or traders living on both side resorted to illegal trade taking advantage of the customery practice of free movement of people and goods of ethnic origin. As the illegal trading continues in the sector, it has become difficult for the customs to guard the entire 1640 km Indo-Myanmar border. On the other hand, this system continued for over 35 years and it is natural that people would not like to shift to a new system overnight. Further, the local traders dealing in trading activities with Myanmar's traders are ignorant of the procedures to be followed in the international trade like commercial documents, regulatory documents and export assistant documents etc.

Secondly the basic infrastructural facilities required for cross border trade like proper road communication, post and telegraph services, telecommunication system, warehouse, export import bank, Directorate General of Foreign Trade (DGFT) branch, Reserve Bank of India branch and also the various departments involved in cross border trade are not started its operation at full extent.

The proposed Indo-Myanmar border trade office at Imphal are yet to open, till today the nearest DGFT and RBI office are at Guwahati, traders have to go long way from Moreh to Guwahati to obtain their Import Export Certificate numbers and other related documents. Further, frequent bandh, economic blockade and insecurity on National Highway, lack of improvement of postal and telecommunication services at the border town are the main obstacles against smooth flow of broder with Myanmar.

The third and most important problem faced by the traders is the non-formalisation of the Indian rupee and Myanmerese Kyat exchange rate. The Myanmerese military government insists that one US $ is equivalent to six Myanmerese Kyats. This is not the internationally accepted rate but just decided by the military junta. If the transaction continues at this rate, then the Indian side becomes the loser. The Indian government insists one rupee is equivalent to 5.84 Kyats. As a result exchange rate is fluctuating 2 Kyats to 10 Kyats per rupee. Delay in finalising of currency exchange rate of the two countries has led to delay in transaction, United Bank of India has been entrusted with this work by the government of India but all the needed facilities have not been given to them.

After opening of Indo-Myanmar border trade, the impact of heroin (Drugs) is also gradually felt in India, where drug addiction is spreading like a malignant growth. In Manipur, the number of drug addicts has risen from 600 in 1988 to an estimated 15,000 in 1991 (*Far Eastern Economic Review* 28th March 1991) most of them are 15 to 25 years age group. But the NGOs working in this area estimated more than 30,000 or more in 1995-96. The health experts of Indian authority estimated in 1990 that within five year. Manipur alone will have 1,600 HIV cases.

Finally the restriction of exchangeable trade items to 22 items has become a crippling impediment in the trade imbalance with trade deficits in favour of India. At present the Indian finished products like fabrics, steel, nail, utensils, bicycles are major export items from the Indian side. On the other hand raw forest produces and some third country products like household items and electronic goods are brought back into India as imports.

Conclusion and Suggested Plan of Action

Though the Indo-Myanmar trade was formally opened on 12th April 1995, still major role is played by the illegal trade between the traders of two countries. To make regularisation of illegal trade in one hand and to boost up the legal trade on the other various preventive, controlling and developmental activities should be undertaken. In this context, both Central and State Governments should take initiative for the establishment of basic infrastructural requirement such as proper road and communication facilities, banking facilities, hotel and lodging facilities and also various departments related to cross border trade within a time framework is highly essential for implementation of various preventive and controlling measures for illegal trade.

Government and Non-governmental organisations should take more initiative for organising seminars, symposium and debating competition as mass awareness programmes and to increase the number of customs and excise check post, providing more securities on the border area, construction of border fencing will enable to check the illegal trade including influx of high grade Myanmar heroin into the border state of North East India.

If all these measures fail to control the influx of drug and also illegal trade, then it is suggested for the modelling the Indo-Myanmar trade in the line of border trade between Myanmar and Thailand on its eastern border and Myanmar and China on its northern border. The trade is thriving on these borders and each accounts for an approximate one billion dollar annually precisely because of complete deregulating of the area and permitting of trans border exchange of commodities without any customs or banking restrictions. At the Yunan Province of China the only item kept on the Watch list is drugs and at the Chiang Mai of northern Thailand trade is again completely opened with vigilence only on transborder traffic of drugs. A similar trade model on the Indo-Mynmar border may be taken up on experimental basis. If it comes to a success, it will enhance trade volume between two countries and also benefit the local traders.

REFERENCES

1. Status paper and agreement on Indo-Myanmar Border Trade, 12th April 1995.
2. IIFT, 1995 Study on Promotion of Border Trade Between India and Myanmar, New Delhi.
3. Industrial Policy of Manipur, 1996.
4. *The Imphal Free Press*, Local English daily, 8th Nov. 11th Nov, 14th Nov. 16th Nov. 19th Nov. 1998.
5. *The Impha! Free Press*, 15th July 1998.
6. *The Imphal Free Press*, 1st December 1998.
7. *The Imphal Free Press*, 8th Jan., 22nd Jan., 29th Jan., 1999.

15

Potentiality of Border Trade Between India and Myanmar

—S.B. Singh & S.N. Goswami

Myanmar shares a common border with India, covering three north-eastern states, viz. Mizoram, Manipur and Nagaland. Myanmar being an underdeveloped country has a consistently unfavourable balance of trade and deteriorating terms of trade. Its trade deficit in 1993-94 amounted to $ 514 million. On the other hand, despite having rich natural resources north-eastern region of the country endowed with poor infrastructure and industrial development as compared to the rest of the country. It resulted into a vicious cycle of low investment, low production, low income and finally, high unemployment and social unrest. Being bordered with Myanmar, the north-eastern states can take the advantage of border trade with Myanmar. In view of the immense potential that exists between India and Myanmar in the field of trade and economic co-operation, Government of India and Government of Myanmar signed an Indo-Myanmar border trade agreement on January 21, 1994. Under the agreement barter trade through the land route would be allowed under the following guidelines, in addition to the regulations of the Reserve Bank of India:

- Export from India to precede imports from Myanmar.
- No monetary transaction to be allowed.

- Consignments to be involved in US dollar, with value not to exceed 20,000 US dollar per transaction.
- Value of goods imported from India to be treated as advance payments for imports into India.
- Banks at Moreh and Champhai designated as authorised dealers for transactions.

The border trade agreement besides attempting to improve India's market share in Myanmar, aims at strengthening the economies of north-eastern states by leading to establishment of export oriented industrial infrastructure facilities in the region. With this objective in mind, Government of India and Government of Myanmar have agreed to open borders in the following sectors:

1. Moreh in India and Tamu in Myanmar
2. Champhai in India and Hri in Myanmar
3. Other place that may be noticed by the two countries by mutual agreement.

However, for getting full benefits of border trade, potential areas should be identified with reference to the strengths and weakness of the north-eastern region in terms of their location, resource base and infrastructure, on the one hand and demand and supply position of various items in Myanmar on the other.

Exports of Myanmar

Myanmar is predominantly an agricultural country with agriculture contributing nearly 40 per cent of the Gross Domestic Product (GDP) of the country. The main crops grown are rice, wheat, millet, beans, pulses, oilseeds, sugarcane, jute and rubber. The country is also endowed with rich forest resources, i.e. covering 51 per cent of the land area. Teak, cane and bamboo are the important forest trees. Infact, Myanmar is the world's largest exporter of teak. Myanmar is also having rich mineral wealth such as tin, zinc, gold, silver, coal, bauxite and dolomite, etc. Because of its rich agricultural and mineral resources, the country posses high export potential. Table 15.1 showed that nearly two-thirds of its exports are primary products. Its exports during 1991-92 was amounted to 488.63 million dollars. Major items of exports were forest products (33 per cent). pulses and beans (15 per cent), rubber (10 per cent) and rice (8 per cent).

TABLE 15.1

Main Exports and imports of Myanmar (1991-92)

Main export items	*Quantity (in %)*	*Main import items*	*Quantity (in %)*
Forest products	33	Consumer Goods	10.86
		Durable goods	4.18
		Food stuffs	3.15
		Textiles	0.72
		Medicines and pharmaceuticals	2.27
		Other consumer goods	0.54
Pulses and beans	15	Raw Materials & Spares for inter-industry use	28.59
		Raw materials	19.42
		Tools & spares	9.16
Rubber	10	Capital goods	29.39
		Construction material	7.13
		Machinery & equipment	8.82
		Transport equipment	11.96
		Other capital goods	0.88
Rice	8	Commodity unspecified	31.17
Others	34		
Total value (in $ million)	488.63	Total value (in $ million)	889.45

Source: Ministry of National Planing and Economic Development, Myanmar.

Regarding exports of Myanmar by country, Singapore

was the leading importer from Myanmar with a share of 19 per cent, followed by China (15 per cent), Thailand (13 per cent), India (1 per cent) and Hong Kong (7 per cent) in 1991-92 (Table 15.2).

TABLE 15.2

Exports and imports of Myanmar by Country (1991-92)

Exports of Myanmar by Country	*Quantity (in %)*	*Imports of Myanmar by country*	*Quantity (in %)*
Singapore	19	Japan	21
China	15	China	17
Thailand	13	Thailand	15
India	11	Singapore	12
Hong Kong	7	Malaysia	7
Japan	6	Korea	4
Pakistan	2	India	13
Sri Lanka	2	—	
Malaysia	1	—	
Other European Countries	24	Other European Countries	21
Total value (in $ million)	488.63	Total value (in $ million)	889.45

Source: Ministry of National Planning and Economic Development, Myanmar.

Imports of Myanmar

The different items which are imported by Myanmar and their share in the total imports are presented in Table 15.1. The main items were classified under consumer goods. raw materials and spares, and capital goods, etc. Its total imports during 199 1-92 was amounted to $ 889.45 million. Capital goods and raw materials together dominated the total imports, accounting for nearly 58 per cent of imports. Under consumer goods, durable goods accounted the highest share (4.18 per cent) followed by food stuffs (3.15 per cent) and medicines and pharmaceuticals (2.27 per cent). Transport equipment, machinery and equipment and construction material are the important imports under capital goods. Regarding imports into Myanmar by country, Asian countries contributed to more than 80 per cent of the total imports into Myanmar (Table 15.2). Japan occupied the highest share of 21 per cent and India being the least with 3 per cent of the total imports of Myanmar. The other important exporters to Myanmar are China, Thailand, Singapore, Malaysia, and Korea.

The foregoing results reveal that Myanmar is an industrially backward country with low level of infrastructure and technological development. Albeit rich in natural resources, they are remained unexploited and underutilised. Its exports are mostly of primary goods and imports are mostly of capital and consumer goods. Despite its long boundary with India, the share of India's exports to Myanmar are minimally low. Moreover India's exports to Myanmar are mostly through Calcutta port and also, a large amount of Indian goods are enrouted to Myanmar via Singapore and Thailand. After the globalisation of the Indian economy since 1991, the growth of industrial product has been increasing more than 10 per cent. Thus, India has got high potential of border trade with Myanmar.

Indo-Myanmar Normal Trade

Table 15.3 indicates Indo-Myanmar trade during the period 1989 -90 to 1997-98. It could be seen from the table that there were insignificant trade between India and Myanmar upto 1992. Since 1992 the bilateral trade between the two country increased significantly. The trade between the two country increased from Rs 894 million in 1989-90 to Rs 2828 million in 1997-98. The large trade deficit with Myanmar was mainly due to the sizable imports of pulses and wood products from Myanmar (Table 15.4). India's exports consist mainly of cement, cycle, drugs and pharmaceuticals, auto parts and accessories, and cotton yarn. The potential available in the capital goods and raw material sectors does not appear to have been, as yet to be exploited by India.

TABLE 15.3

Indo-Myanmar Normal Trade (Million Rupees)

Year	*India's Exports to Myanmar*	*India's Imports from Myanmar*	*Total Trade*	*India's Balance of Trade*
1989-90	12.9	881.3	894.2	-868
1990-91	33.4	1534.6	1568	-1501
1991-92	94.6	1256.2	1350.8	- 1161
1992-93	204.5	3222.4	3426.9	-3017
1993-94	652.5	3782.4	4434.9	-3129
1996-97	596	2488	3084	-1892
1997-98	300	2528	2828	-2228

Source: DGCI and 5, Calcutta.

Review of Foreign Trade, CMIE, Bombay.

India-Myanmar Border Trade

As had already been mentioned that border trade between India and Myanmar takes place in three border points, viz. Moreh in Manipur. Champhai in Mizoram and Lungwa in Nagaland. Of these, only Moreh is officially declared open for trade, to be followed by Champhai, once the formalities are completed. Preliminary work on Lungwa area is yet to begin.

Moreh

Based on information given by custom officials, members of the merchants association and officials of the BSF, it was estimated that border trade amounted to Rs 1600 crores per year. Major items entering India are blankets, electronic goods, betel nuts, pulses, teak, groundnuts, iron scrap, gold, silver and precious stones. Main items entering Myanmar from

India are cotton yarn, cycles, food products, textiles, kerosene, diesel and drugs and pharmaceuticals.

TABLE 15.4

India's imports from and exports to Myanmar (1993-94)

Importing Items	*Value (in Rs. million)*	*Exporting items*	*Value (in Rs. million)*
Pulses	2192.9	Drugs & pharmaceuticals	14
Metaliferous ores & scraps	9.9	inorganic/organic material	6
Wood and wood products	1418.1	Cosmetic/toiletries	4
Machinery (except electrical & machine tools)	0.1	rubber manufactured products	22
Coal, coke & briquettes	1.8	Paints. Enamels, varnishes. etc.	
Other commodities	180.2	Glass. Glassware, ceramics refts/cement	130
—	—	Plastic & linoleum products	2
—	—	Residual chemical & allied products	0.4
—	—	Manufactures of metals	55
—	—	Machinery & instrument	8
—	—	Transport equipment	16
—	—	Iron & steel bars	143
—	-	Primary & Semi-finished iron & steel	243
—	—	Cotton yarn, fabrics & made ups	1
—	—	Jute manufacturers	0.8
Total	3782.8	Total	652

Source: DGCI & 5, Calcutta

Champhai

According to a study conducted by Indian Institute of Foreign Trade, New Delhi, the total amount of trade through Champhai was estimated at Rs 500. Most of the items entering into India are of electronic goods. Main items moving from India are cotton yarns, medicines and food items like Maltova, Horlicks and various baby food products.

Lungwa

The same study reported that trade through Lungwa (Nagaland) amounted to Rs 100 crores per annum. The main items include textiles, electronic goods and teak from Myanmar and medicines, food items, kerosene and diesel from the Indian side.

Potentials of Border Trade

As discussed above Myanmar is an underdeveloped country with poor infrastructure and technological development. Its main exports are mostly of primary products while imports are of capital goods, consumer goods and raw materials. On the other hand, existing border trade between India and Myanmar is charaterised by reexporting of consumer goods from Myanmar and importing daily necessities from India. Commodities being traded in the border areas are mostly not of north-east origin. Although the value of border trade was estimated as high as 2000 crore per year, official trade statistics do not reflect the substantial border trade that takes place between the two countries. Thus Indian Government in general and north-eastern states in particular get little benefits out of border trade. It is due to domination of illegal border trade that exists in the border. Commodities worthing more than 10 crores of rupee were seized every year by the custom department at the India-Myanmar border. The ongoing authorised bilateral trade between the two countries was mostly enrouted to Calcutta port. It may also be noted that a variety of products, particularly of Indian origin, are reportedly entering Myanmar through Singapore and Thailand. Therefore, direct trade between India and Myanmar through Indo-Myanmar border should benefit the north-eastern states in terms of increasing income and employment. The north-eastern states, particularly those bordered with Myanmar, are landlocked and totally isolated from the other parts of the country because of their geographical entity. Bringing exporting commodities from other parts of the country, thus would escalate the cost and ultimately, the price could not compete in the international market. Therefore, identification of both export and import oriented investment areas in the north-eastern states would finally help in getting full benefits from border trade.

Potential Areas of Export Oriented Investment

1. North-Eastern states being rich in medicinal plants and herbs, a pharmaceutical unit can be set.up for commercial exploitation as the demand for pharmaceutical products is very high in Manmar.
2. Tea based post-harvest industry should be set up in Assam as the domestic demand of Myanmar is completely met by imports.
3. Manipur being famous for handloom products, it should be commercialised as the demand is high in Myanmar. Sericulture based handloom products also should be encouraged.
4. Post-harvest agro-based industry for fruits and vegetables should be set up as the demand for processed food is high in Myanmar.
5. Since cycle is in great demand in Myanmar, the existing cycle producing unit in Manipur should be encouraged. Cycle parts such as tubes can be manufactured in Tripura and Manipur as the rubber is produced abundantly.
6. Paints and varnishes industry should be established

in Manipur as the forest based raw materials are abundantly available.

7. Since north-eastern states are having a large number of river and riverine, power industry can be set up for supply of electricity to Myanmar.
8. Since Assam has got all the requirements for industrial development, Assam can be developed into an industrial park for the north east for producing both consumer and capital goods.

Potential Areas of Import Base investment

1. Myanmar is one of the main exporting countries of rice, pulses and beans, these items can be imported from Myanmar to the hilly states and thus, the cropping pattern in the hilly region can be diverted to high value crops such as fruits, vegetables and forest trees.
2. Since Myanmar is the largest exporter of teak, teak processing industries can be set up in border areas of Manipur, Mizoram and Nagaland. It can become a central point for supplying the entire demand for wood and furniture in the country.
3. Cutting and policing of precious stones can be set up in the border area for supply.
4. Polishing and milling of pulses can be done in the border area.

Problems and Constraints

1. Poor development of infrastructure such as transport, communication, electricity and financial institutions.
2. Law and order problem in the region is deteriorating.
3. Poor demarcation and protection of border areas.
4. Restricted trade laws and regulations.

REFERENCES

Centre for Monitoring Indian Economy (1994), *Basic Statistics Related to the Indian Economy*, CMIE, Bombay, Vol. 7.

Centre for Monitoring Indian Economy (1998), *Monthly Review of the Indian Foreign Trade*, CMIE. Bombay, Vol. 7.

Pal, Suresh (1992). Agricultural exports of India: Issues of Growth and Instability, *IJAE*, 47 (4): 18 5-87.

S.K. Agnihotri (1993), Border Trade with Bangladesh. *JNECSSR*, Vol 17 (2): 29-42.

PART IV

CONTEMPORARY TRADE: NORTH-EASTERN REGION AND BANGLADESH

16

Economic Impact of Exposed Indo-Bangla Border: A Case Study of Karimganj Region

—Sukhendu Shekhar Dutta

The social scientists of the present century have achieved remarkable progress in ascertaining the causes of various socio-economic problems of the world and suggesting solutions thereof. Models have been framed for accelerating the rate of economic growth and measures have been suggested to get rid of the incidence of poverty and all that. But there has been little attention to look into the multifarious issues and problems connected with international borders. Gunnar Myrdal, in his *Asian Drama,* has dealt with some border conflicts only, but he has not taken into account host of other socio-economic issues of immense significance relating to inter-national borders.

In this paper I propose to put the spotlight only on one aspect of unholy border trade and its economic consequences. My observation is that the inflow of commodities from Bangladesh leads to an outflow of money. It is difficult to ascertain the quantum as well as the money value of foreign goods entering into Karimganj. Even then a permanent resident of Karimganj town knows that almost in every house there is either a V.C.P. or a camera or a tape-recorder or some other electrical appliances of foreign make. The value of such items can be calculated on the basis of the prevailing prices, as reported by the sellers or purchasers. A Japanese V.C.P. (Funai Brand) is sold in Karimganj at a price of rupees seven to eight thousand, tape-recorders at a price of rupees one thousand or more, camera at a price of one thousand or so. Evidences collected from the sellers of these items as well as from other sources indicate that they make transactions worth rupees three or four crores every year. The correctness and authenticity of the estimated figure can be further substantiated if one looks into some of the cases detected by the Department of Central Excise and Land Customs in recent years. Table 16.1 exhibits the position.

TABLE 16.1

Goods Smuggled in and Their Money Values

(Rs. in crores)

Year	*No. of cases*	*Gold*	*Narcotic*	*Others*	*Total*
1992-93	3144	0.4	0.35	0.62	1.37
1993-94	1369	0.16	0.31	0.71	1.18

Source: Central Excise and Land Customs, Govt. of India, Karimganj.

According to the statement of the customs officials, the percentage of detection is generally not more than 30 per cent of the actual quantum of goods smuggled into Karimganj. If this is taken as the base, it is apprehended that the total money value would be around rupees 3 to 4 crores. Thus, a huge amount of money is going out of our income stream every year enhancing the probability of cumulative loss.

Observation in this regard can also be stretched to other fields of activities. The total number of rickshaw permits issued by Karimganj Municipality, Badarpur Town Committee and Gaon Panchayats of Karimganj is around one thousand. Moreover, if only ten per cent of the rickshawallas are from Bangladesh, then the total number shall not be less than 100. If it is presumed that such rickshaw pullers earn Rs. 60.00 to

Rs. 80.00 per day, total income of this group of people per month would be (70 × 25 × 100) Rs. 1,75,000/- assuming that they work on an average twenty five days a month (Rs. 70,00 is taken as the mean of Rs. 60.00 – Rs. 80.00). Therefore, the annual outflow value of this would be (1,75,000 × 12) = Rupees, 21,00,000.

In the opinion of the police and custom departments (Karimganj) gold and narcotic drugs came in such a huge quantity that their money value per annum can not be ascertained with certainty. However, if the customs Department seizes only 30 per cent of such commodities, as mentioned earlier, and if the money value of 30 per cent of only two seized articles comes to Rs. 1.37 crore in 1992-93 or Rs. 1. 18 crores in 1993-94 (Table 16.1), then the money value of 100 per cent seizure will be Rs. 4.6 crore or Rs. 3.93 crore in 1992-93 and 1993-94 respectively. To these figures will be added the money value of electronic products and many such articles. Thus, taking together the money income of Bangladeshi rickshaw pullers, unskilled workers etc., and the value of different types of commodities as well as the unauthorised outflow of money capital, the total amount of drainage, through Karimganj border shall be more than 10 crores of rupees per annum.

The impact of this outflow of income will be taken up for economic interpretation in what follows.

The amount of money going out of the country through illegal and immoral activities has its disastrous consequences on the economy of the country. Normally, an increasing level of income leads to an increasing volume of investment and promotees economic growth via operation of the principles of multiplier and acceleration. Similarly, any diminution of income leads to diminution of investment due to the reverse combined action of multiplier-acceleration. In this study only the multiplier impacts have been taken into considerations.

Reverse Operation of Multiplier

The multiplier operates backward or forward, depending on the direction of the initial change in investment. In this study, an annual drainage of Rs. 10 crores leads to a corresponding decline in investment. If investment decreases by Rs. 10 crores, those engaged in the production of consumer goods will have that much less income than before. With a marginal propensity to consume of one-half and a multiplier of 2, consumption expenditure would keep declining on a 50 per cent basis in each round until aggregate income decreases by Rs. 20 crores. Thus the initial reduction in investment precipitates the reverse operation of the multiplier. With a marginal propensity to consume of four-fifths or 80 per cent, the ultimate decline of income would be Rs. 50 crores. In a backward economy like that of Karimganj, the marginal propensity to consume is generally high. Naturally, the quantum of decline in income is likely to be quite high. Thus the higher the marginal propensity to consume the greater the value of multiplier and the greater also the cumulative decline of income. In other words, a community with a high propensity to save is hurt less by the reverse operation of the multiplier than one with a low propensity to save. The effects of the decrease in investment on income in this two cases are shown in 16.1A and B. transposed in the light of marginal propensity to consume, etc. of Karimganj as assumed.

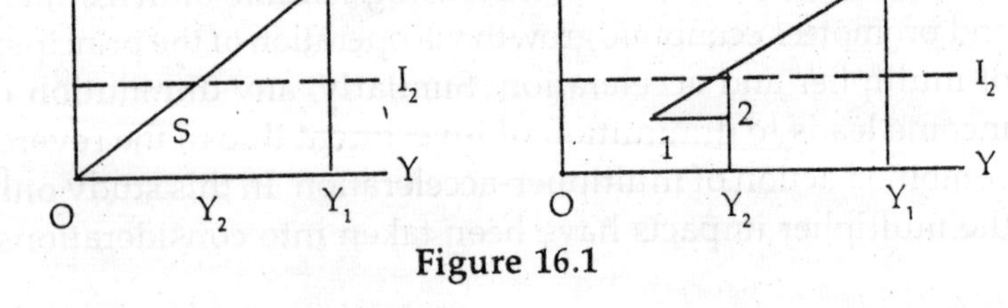

Figure 16.1

Effects of the Decrease in Invest on Income, with Different Marginal Propensities to Save

In figure 16.1 A and B the investment schedules are drawn to be horizontal which indicate the autonomous nature of investment. In figure 16.1(A), the savings curve slopes upward in such a way as to indicate a marginal propensity to save one-half, and in 16.1(B), it is flatter to designate a marginal propensity to save one-fifth. In both cases the decline in investment is assumed to be the same, as measured by the distance between the investment curves, I_1 and I_2. The equilibrium level of income given by the intersection of the savings curve and the new dotted investment curve is much lower down from the initial level in B than in A. With a marginal propensity to consume of four-fifths or 80 per cent (inverse of the marginal propensity to save one-fifth), the ultimate decline of income would be Rs. 50 crores. On the other hand, with a marginal propensity to consume of one-half, or 50 per cent (inverse of the marginal propensity to save of one-half), the ultimate decline of income would be Rs. 20 crores. The decline of Rs. 50 crores in income corresponds to the horizontal length of Y_1 Y_2 in figure 16.1(B), and Rs. 20 crores decline in income is reflected in the distance between Y_1 and Y_2 in figure 16.1(A). These declines in (A) are on the assumption that the initial decline in investment is Rs. 10 crores in both cases, as measured by the distance between the old; solid investment curve and the new; dotted investment curve. The horizontal length Y_1Y_2 in 16.1(A) will be found to be exactly twice the vertical distance between the two investment curves. This conforms to the previous explanation that, with a marginal propensity to consume of one-half and therefore, with the multiplier of 2, Rs. 10 crore investment outlay leads to an ultimate income of Rs. 20 crore. Similarly, the horizontal length I_1I_2 in 16.1(B) equals five times the vertical distance between the two investment curves. This is so because, the marginal propensity to consume is equal to four-fifths and corresponding multiplier involved is 5.

Thus it can be said that the initial decline in investment will have a more depressing effect on the levels of income and employment when the marginal propensity to consume is high (or when the marginal propensity to save is low) than when the marginal propensity to consume is low (or when the marginal propensity to save is high). It follows that the cumulative decline of income is likely to be greater with a given decline in marginal propensity to consume exhibits an upward trend than when and where it tends to fall.

From the above analysis it appears that the estimated drainage of Rs. 10 crores per annum from Karimganj, definitely acts as a drag on the development process of the region. Such a consequence is the obvious outcome of the vulnerable Indo-Bangladesh international border. Had there been no such loose and often uncared for international border, there would have been no such drainage or no such economic loss. Rather, the economy could enjoy the benefits of forward operation of multiplier and experience an increase in income. A persisting outflow of money through the international border has retarded the economic progress of Karimganj to a considerable extent.

Thus the exposed Indo-Bangla border has crippled the economy of Karimganj, as smuggling plays a dominant role in distorging economic functioning. Before partition, Karimganj was a prosperous commercial centre catering to the needs of Tripura, Manipur, Mizoram and the entire Barak valley. But partition and the consequent emergence of a new international frontier changed the commerce oriented economy of Karimganj into a smuggling-oriented economy. Bangladesh market being flooded with foreign goods of better quality got an outlet through the border and reached Karimganj in huge quantities. Consequently, a huge amount of money is perpetually being drained out of India through Karimganj border. The situation is very much perplexing. It is difficult to get rid of such a state of affairs.

However, the continuous drainage of money outflow can be tackled by introducing Free Trade Zone or by legalising border trade. Such a policy may help us to get rid of the inherent vices of smuggling to a considerable extent.

17

Coal Export from Meghalaya to Bangladesh: A Case Study of the Barsora Trade Route

—Rajesh Dutta

Meghalaya and Bangladesh share a common border covering a distance of around 423 km. Trade existed even before India's Independence between the people residing in these remote areas. But trade came to a halt after India's independence when the central Government withdrew these facilities. Discontentment among the border people led to the emergence of unofficial trade. Border trade was subsequently opened up when its importance was recognised. Today border trade is carried out at certain specified hats under the B.S.F. supervision.

Given the geographical location of Meghalaya and the fact that very few indigenous industries exist, most of her mineral resources have found their way to neighbouring states and countries. However, since these neighbouring states and countries are also at their initial stages of development, the level of trade is insufficient to contribute significantly to the economic development of the people and the regions possessing the mineral resources.

With the above in mind the study focuses on certain issues related to the largest export item from Meghalaya, i.e. coal. Even though the study confines itself to coal trade along the Barsora trade route in West Khasi Hills, the issues discussed are neither exhaustive nor unique. The sources of information for this study are secondary as well as primary data.

Objective of the Study

Due to time constraint, this paper focuses on the following issues:

(a) Establish the importance of the Borsora trade route,
(b) Modus Operandi of coal trade,
(c) Show the existence of voluminous unofficial trade,
(d) Impact of trade on the region; and
(e) Problems hampering trade and measures.

(A) Importance of the Borsora Trade Route

Borsora, a traditional trade route for coal, is situated in the West Khasi Hills District about 140 km from Shillong. It is also situated in the Langrin Coal Field near the Bangladesh border. The Langrin Coal Field has an estimated reserve of 97.61 million tonnes or 59 percent of the total Khasi Hills reserves of 164.5 million tonnes. This coal field is bound by the Kynsi river on the east, Moheskhola river on the west and the Umbytit river on the north. Hence, the only economically viable route for exporting coal from this region is via Borsora to Bangladesh.

The important coal producing areas in the Langrin coal field are Nongjry, Nonghyllam, Rajaju, Tipul, Lailad and Sawnumber. Of these Nonghyllam and Sawnumber are the major coal exporting areas. Mining was first started in this region by the Assam Bengal Cement Company for the Chattak Cement Plant but was discontinued in the 1960s.

The other coal field in West Khasi Hills is the East Darangiri Coal Field. Coal from this reserve finds its way to Assam via Sonapahar and Boko.

(B) Modus Operandi of Coal Trade

According to Directorate of Mineral Resources (DMR) sources, although there are over a 100 supplier/exporters, only 28 individuals and groups are exporting coal regularly. Group members range from 2 to 8.

There are three classes of individual traders:

(a) those with mines and export licences,
(b) those with mines but no licences; and
(c) middlemen — no mines and no licences.

A newly established exporter has on an average 4 mines engaging 4 labourers per mine. Daily extraction of coal from the new mines is around 5 to 6 tonnes per mine. Well established exporters have on an average 20 or more mines engaging 12 to 15 labourers per mine. Daily extraction from these mines is about 20 to 25 tonnes. The minimum labour cost (extracting, loading and unloading) works out to around Rs.300 per tonne.

The above information is depicted in Table 17.1.

TABLE 17.1

Features of Coal Mining in Borsora

Classification of Exporters	*Average No. of Mines*	*Labour Engaged Per Mine*	*Daily Extraction of Coal per Mine (in tonnes)*	*Minimum Labour Cost per*	*Total Labour per day per mine*
Newly Established (Less than 5 years)	4	4 (16)	5 to 6 (20-24)	Rs.300	Rs.1500-1800 (Rs.6000-7200)
Well Established	20 or more	12 - 15 (240-300)	20 to 25 (400-500)	Rs.300	Rs.6000-7500 (Rs.120000-150000)

Note: (a) Figures within parentheses indicate Totals.
(b) The number of mines in the table refer to the regular suppliers only.

Table 17.1 reveals that the daily expenses are high and this is a likely reason for the small number of regular exporters.

Export Procedure

An exporter receives a Letter of Credit (LOC) from an importer. This LOC states the quantity of coal demanded at the officially determined rate per tonne. The exporter then produces the LOC at the DMR office in Shillong and obtains challans after paying a royalty of Rs. 120/- per tonne for the coal that is to be exported. Challans are issued on the basis of tonnage per truck. Permissible tonnage per truck has been increased from 6 tonnes to 7 tonnes in 1997-98. Challans are presently worth Rs.840/- (earlier Rs.720/-). One LOC was equal to 100 tonnes, now reduced to 50 tonnes. Challans are produced at the LCS in Borsora when coal is exported. Not much is known about the use of imported coal, except that it is used for domestic purposes and for brick burning.

TABLE 17.2

Coal Production in West Khasi Hills Exports Through Borsora (in Tonnes)

Year	*West Khasi Hills*	*Export*	*Through Borsora*
1989-90	60,900	1000	(1.6)
1990-91	54,300	973	(1.8)
1991-92	50,500	1500	(3)
1992-93	62,900	1346.42	(2.1)
1993-94	43,900	3420	(7.8)
1994-95	91,700	33258	(36.3)
1995-96	182,100	28500	(15.2)
1996-97	106,500	52750.35	(50)
1997-98	112,800	33308	(39.3)
Total	765,600	167055	(21.8)

Source: DMR

Note: Figures within ( ) indicate the annual percentage of production from the Langrin Coal Field to total production in West Khasi Hills.

The following table gives the total coal production in West Khasi Hills alongwith the quantity of exported coal through the LCS at Borsora for the period 1989-98.

The above table reveals that total production has fluctuated over the years and also that total production exceeded one lakh tonnes from 1995-96. Exports through Borsora remained low until 1993-94. Since then exports increased significantly inspite of fluctuations. This increase in exports may be due to the liberalisation process/export promotion or due to devaluation/depreciation of the rupee vis-a-vis the dollar. It could also imply that exporters were better established and hence output extracted had significantly increased

(C) Existence of Unofficial Trade

Using the export figures through the LCS at Borsora, the number of trucks plying per annum and per day have been calculated in Table 17.3.

TABLE 17.3

No. of Trucks Per Annum and Trucks Per Day Through Borsora

Year	*Export (In Tonnes)*	*Trucks Per Annum*	*Estimated Trucks Per Day*
1989-90	1000	167	< 1
1990-91	973	162	<1
1991-92	1500	250	1
1992-93	1346.42	224	1
1993-94	3420	570	3
1994-95	33258	5543	26
1995-96	26500	4750	23
1996-97	52750.35	8792	42
1997-98	44308	6330	30

Notes: 1. No. of trucks per annum have been calculated using the following:

Period : 1989-97 : tonnage per truck = 6

1997-98 : tonnage per truck = 7

2. Estimated trucks per day have been calculated by assuming 7 working months, i.e. Jan.-April and Oct.-Dec. or 210 days.

Primary data, however, reveals a different picture. According to unofficial sources, the number of trucks plying per day was estimated at 120 at the time of this study. This would mean 25,200 trucks (120 × 210) per annum exported 1.76.400 tonnes (25.200 × 7) of coal in 1997-98.

This information leads to 3 conclusions:

(a) official data relating to quantity of trade is underestimated,

(b) unofficial trade of 1,32,092 tonnes (1,76,400-44,308) took place in 1997-98 and this volume is around 3 times larger than the official trade,

and (c) huge revenue loss amounting to Rs.1513.5 lakhs (1,32,092 x Rs.120 per ton) to the DMR in the form of royalty payment.

It has also been learnt that the actual trading price of coal per ton is less than the officially determined rate. This leads to 2 conclusions:

(a) official data relating to revenue from exports is overestimated,

and (b) net profit per truck is also overestimated.

The table 17.4 makes both the conclusions clear.

This section is based on observations made during my visits to the study site.

The obvious impact of trade is that the coal reserves have been partially exploited and exported and income and employment generated in the process. But the gains of trade have gone to a few leading to income disparities. Majority of the exporters do not belong to the region. The local inhabitants, the Hashahs, being poor did not and still do not have the means to exploit the coal reserves. So they have either sold or leased their lands to people from other regions.

TABLE 17.4

Projected and Actual Gross and Net Profit Per Truck

Revenue Per Truck	*Cost Per Truck*		*Net Profit Per Truck*
1) *Projected*	1) Minimum Transport	- Rs. 2500	1) *Projected*
	2) Payment to the		
7MT x $ 40 = 280$	King/Syiem at		Rs. 5105
or Rs. 11760	Check Gate	- Rs. 165	
	3) Royalty on Leased		2) *Actual*
2) *Actual*	Mines @ Rs. 150		
	Per Tonne	- Rs. 1050	Rs. 2165
7MT x $30 = 210$	4) Minimum Labour		
Or Rs. 8820	Cost Per Truck	- Rs. 2100	
	5) Royalty to Govt.		
	(Challan) @ Rs. 120		
	Per Tonne	-Rs. 840	
	Total Cost	- Rs. 6655	

Notes : (1) Tonnage Per Truck = 7
(2) Officially Determined Rate Per Tonne = $40
Actual Selling Rate Per Tonne = $30
(3) Current Exchange Rate $1 = Rs. 42

(D) Impact of Trade on the Region

Inspite of several years of mining, the process remains unscientific. Surface mining method/rat hole method is practised to extract coal. Since quantity extracted is small and tedious the labourers have to work for longer hours. Moreover, the absence of electricity prevents the use of modern mining equipment.

There is also no evidence of a developing town with modern amenities in Borsora. A few shops and tea stalls are all that exist at the customs check gate. The road leading to Borsora from Ranikor is in poor condition. Communication is largely underdeveloped.

The labourers live in pitiful and unhygienic surroundings. Many suffer from ailments associated with mining such as back pains, chest pains., joint pains etc. apart from the common malaria sickness in the region. Living costs are high in Borsora and this leaves the workers little or nothing to save.

There is also no evidence of ploughing back of profits apart from that in expanding mining and trade operations. This implies an outflow of income from the area. In short, there has been little economic development in the region inspite of trade over the years.

(E) Problems and Measures

Profit incentives push trade to higher levels and this is reflected by the increasing quantity of exports over the years, inspite of several constraints.

The primary and most significant problem facing exporters is the trade route. Poor road conditions have led to delays in the movement of coal, higher transportation costs (due to greater depreciation of trucks) and hence smaller net profits. Smaller next profits via official trade have led to voluminous unofficial trade. Also, the existing road condition makes possible the usage of trucks of smaller carrying capacity (7 tonnes, instead of 10 or more tonnes). Certain coal reserve areas are inaccessible due to the complete lack of roads.

The surface mining method and the absence of electricity for adopting modern mining technology have kept extraction of coal at low levels. Lack of finance lending institutions have led to erratic supply from small exporters due to high operational costs. Corruption/kickbacks along various points of the trade route have discouraged the smaller exporters and also promoted unofficial trade in a big way.

Earlier there was the problem of obtaining challans from the DMR office in Shillong all the way from Borsora. This problem has been solved by issuing challans from the LCS in Borsora.

Another problem is regarding the administered price of coal by the Central Government. The official rate is higher than the actual traded rate. Administered rates make the supply price of coal uncompetitive. In this regard, it has been learnt that Australia currently supplies coal to Bangladesh at a much cheaper rate.

The measures emerge from the nature of the problems. Proper roads and communication, electricity and scientific mining are necessary to reduce wastage of time, reduce costs and increase the output. Corruption/kickbacks need to be checked and official trade promoted. Administered prices need to be done away with. There measures would lead to grater revenue for the State Government. The Government, in turn, should utilise the revenue earned for creating the necessary infrastructure and climate favourable to trade. The measures should be such that it promotes trade in many commodities. Then border trade would be on a larger scale, comprising many commodities and affecting a wide range of occupations and people.

Measures should also be taken to ensure that the land resources are made inalienable from the local inhabitants. The locals should be made shareholders in the production process to ensure that they get income on a regular basis.

In 1993 the Meghalaya Mineral Development Corporation (MMDC) was bestowed with the status of Export House to assume the catalytic role of export promotion. Given the prospects of international trade, the MMDC has been entrusted with working out a detailed strategy based on the ground reality of the state. The results are still awaited.

18

An Empirical Investigation into the Cross Border Indo-Bangladesh Trade: A Case Study of South Assam

—Keya Sengupta & Harun Rashid Laskar

I. Introduction

No nation in modern times can afford to live in isolation and this is more true particularly for smaller nation. The basic idea of international trade is based on the fact that no nation is endowed with all the requisite resources, which may help to produce all the required goods necessary to survive in a civilized society. Interdependence among nations through trade, therefore, is most essential for attaining a higher level of consumption. It also helps in the optimum utilisation of factors. Since resources can be allocated to sectors according to the needs of international trade, rapid growth of the economy by maximum utilisation of its productive potential is, thus, facilitated. While there is very little debate relating to the importance and necessity of interdependence among nations through international trade, differences arise on the extent, type and nature of this interdependence. International trade is one of the oldest branches of economics, the idea of which developed way back in the 16th century. In fact, the very foundation of economics—the principle of "Law of supply and demand" was first propounded by Mill, to explain price determination in international markets. The issue which brought international trade in focus still continue to dominate economic thinking with greater intensity and strength, paving its way to the modern idea of globalisation and global integration.

II. Benefits and Problems of Trade Between Nations

Trade between nations are advantageous mainly because technological benefits originating in one nation can be shared by the trading partners, this is possible through the exchange of goods, which embodies modern technology or directly through technological transfer. International trade also facilitates transfer of capital so that the excess capital of the developed nations can be invested profitably for the development of the less developed nations supplementing domestic savings. Added to these advantages, the major thrust of international trade lies in the optimum utilisation of factor. Input of the trading nations. This allocative function of international trade maximise factor reward resulting in stimulating national income, employment opportunities, and consumption level of trading partners. These motivating factors in turn gears up the national economy with the positive impact on the major macro economic variables of the nation.

However, a number of hesitancy marks international trade which results in numerous debates and discussions relating to the nature and magnitude of international trade. Consequently trade between nations are often restricted resulting in less than optimum benefits from international trade. Global interaction through international trade may influence domestic employment and growth rates which may be transferred from one nation to another through international transactions. This in turn has its impact upon domestic monetary and fiscal policies formulated not only to maintain external balance but even for the achievement of domestic goals. This necessitate knowledge of the trading partners, economic policies on agricultural and industrial sectors, which in turn may influences international prices for these products.

Their policies and exchange rates, tariffs and custom duties are also of crucial importance. The role of such policies assume greater significance when the trading partners is an economically strong nation. Experience also reveals that too much dependence of the smaller nations on the economically advanced nations may also give way to political dominance where the domestic policies relating to economics and politics, may be dictated by the dominant trading partners. The smaller nations under such circumstances are under a much greater hesitancy and doubt to enter into trade contract with larger nations.

III. Trade Relation Between India and Bangladesh

Keeping the benefits of trade in mind particularly between neighbouring nations, that we make an attempt to examine the border trade relation between India and Bangladesh. Trade is encouraged and hurdles of international trade removed when the pairs of trading nations are endowed with similar factors and have similar customs and culture. Geographical closeness of neighbouring trading nations reduced transport cost and boosts up border trade. All these features prompts us to investigate the trade relation between India and its neighbour Bangladesh, the two nations which are located in close proximity with uniform custom and culture, particularly with those states of India bordering Bangladesh. In this connection we shall focus attention to the border of South Assam Through which a substantial portion of transaction between this nation is carried on.

An important aspects of India-Bangladesh relationship since the emergence of Bangladesh in 1971 was economic co-operation and high level of trade which was expected to enhance not only better understanding between the two nations, but was also expected to pave the way for long term economic development based on trade. The emergence of Bangladesh as an independent nation and closer political ties between the two nations had brightened the prospects of

Indo-Bangladesh trade. It was expected that exports from India would include consumers items, drugs, medicines, raw materials and light equipments like steel products, ferry engines, power generation and transmission equipments and petroleum and petroleum products. It is to be noted here that most of these items were either produced in India for export to other nation or produced as import substitution or even imported from other nations to be re-exported to Bangladesh, and entailing substantial loss of foreign exchange.

The economic reforms of 1991 in India contained important trade policy components, which had been motivated by a full recognition of the important role that trade can play in promoting growth. Since 1991 India has made steady progress in eliminating quantitative restrictions and imports of capital goods, raw material and components have been delicenced and rates of tariffs reduced drastically, Exim policy 1992-97 has been reviewed and revised in several ways during the current year to further phase out quantitative and qualitative restrictions. Attention has been focused due to the various SAARC meets to improve border trade with Bangladesh, keeping in view the tremendous potentiality of trade between these two nations.

Economic reform introduced in Bangladesh between 1983-1995, with intensive reforms measure from 1990-95 have put special emphasise in boosting up the export sectors. Bangladesh was been experiencing vibrant export growth since 1980. The improved export policy framework coupled with a favourable trading environment in India for Indo-Bangladesh trade is expected to raise the extent and volume of trade in both these nations. This in turn is further expected to raise the national income and economic welfare in these respective nations.

IV. (I) Empirical Analysis

In view of the immense role which Indo-Bangladesh trade can play for the economic development of the respective nations, it is interesting to review the trend of trade between these two nations. The analysis shall be devided into two parts. The first part shall explore the Indo-Bangladesh trade relation with the help of official figure and the second part of work will deal with similar work based on unofficial figures relating to Indo-Bangladesh trade carried on through the border of South Assam.

TABLE 18.1

Percentage of Indian Export and Import from Bangladesh

Year	*Export*	*Import*
1992-93	0.019	0.00035
1993-94	0.019	0.00076
1994-95	0.034	0.00133

A perusal of table 18.1 reveals that both in 1992-93 and 1993-94 the level of export from India to Bangladesh recorded a paltry 0.019 per cent increase rising marginally in the following year to 0.034 per cent. Examination of corresponding figure for import from Bangladesh presents a still more miserable picture. The proportion of import from Bangladesh to total import stands at 0.00035 per cent in 1992-93 rising marginally to 0.00076 per cent and 0.00133 per cent in the following year. These results reveal that the trade understanding between these nation and the efforts at global integration has failed to have any significant impact on the Indo-Bangladesh trade regime, inspite of having vast scope of improving trade ties between two nations.

It is also interesting to examine in this connection the increase in value terms of Indo-Bangladesh trade, as against the over all trade in India. This would enable us to grasp the position and importance of Indo-Bangladesh trade. Examination of table 18.2 reveals that while export to Bangladesh increased by Rs. 320 crores and Rs. 1475 crores in 1992-93 and 1993-94 respectively. Total export for the corresponding period in India increased by Rs. 16063 and Rs. 12923 crores. The value of import from Bangladesh has gone up, by even a smaller amount. While it increased by Rs. 34 crores in 1993-94, from 1992-93 it rose marginally to Rs. 64 crores, in the following year. Total import to India for the same period increased by Rs. 9726 and Rs. 16870 crores. Examination of the trend of trade with Bangladesh therefore reveals that trade between these two neighbouring nations leaves a lot to be desired.

TABLE 18.2

Trend on Indo-Bangladesh Trade

(Rs. in Crores)

Year	*Growth of Indias Export*		*Growth of Indias Import*	
	To Bangladesh	*All other countries*	*From Bangladesh*	*All other*
1993-94	320	16063	34	9726
1994-95	1475	12923	64	16870

The above analysis of the trend of trade between these nations has further prompted us to examine the foreign trade multiplier or the export multiplier of trade between these two nations. Such multiplier can draw the broad contours of growth of the domestic economy, due to operation of export sector. This possibility arises not only due to the direct impact of export on economic welfare, but by working out the secondary effects, the export multiplier can indicate the exact amount which the total national income of the domestic sector may be pushed up due to export.

For estimating the export multiplier the economy is assumed to be an open economy which maintains equality between saving and investment on one hand and export and import on the other. A change in any of these variables would automatically effect the other variables. However for our purpose we will assume that saving which equals investment are fixed so that we shall consider only the effects of changes of export on National Income. Consequently we shall consider the following model.

$$\Delta Y = \frac{1}{K_f} \quad \Delta X$$

$$\text{Where, } K_f = \frac{1}{s + m} = \text{the foreign trade multiplier.}$$

$$s = \frac{\Delta S}{\Delta Y} = \text{Marginal propensity to save.}$$

$$m = \frac{\Delta M}{\Delta Y} = \text{Marginal propensity to import.}$$

ΔS = Change in saving

ΔM = Change in import.

ΔY = Change in National income.

ΔX = Change in export.

Savings and imports are considered to be direct leakages from the stream of nation's National Income and therefore, they do not facilitate the growth of domestic income. The Marginal propensity to import establish linkages between domestic and foreign sectors of the economy. Here we shall firstly analyse the effects on National Income of an increase in export to Bangladesh by the estimation of foreign trade multiplier (making the drastic assumption that trade with other nation is fixed).

The results of our estimation reveals that the foreign trade multiplier of export to Bangladesh had the ability to increase India's National Income, through the operation of export multiplier, to the extent of Rs. 890 crore in 1993-94, and Rs. 3317 crore in 1994-95. In the contrast the total foreign trade multiplier in India had the capacity to increase India's

National Income by Rs. 44655 crore in 1993-94 and Rs. 29076 crore in 1994-95. The analysis goes to suggest that the vast potentiality of Indo-Bangladesh trade not withstanding trade between these two neighbouring nations constitute a very insignificant proportion of the total volume of trade in India. The various understanding and memorandum of economic co-operation and trade between these two nations atleast did not benefit India significantly.

TABLE 18.3

Potential Impact of Foreign Trade Multiplier on India's National Income

Year	*Bangladesh (Rs. in crores)*	*World (Rs. in crores)*
1993-94	890	44655
1994-95	3317	29076

IV. (ii) Empirical Analysis

Due to the existence of tremendous potentiality of export to Bangladesh and its concomitant impact on Indias National Income coupled with the fact that it is an accepted fact that close border encourages unofficial trade, we have made an attempt to investigate the extent of such unofficial trade or as it as termed as "smuggling" across the border. We have selected the border areas of South Assam for this purpose. As can be well understood obtaining data for such purposes is associated with a lot of resistance and difficulties. However, we have attempted to the best of our ability to derive the requisite information. Our data reveals that the major items smuggled out of India through the border of South Assam are sugar, salt, rice, bidis, kerosine oil, medicines, shaving razor, blade, torch battery, chillies, textiles and fruits. In contrast, the items that reach India from Bangladesh are fish, chappals, soap, and mustrad oil.

TABLE 18.4

Official and Un-official Trade from India to Bangladesh Through South Assam

Year	*Un-official (Rs. in crores)*	*Official (Rs. crores)*
1997	365.2	2215
1998	967.00	2506

Among the items going to Bangladesh from India, rice constitutes the bulk of the value of goods followed by sugar, bidies and blade. Estimation of the total value of the produce from India, finding its way across the border to Bangladesh through South Assam, stands at Rs. 365 crores in 1997 and Rs. 967 crores in 1998 (till October). As against this values, the official tradc across the same border for the corresponding period stands at Rs. 2215 and Rs. 2506 crores respectively. It is interesting to observe that while official level trade increased by 11.6%, the unofficial trade jumped by 62.2% in the same period, reveals the increasing attractiveness of unofficial trade over official trade. It is further observed that items like, rice and chilly, come under both categories of trade, official as well as unofficial. While India earned Rs. 1460 crores in 1998 through export of rice alone, as per official statistics, earning from unofficial trade for rice for the same period amounted to Rs. 6204 crores. Reasons could be the unprecedented floods in Bangladesh in 1998 destroying their standing crops and necessitating immediate imports from India. Similarly while export earning from chilly was Rs. 3.83 crores in 1997, it was 7.3 crores through smuggling in the same period.

It can therefore be maintained from the examination of these trade figures that unaccounted trade has become a characteristic feature of border trade through South Assam, pushing the official level trade to the back ground.

TABLE 18.5

Potential Impact of Foreign Trade Multiplier on India's National Income (for Trade Both Official and Unofficial Through the Borders of South Assam)

(Rs. in Crores)

Year	*Through official trade*	*Through unofficial trade*
1997	6157	1016.4
1998	5613	2174.9

The above analysis has warranted the estimation of foreign trade multiplier of both official and unofficial level of trade, so as to capture the growth potential of the Indian economy due to her export to Bangladesh. Using the same method for the estimation of foreign trade multiplier as before, perusal of Table 18.5 reveals that the increase in — National income in India, due to the operation of export multiplier through official export across the South Assam Border is Rs. 6157 crores and Rs. 5613 crores respectively in 1997 and 1998. On the other hand for the same period the income generating through export multiplier, estimated on the basis of unofficial trade works out to be Rs. 1016 crores and Rs. 2174 crores respectively. Absence of illegal trade could have succeeded in adding this amount to the income generation capacity through legal trade. The nation is therefore loosing the income creating capacity every year by this huge amount through illegal trade only through South Assam. If similar estimates are made for the entire volume of cross border trade, for all the borders with Bangladesh for the other entry points as well, the loss to the Indian economy not only by way of foreign exchange alone but also numerous other ways is too high a price which our nation can hardly afford at this stage.

If income to the extent of Rs. 1016 crores and Rs. 2174 crores could have been generated through recognised legal channels of trade, the economic scenerios of South Assam might have been totally different. The region is industrially backward, added to which its geographical, isolation and unfriendly communication system, has hampered seriously the economic progress of the region, particularly after the partition. Development of this region had received a serious set-back after the partition, which has a tremendous negative impact on its economy. Limited market demand in the region, high transportation cost and diseconomics of large scale production has discouraged industrial development on a massive scale. Inability to fully harness, the developmental potentials of the region both in the agricultural and industrial sector has led to the systematic blunting of its growth capabilities. Examination of the unofficial level of trade between Bangladesh and this region reveals that agricultural items like rice, chilies and fruits of various types from this region are in high demand in Bangladesh. Trade at the official level could have encouraged agricultural and horticultural sector of the region, which in turn could have provided strong base, for the future developmental prospect of the region. Unofficial trade of these items however has prevent such a prospect. A major portion of the smuggled out items from this region arrive from the other parts of India, meant for the consumers of this region. However, smuggling of these items to Bangladesh not only entails loss of consumers welfare in this region by way of reduced consumption, but also by way of higher prices which consumers of this region have to pay mainly due to the artificial shortage of such items of consumption.

Besides agricultural and horticultural products industrial items which can be produced in the Small Scale sector such as bidis, blades, razors, torch battery, by the establishment of Small Scale units, could also have been geared up in this region. This would not only have increased earnings of foreign exchange, but, through the secondary impact of foreign trade multiplier, could have created huge employment opportunities, in these sectors, and subsequently could have boosted up production and further employment in consumers goods industries as well through the export multiplier. Failure in harnessing these opportunities has resulted in misallocation of our resources and less than their optimum utilisation.

Though the study has confined itself only to that aspect of international trade dealing with foreign trade multiplier, attention has also to be focussed on the fact that unaccounted trade to the extent of Rs. 365 crores and 976 crores in 1997 and 1998 respectively across the border of South Assam also entails loss of govt. revenue by way of tariffs and duties. It is also maintained that every successful nation attempts to synchronize their domestic policies with the trade policies of the nation's external sectors but such massive volume of unaccounted trade falls totally outside the purview of our trade policies. This disturbing feature if allowed to continue unabated will not only lead to the failure of our domestic policies, but may also come in direct confrontation of our internal policies throwing a substantial part of our aims and objective of development based on foreign trade, totally out of gear.

It is also evident that such illegal trade which is totally monopolising the Indo-Bangladesh trade scenerio, if not immediately arrested may prove to be extremely harmful particularly from the future growth prospects of the sate bordering Bangladesh. This is more true for an isolated region like South Assam, which may find it very difficult to develop her economy by a total dependence on internal domestic policies and resources alone. South Assam thereby may continue to remain backward, despite having tremendous potentialities of growth, through a significant dependence on Indo-Bangladesh trade. This in the long run will surely proved to be a very important means of progressive stimulus to its development efforts only if given a proper chance.

V. Conclusion

However, all is not steeped in total pessimism. The Central

Govt. has recently agreed to a proposal by the State Govt. to set up a free trade centre at Suterkandi, 18 K.M. away from Karimganj Town, which is the main area through which unofficial cross border trade is carried on. Setting up of the proposed centre, which is expected by the year 2001 may go a long way in checking illegal trade, added to this effort some concrete steps have also to be undertaken immediately to have a direct control ever such unofficial trade. The proposal of carrying out the entire transaction in Dollar may also mean the possibility of some positive impact on the Indian economy, since total export to Bangladesh far exceeds, Indias import from Bangladesh, both at the official as well as unofficial level. It is thus evident that India had failed to take advantage of the immense potentialities of Indo-Bangladesh trade relation, which unfortunately has so far remained unexplored and unexploited.

REFERENCES

1. *Economic Survey:* Govt. of India, various issues.
2. Feder, G., (1982), "On exports and economic growth," *Journal of Development Economics.*
3. Heller, R.H., (1974), *International Monetary Economics,* Englewood Cliffs, Prentice Hall.
4. Keesing, D., (1967), "Outward looking, policies and Economic Development," *Economic Journal.*
5. Michaely, M., (1977), "Exports, and growth: An Empirical investigation", *Journal of Development Economics.*
6. Quibria, M.C., (Ed.), 1997, *Bangladesh Economy in Transition,* Oxford University Press, New Delhi.
7. Sen, Sunanda, (1972), Indo-Bangladesh Trade: Problems and Prospects," *Economic and Political Weekly,* issue 15, Vol. VII.
8. Srinivasa, Madhu, (1994), "Trade and external sector reforms in Developing Asia," An overview, *Economic and Political Weekly,* issue 6, Vol. XXIX.
9. *Statistical Outline of India, 1996-97:* Tata Service Ltd., Department of Economics and Statistics Mumbai.
10. *Telegraph,* Oct 26 (1998), Second border trade Centre in region cleared.

19

The Impact of Cross-Border Human Traffic: A Case Study of Karimganj District

—P.C. Dutta & N. Roy

Karimganj district with an area of 1839 sq. km. is situated in the southern part of Assam. Geographically, the district is vulnerable as it is surrounded by Bangladesh in north and west covering an area of 94 km. long international border. Of this total length, 54 km is land border and 40 km is riverine border. The southern boundery of Karimganj is Tripura and Mizoram and the eastern boundery is other two districts of Barak Valley viz. Cachar and Hailakandi.

Karimganj, the extreme southern district of Assam is situated between longitude 92 15′ and 92 35′ East and between 24 15′ and 24 55′ East latitude. The north and north-eastern parts of the district are plain areas while the south and south-western parts are covered by dense forests.

Before independence, next only to Guwahati and Tinsukia, Karimganj was one of the most flourishing trade centres in the province of Assam. This commercial importance of Karimganj suffered a set back primarily due to disruption of easy communication link with the rest of India.

In the context of economy of Karimganj, the hard reality is that there is neither any scope to transfer the surplus manpower from the farm sector to some other sector nor there is any possibility of bringing about any change in techniques when the economic structure itself is more or less primitive.

As the labour class from Bangladesh agree to do work at a lower wage rate and as also they do not hesitate to do work even under adverse climatic conditions even in remote interior places, the businessmen and contractors of Karimganj prefer those Bangladeshi labour. It is a fact that efficiency level of those workers is higher than that of the local workers. It is their ability and mobility which give them the opportunity to take place easily into the employment market.

The Table 19.1 reveals the fact that the density per square km. in Karimganj district is much above the all Assam and all India level which supports the fact of growing infiltration in Karimganj due to the peculiar border area. It is observed in some places that an international border line passes through a house. As a result the family belong that house is considered as neither the citizen of India nor the citizen of Bangladesh or the both which creates a problem.

TABLE 19.1

Density Per Sq. Km.

Census year	*1971*	*1981*	*1991*
Karimganj	317	439	457
Assam	186	254	184
India	177	216	267

Source: Statistical handbook of Assam. 1976, 1992.

A close look at the Table 19.2 reveals that the natural growth rate of population in Karimganj is higher than the all India level. No significant event — social, political, economical or climatic took place in Karimganj in Twentieth Century which might have its impact on the natural growth rate of population except the freedom of India (1947) and Independence of Bangladesh (1971).

TABLE 19.2

Percentage Decadal Variation in Karimganj

Census year	*Karimganj*	*Assam*	*India*
1901-11	12.94	16.99	5.75
1911-21	3.19	20.48	–0.31
1921-31	5.91	19.91	11.00
1931-41	9.52	20.40	14.22
1941-51	29.87	19.93	13.31
1951-61	22.96	34.98	21.51
1961-71	25.15	34.95	24.80
1971-81	36.20	23.36	24.66
1981-91	31.82	23.58	23.50

It is observed that there are two sudden jumps in decadal variation in Karimganj one is from 9.52 in 1941 to 29.97 in 1951 and the other is from 25.15 in 1971 to 36.20 in 1961. This may due to the fact that after independence (1947) people came here from Bangladesh for their safety and shelter in all respects. The same drama repeated again in 1971-81 due to independence of Bangladesh (1971).

Table 19.3 shows the number of persons detected by the police and these figures forms only a very little fraction of the total number of Bangladeshi persons working in Karimganj. There is no elaborate and scientific machinery for proper detection of all such persons. Some persons are detected only when the police initiate a drive against unlicensed rickshaw pullers. So these migrants are depriving the bonafied workers from the benefit of employment and earnings It is due to the fact that economic crisis in Bangladesh have compelled them to come over here in search of bread and clothing.

The partition of India brought about a total disruption in the transport system of Karimganj and posed a challenge to the security as well as economy of the valley.

TABLE 19.3

Detection of Unlicensed Rickshaw Puller

Year	No. of persons ('00)
1990	483
1991	499
1992	448
1993	377
1994	421
1995	478

Source: Office of the Superintendent of police, Karimganj

It is observed that a good number of students and youth of Karimganj are running madly after money after influenced by the immigrants. The easiest method of earning is to get one self involved in the under world activities for which ample opportunities are available at hand. Once they get accustomed to hot earnings, they do not hesitate to indulge themselves in more crimes like snatching and decoity etc. The prospect of easy earning through smuggling has already created a sort of temptation among the young stars specially teenagers.

So it is a high time that social scientists may try to locate in depth the causes of this social degeneration to other factor quite unconnected with international border. Infact, social degeneration and corruption are global phenomena.

The influence of crime related activities is so intense on the teenagers of Karimganj district that they have accepted it as a challenging opportunity for them to earn any amount of money within a very short period.

A cursory view at the Table 19.4 reveals the fact that the percentage of people living on Agriculture has declined from 36.2 per cent in 1986 to 33.4 per cent in 1997, while the percentage of daily labour has increased from 10.1 per cent to 12.2 per cent in the same period. One of the important reasons may be that the illegal migrants from Bangladesh, who have taken shelter here preferred the short term daily works (daily labour) instead of engaging themselves in medium or long term agricultural activities.

TABLE 19.4

Occupation Distribution of Population (In per cent)

Occupation	*1988-89*	*1997-96*
Agriculture	36.2	33.4
Service	35.3	34.4
Business	12.2	13.5
Mixed	6.2	6.5
Daily labour	10.1	12.2
Total	100.0	100.0

It can be inferred that the potential cause of the high population growth in Assam, in general, and in Karimganj in particular, is the high influx of people from Bangladesh. This is due to easy entry routes all through 94 km. virtually uncared for international border line. As a consequence the district of Karimganj has to feed additional mouths in all respects viz housing, medical facility, education etc. Such a situation definitely act as a drag and pulls down all sorts of development efforts in Karimganj.

A higher level of retail price in Karimganj has also received a push upward due to the existence of unaccounted easy money generated by smuggling. The uncontrolled smuggling activities in Karimganj act as a booster to the parallel economy already generated in India.

A sizable addition to the rural population of Karimganj has significantly intensified the problem of disguised unemployment. There is a disproportionately high growth rate of muslim population due to unchecked infiltration. In the context of inherent backwardness of Karimganj, the disguised unemployed persons have very little scope to shift elsewhere and find out alternative source of employment. The Indo-Bangladesh peculiar border passing through Karimganj is responsible to some a extent for bringing about degeneration among the people, particularly among the younger groups.

20

Prospects of Indo-Bangla Border Trade in Horticultural Sector of North-Eastern Region

—S. N. Goswami, G. Medhi & S.B. Singh

Horticulture development can play a dominant role in the economic upliftment of tribal farmers of North Eastern region. Fruits and vegetables are the important horticultural produce of the region. Fruits and processed fruit products constituted a significant share of the global trade and thus, represents an important foreign exchange earner for many agricultural based economies. In the fresh fruit segment, the main fruit exported from India are mango, banana, grapes, citrus fruits, guava, apple, litchi, pineapple and papaya. Of these, the main fruits being cultivated in the north-eastern region are pineapple, citrus fruits, guava, banana, sapota, litchi and apple. Grapes and mango, which form the bulk of Indian export, are not prominent in the region. Though horticultural sector of the region is not developed, still many fruits and fruit products are exported to Bangladesh through various border points. The export market of north-eastern region as regards to horticultural sector to Bangladesh is discussed in this paper.

The North-Eastern region of the country, comprising of the seven states, is a land locked area which is bounded by Bangladesh, Myanmar and China. The northern stretch is bounded by the Himalayan mountain ranges and the region, otherwise, comprised of undulating terrain, in the form of mountain ranges and hills. Hence, the connectivity of the region with other regions is very low. Even the inter-state connectivity is low because of hilly terrain. Therefore, the land routes are not well developed in these seven states. Traditionally, however, due to geographical contiguity this region was bound by centuries of trading between the neighbouring countries. In terms of proximity, the export market with reference to the north-eastern region of the country, may be divided into the following categories:

Border Nations : Bangladesh and Myanmar.

South/South-East Asia: Bhutan, Hong Kong, Malaysia, Maldives, Nepal, Philippines, Singapore and Sri Lanka.

Middle East: Saudi Arabia, UAE, Kuwait, Qatar and others.

Europe: Comprising of the nations in the European Union.

Others: Including the US, China and Japan.

For processed fruit products to the South Asia, South East Asia and Border nations, the combined market currently contributes less than 15 per cent of the Indian processed fruit exports. But it has exhibited a high growth rate of 81 per cent over the last year. Hence, the market has potential to develop further for the Indian exports.

Apart from land routes, where considerable difficulties are to be faced, the other likely option is the Calcutta port (air and sea route) for North-East. However, in value terms, exports from Calcutta contribute only about 5 per cent of India's export. Of these, the products being sourced from the North East are negligible.

Though some of the entrepreneurs are exporting oranges to Bangladesh, they are not sourcing their products from the

North-East. The oranges are sent by land routes to Bangladesh. They are brought from as far as Nagpur, Amrabati and Bhutan, or Siliguri The major reason for neglecting North East region as a potential source of supply is the price differential between the products. Oranges from Assam are costlier as compared to the others and they rarely find their way outside the North East. Additionally the reliability of supply is not there with longer delivery times. For the North East products, the supply situation of Calcutta market and the existing price differential acts as a major obstacle towards growth of export.

Trade with Bangladesh

Bangladesh has a geographical location such that it is bordering the Indian states on all sides. While it border with West Bengal in the West; the rest of it is enveloped by the North Eastern states. It has a 889 kms. border with Tripura and 443 km. border with Meghalaya. It also borders the State of Assam for another 200 km. Aided by this geographical location, trade between the two countries has been regularly carried out.

The Border Trade Agreement between India and Bangladesh, first signed in 1972, laid the foundation for state regulation of trade in the border regions, to meet the day-to-day requirements of the people. This was to cover to stretch lying within a 16 km. belt of the border, on either side.

Trade with Bangladesh takes place from the following border points.

a) **Meghalaya** - Dawki, Bholaganj
b) **Assam** - Karimganj, Steamerghat and Sutarkandi
c) **Tripura** - Manu, Agartala and Srimantapur.

During 1996-97, the total value of horticultural trade carried out in the region through these points amounted to Rs. 149 Lakhs (Table 20.2). Of this, nearly Rs. 113 Lakhs was earned through the export of oranges. Of these points, the maximum export takes place through Karimganj and Steamerghat, which accounts for 62 per cent of to total border trade in the region. The border point ranking second in terms of export value is Dawki accounting for 16 per cent of the trade.

During the previous year, till September 1997, to total value of horticultural products traded has been to the extent of Rs. 47 lakhs. The maximum export has taken place through Dawki and Karimganj, accounting for 60 per cent and 37 per cent of to total export respectively.

TABLE 20.1

Estimates of Production, Consumption and Surplus of Horticultural Crops in Meghalaya by 2000 AD.

(In '000 tonnes)

Crops	*Production*	*Consumption*	*Surplus*
Pineapple	72.12	21.63	50.48
Banana	61.80	30.90	30.90
Citrus	55.34	11.07	44.28
Other fruits	47.07	11.77	35.30
Potato	283.20	84.96	198.24
Ginger	52.37	5.24	47.13
Turmeric	2.08	0.42	1.66

a) Meghalaya

The production of horticultural crops has assumed great importance in Meghalaya in view of the topography, climatic conditions and agricultural practices prevailing in the State. At present approximately 29,000 hectares of land in Meghalaya is under horticulture. Major horticultural crops in the state are pineapple, banana, citrus, pear and stonefruits. The total area under these crops is estimated to be approximately 17 thousand hectares. The average productivity is approximately 8 tonnes per hectare. The total production of ginger in the

TABLE 20.2
North East Export to Bangladesh (1996-97)

Sl. No.	*Border Points*	*Items*	*Quantity*	*Value (in Rs)*
1	Dawki (Meghalaya)	Citrus fruits	71855 kgs	369188
		Orange	297141 kgs	2026736
2	Bholaganj	Citrus fruits	86220 nos	41445
	(Meghalaya)	Pears	131700 nos	32266
3	Karimganj Steamerghat (Assam)	Orange	7860415 nos	6909420
		Apple	1100 kgs	22000
		Mango	7675.5 kgs	76161
		Citrus fruits	2215770 nos	2011442
		Grapes	6207 kgs	150473
		Pears	12.99 MT	35970
4	Sutar Kandi (Assam)	Orange	9245 kgs& 1612316 nos	1547121
		Citrus fruits	10500 nos& 22.5 MT	40594
		Apples	3290 kgs	59220
		Grapes	7440 kgs & 0.33 MT	44208
5	Manu (Tripura)	Citrus fruits	17700 nos	10683
		Orange	199387 nos	154385
		Apples	2400 kgs	3600
6	Agartala (Tripura)	Jack fruit	10 MT	7700
		Grapes	2.825 MT & 600 kgs	75005
		Orange	78.41 MT	483131
		Apples	3.75 MT	65057
7	Srimantapur (Tripura)	Grapes	17.875 MT	190473
		Jackfruit	109.5 MT	62829
		Apples	143.75 MT	220560
		Orange	43.25 MT	246443
		Marmelos	21 MT	22572
		mango	1.4 MT	3675
		Bananas	2.0 MT	1750
	Total (Rs)			149,14107

Source: APEDA

State is approximately 32,000 MT per year. About 85 to 90 per cent of the total production could be exported. It could be done either in the raw form or in the form of dry ginger and ginger products. The state is also producing high quality turmeric. The production is estimated at 2,500 MT of day turmeric. The possibility of exporting quality turmeric powder to Bangladesh could be explored. Besides, there is surplus in production of potato which is estimated at 1 lakh MT during the harvesting season. The estimated surplus of different horticultural crops available in the year 2000 calculated on the basis of the population as per 1991 census are given in Table 20.1.

It could be seen from the table that there is considerable scope for exporting high quality horticultural crops specially fruit products from Meghalaya. Besides these facts the total value of existing border trade of horticultural crops in the State is exceptionally low. The border point is at Tamabil, a kilometre away from Dawki. The export trade at Dawki during 1996-97 was to the extent of Rs. 53 crores. The primary commodity exported is coal which accounts for nearly 97 per cent of the value of export. Horticultural products constituted less than one per cent of the total exports and the main horticultural product exported is citrus. During the year, 537.2 million tonne of oranges were exported, valued at Rs. 36 lakhs. The quantity of other citrus fruits was 137.3 metric tonne, earning an amount of Rs. 3.7 lakhs. The export of orange is seasonal, from November to February. During the previous year, orange exports had been higher upto Rs. 90 lakhs though other citrus fruits were only for Rs. 2.3 lakhs. Grapes and apples had also been exported during the year. The apples from Himachal Pradesh and apples and oranges from Bhutan are often traded across to border. However, to fruit processing industry in the State is yet to be developed.

The reason is due to inadequate market infrastructure and necessary post harvest technologies which resulted into lack of international competitiveness of horticultural produce. There are at present two small fruit processing units operated by to Department of Agriculture. Their capacity is 60 MT and 40 MT of finished product at Shillong and Dainadubi respectively. In addition, there are two private fruit processing units located at Burnihat. It is felt that the existing processing units in to State are not in a position to cope with the processing of surplus fruits and vegetables produced in the State. Steps should, therefore, be taken for setting up of an economically viable and commercially viable and commercially run fruit processing industry would be a pre-requisite for export trade in processed fruit products

TABLE 20.3

North East Export to Bangladesh (1997-98 up to September 97)

Sl. No.	*Border Point*	*Items*	*Quantity*	*Value (in Rs)*
1	Dawki (Meghalaya)	Citrus fruits	78931 kgs	2219169
		Pears	298272 kgs	596544
2	Karimganj	Citrus fruits	1727365 nos	1717752
	Steamerghat (Assam)	Orange	27040 nos	17573
3	Starkandi (Assam)	Grapes	150 kgs	3750
		Orange	3000 nos	2999
4	Manu (Tripura)	Citrus fruits	37547 nos	37547
		Orange	18083 nos	35830
5	Srimantapur (Tripura)	Jackfruit	17 MT	24095
		Pineapple	20 MT	69922
	Total (Rs)			47,25181

Source: APEDA

b) Tripura

Two land custom stations are operational, viz. at Akhoura and Sonamura, out of the eight notified by the Government of India. Official export trade ranges round Rs. 1 crore, consisting of local produce (pineapple, orange, jack fruit, seed potato, ginger, plywood) and other items from other states (auto parts, coal from Meghalaya, apple and grapes, etc.) Imports consists of Hilsa fish and Jamdani sarees.

A study conducted by Indian Institute of Foreign Trade estimated that the unofficial trade with Bangladesh exceeds Rs. 100 crores, with which the state has a border about 339 kms. The Tripura Government has proposed border trade, within 5 kms of the border, at 11 Les/villages. It has also been proposed that traders with license issued by the state government be allowed to carry on the trade, with supervision of the Customs Authority and BSF. And that the national currencies be allowed for such trade, and mode of transport to be road/river. The distance between Agartala to Calcutta is about 350 kms, about 10 hours by road. If this route through Bangladesh is opened up, it will help trade with the rest of the domestic Indian market and will help to integrate the State economy with the Indian economy.

From the above discussions it could be concluded that the feasibility of Indian horticultural export from the North East region of the country would depend largely on the following key issues:

* Quality of the product - whether the region can match the international quality requirements.
* Scale of operation - whether the cost efficiencies of large scale production can be achieved.
* Domestic competition - Whether the States in the region can take on the competition export market from other states, through state initiatives and focused support to the sector.
* International competitiveness — whether the products from the region, after passing through the various stages, would be able to remain competitive in the international markets in terms of price.

Therefore, the export market can be tapped profitably provided the exportable commodities fulfilled the two critical requirements of quality and price. However, at present the regional expert potential of horticulture is not overwhelmingly favourable. For certain products opportunities do exist which can be tapped in the future, but only certain pre-requisites are complied with. However, with the establishment of processing industries and development of marketing infrastructure and communication net-work the export potential of horticultural product from the region could be increased to a great extent.

REFERENCES

Agricultural Finance Corporation Limited, Study Report on Marketing of High Value Crops in Assam. 1998. pp 27-50.

Agricultural and Processed Food Products Export Development Authority (APEDA), Export Potential Assessment of Horticulture and Floriculture Products for the North Eastern States. 1998, pp. 6-20.

Spices Board, Report on the Production and Marketing of Ginger in Mizoram, 1998. pp 20-23.

PART V

BORDER TRADE PROSPECT IN ARUNACHAL PRADESH

21

Indigenous Trans-Himalayan Trade: A Study of the Tribes of Western Arunachal Pradesh

—Bibhash Dhar

Arunachal Pradesh is the largest state in the Northeast region of India in terms of area. It is the habitat of about twenty-five major tribal community divided into a number of sub-tribes. The state is strategically located as it borders China (Tibet) on the North, Bhutan on its West and Myanmar to its east. The Southern part of the state runs into the plains of Assam. It is all through a mountainous state with a number of snow covered sierra, criss-crossed by innumerable mountain rivers and rivulets.

Interestingly enough, though the British-Indian regime was successful to a certain extent to contain the tribal people within the boundary restrictions of NEFA but the British-Indian officials had little or no information about the social and commercial linkages the people hitherto developed through the trans-Himalayan trade routes that extended to Tibet and even upto Assam. Tribal people used to move with their pact animals in the winters through the mountain passes that appeared inaccessible to British-Indian officials. It needs a mention that the terrain of the Western region of Arunachal Pradesh was found to be favourable for movement of the pack animals even though the mountain braes are steep. Furer-Haimendorf (1982: 146) in this context observed,

> "This region which adjoins to the west the mountain kingdom of Bhutan, differs from the rest of Arunachal Pradesh both topographically and culturally. Whereas elsewhere the nature of the terrian had prevented the development of caravan route suitable for pack animals, in the western-most part of Arunachal Pradesh there are climatic and geographical conditions which favoured the opening of trade routes linking the territory both with Tibet and with the plains of Assam."

The township of Tawang, strategically located on western-most part of the state which is the headquarters of the district also known as Tawang, happened to be the nerve centre of the trans-Himalayan indigenous trade. It was through the present day Tawang town the important caravan route connecting Tibet with the plains of Assam passed. In this context, Gupta (1974: 30) observed, "Also through the Tawang Tract, which extended from the Tibetan plateau right down to the Assam plains, just north Udalguri (Assam), ran an important trade route between Indian and Tibet."

The tribal communities of the western Arunachal Pradesh are primarily agriculturists with the exception of a few pastoralists found near the MacMohan Line in the Tawang district. Most of these tribes since time immemorial used to subsidise their economy through the inter-ethnic indigenous trades. The Monpas, the major tribesmen of the districts of Tawang and West Kameng are considered to be one of the expert group of traders in the Arunachal Himalayas and since long are better known for their tradition of long distance trade in the markets of Bhutan, Tibet and Assam. Similarly, the Mijis, another tribesmen group of the Nafra sub-division of the west Kameng maintained a network of indigenous trade transactions with the Monpas, Akas and with the plains of Assam. The Akas, found in the Thrizino sub-division of West Kameng had trade relation with the plains of Assam. The Pangchen-pas and the Thingbu-pas on the MacMohan Line in the Tawang district are the only tribal communities so far identified with the economy of livestock rearing. They had trade relations with the Tibetans since time immemorial but at the same time they used to have commercial exchanges with the Bhutanese and Monpas of lower altitude which they still continue. The Sherdukpens, found in the Rupa-Shergaon (Shargong) area of the Bomdila sub-division of the West Kameng are a small group of tribal community that had indigenous trade relations with the Monpas, Akas and with the plains of Assam. The Bangnis, a strong group of people in the East Kameng district and known widely for the heavy-handedness also had commercial links with the people of Assam along with the other neigbouring tribes, such as, the Akas, Mijis, Nishis. The Sulungs of the Chayantajo sub-division are a group of very submissive and shy type of people and since quite sometime they are the virtual slaves of their stronger neighbours. It has been, however, ascertained that long back even the Sulungs had trade relations with the Monpas of Tawang area. Nishis of the Lower Subansiri are another group of fire-brand people and they had indigenous commercial relations with the Bangnis, Apatanis and with the people of the foot hills of Assam. Last but not least, the Bangros a small group of the highland people of the Koloriang sub-division of the Lower Subansiri had trade relations with the Tibetans and the other neighbouring tribes of the region.

The Monpas

The Monpas are the major tribesmen of the West Kameng and the Tawang district are expert in mountain agriculture and excellent carpet weavers. The people are Buddhist by religion and belong to the Mahayana division of the Gelukpa sect of the Tibetan-Lamaist Buddhism. As per the Census of India (1981) the population of the Monpa has returned as 33,661. The Monpas since the very early days had an old tradition of commercial intercourse with the different communities of Assam through the various markets in the foothill region. In those olden days a fair used to be held somewhere near Udalguri in the Darrang district, Assam and traders from Tibet, Bhutan, Assam, Bengal and other adjoining areas used to take part. Merchants from Tibet and other nearby areas used to come down with mineral salt, gold dust, woolens, musk, horses, Chinese silk and other noticeable items. The Tibetan and Bhutias, which included the Monpas, used to return to their habitats with Assamese silk, buffalo horns, pearls, iron and lac and corals brought by the traders from Bengal. Choudhury (1978:26) referred about three annual fairs at different centres namely; Udalguri, Daimara and Sadiya. These fairs were chiefly attended by the Monpas of Tawang and in less number by the Akas and Daflas (Bangnis and Nishis). The Monpas who used to rear ponies, yaks and horses used to earn handsome amount of money by engaging the animals in caravans covering trade trips over Tibet, Bhutan and Assam. Apart from Assam the Monpas ventured into the markets of Bhutan on the west, Tibet on the north and Miji and other tribes on the east and south. The people traditionally used to produce certain items in surplus, such as, chilli, orange, maize, vegetable dye, apple, wooden bowls, handmade paper and incense. On the other' hand they were in need of *Churpi* (hard cheese-like milk produce), dried meat, wool and woolen cloth, mineral salt, yarn, brass and bronze utensils and other items of day to day need. Accordingly, the Monpas in general and those of Tawang in particular used to undertake trade journey to Tsonadzong in Tibet, the markets, of Merak and Sakten in Bhutan and the different markets in Assam. Furer-Haimendorf (1982: 176) also noted the intensive trade relation of the Monpas, "For three measures of rice they obtained about two measures of salt from Tibet which was in great demand among the tribal population of Arunachal Pradesh. In the months of December and January many Monpas and Sherdukpens used to go to Assam where they bartered Tibetan wool and blankets for rice." The Monpas used to visit the markets at Udalguri, Rangapara, Lokra and Charduar mostly. The caravans used to start for the markets in Assam in *Dawa Gupa* (October-

November) and used to follow the stream Amatala-Ri, the principal stream in Khalegthang area, which confluences at Bhairabkund in Assam.

The Pangchen-Pas

The Zemithang administrative circle of the Tawang district is the habitat of the Pangchen-pas. The country of the Pangchen-pas borders Bhutan on the west and China (Tibet) on the north. It is through the habitat of the Pangchen-pas the traditional caravan route to Tibet passes but still since the very early days the Pangchen-pas were relatively less interested in the indigenous trade. However, the Pangchen-pas used to visit the Tsonadzong Monastery in the Tibet during the three Yearly fairs known as *Ngapa Tsongdi* held in *Dawa Ngapa* (June-July), *Dunpa Tsongdi* held in *Dawa Dunpa* (August-September) and *Chukchipa Tsongdi* held in *Dawa Chukchipa* (December-January).

While on a visit to such fairs the Pangchen-pas used to carry with them loads of green chilli, vegetable dye, baskets, bamboo mats, paddy and *chhang*, the indigenous millet beer. They used to bring back from Tibet loads of mineral salt, dried meat, wool and Tibetan currency. The Pangchen-pas had trade relations with the Bhutanese of Tashigong and Ngalagong with whom they used to exchange milk products for millet and rice. The people had a similar trade relation with the Monpas of Lumla area.

The Thingbu-Pas

The Thingbu circle of the Tawang district is the habitat of the Thingbu-pas. They are found in only one village which is known as Thingbu and their total population is 174. The Thingbu-pas had well organised indigenous trade relations with Tibet on the one hand and with the Monpas of Tawang and Dirang on the other. In the *Dawa Gyepa* (September-October) the Thingbu-pas used to march out for Tibet with their caravan loads of dry chilli, cane ropes, bamboo baskets and maize. The route they followed was Thingbu to Mago and Mago to the border post of Thulung-La and then Minnang and finally to the Jhorakharda monastery in Tibet. From Jhorakharda the Thingbu-pas used to bring back mostly dried meat, mineral salt and wool. The trade with Tibet continued till 1962. The Thingbu-pas, at present, give much stress towards the trade with the Dirang Monpas of Nyikmadung area and the Tawang Monpas of Jang and other nearby villages. For trading with the Monpas the Thingbu-pas descend from their habitat in the *Dawa Chupa* (November-December) and in *Dawa Chukchipa* (December-January) with caravan loads of milk products. They exchange the milk products mainly with millet and maize and walk back to Thingbu.

The Nishis and the Bangnis

The Nishis and the Bangnis are the same stock of people and in the pre-Independence period they were known as the Daflas. However, the people at present consider the term Dafla derogatory and those who have made the East Kameng district as their habitat, introduce themselves as Bangnis while those who are found in the adjacent district of Lower Subansiri are known as the Nishis. Both the communities are largely jhum cultivators. The people claim that in the early days they had indigenous trade relations with the Tibetans.

In the winters the people used to move out for the Tibetan villages with musk, animal skin, cane and cane ropes mostly. They used to return with mineral salt and beads. In the drier months of the year the Nishis and Bangnis used to visit the markets near the foot-hill region of the state, namely, Harmoti, Itakhola, Charduar and North Lakhimpur in Assam. They carry with them musks, cane and cane ropes mostly and carry back utensils, cloth Assamese silk and iron implements. From the Monpas of Dirang area they generally bring maize and yeast in return of musks and cane. From the Mijis, Akas and Apatanis the Bangnis and Nishis obtain local variety of cotton paddy and Maize in exchange of *mithun* and musks.

The foregoing facts quite clearly indicate that the tribal societies of Arunachal Pradesh were able to interact closely between themselves as well as with the others outside the boundary inspite of the restrictions imposed by the British-Indian regime. The interaction could take place through the multiple trans-Himalayan trade routes with a view to exchange the indigenous surplus produces for the products that were needed in everyday life but were never manufactured or produced by the tribal communities. Thus to procure those items the tribal communities took all the pain to walk past the difficult mountain terrains to reach Assam, Bhutan and Tibet in the drier season of the year. It is also noticed that the tribal groups of Lower Subansiri and East Kameng showed lesser interest towards the indigenous trade mainly because of the unfriendly terrain compared to the western part of Arunachal Pradesh. It is also noticed that the traders from the plains, namely the Assamese, never visited the habitats of the tribals but welcomed the tribal traders to their markets in the plains. However, the tribal traders visited and still make trips to each others habitats and such trips are the periodic sources of socio-economic support for each other. It also remained a fact that through such exposures the tribal socio-cultural life failed to usher in noticeable changes because the Tibetans, the Bhutanese and the Assamese were as traditional and home spun as the tribals themselves were. Subsequently, with the Sino-Indian border conflict of 1962 the trade transactions and other socio-cultural activities of the people suffered a major set back due to the closure of the borders with Tibet. To make up this loss most of the tribal lots of the state tried to establish greater economic links with the Assamese in the plains of Assam and other indigenous markets in the mountains. It could, however, be safely stated that inspite of the diverse contact of the people the tribal communities of the state could maintain their traditionality to a large extent barring some spontaneous changes. People have taken to mill-made clothe and more importantly have picked up Assamese and Hindi languages which they require every moment they remain outside their respective habitats.

REFERENCES

Choudhury, D. P., 1978, *The North East Frontier of India*, 1865-1914, the Asiatic Society, Calcutta.

Furer-Haimendorf, C. Von, 1982, *The Highlander of Arunachal Pradesh*, Vikas Publishing House, New Delhi.

Gupta, K., 1974, *The Hidden History of the Sino-Indian Frontier*, Calcutta.

Luthra, P. N., 1971, *Constitutional & Administrative Growth of the North East Frontier Agency*, NEFA. Shillong, p. 11.

22

Border Trade Issues in Arunachal Pradesh: An Overview

—M.C. Behera

Issue and Setting

In the era of 'globalisation' and 'liberal regime' the issue of border trade has attracted the attention of planners, bureaucrats, politicians and academics alike in northeastern region. Shukla Commission Report (Transforming the North-East: 1997), interalia, has also recommended cross-border trade for economic development of the region. In its survey report on Export Opportunities in Myanmar, the Indian Institute of Foreign Trade (IIFT) has also made recommendations and suggested action plans for immediate processing so that obvious trading opportunities are not lost by default.

The region earlier had cross-border free trade relations which came to an end after 1947. Almost all the tribal groups of Arunachal Pradesh along present border had trade relation with people of neighbouring areas across it (Cooper: 1873 230; *Gazetteers of Lohit, Tirap, Siang, Subansiri and Kameng*). With the extension of administration by the Government of India attempts of economic integration by making consumer goods available and as a fall out of Indo-Chinese border conflict in 1962, the trade with neighbouring people across the border discontinued.

Presently there is a desire at various levels on the issue

of revival of border trade not only in other N.E. states but in Arunachal Pradesh also. This paper attempts to discuss the issue in the context of Arunachal Pradesh. The main objective is to understand the impact of such a trade on the people of the state in general. As a corollary to it, the study will focus on the extent of participation by Arunachalees because it has been identified in the Human Development Report (1993) as a key to human development. Besides the study will also focus on the development issues that weaves development around people, not people around development.

The analysis of this paper has been stylized dialectically by eliciting information from local scholars and common people in the state. Local scholars belonged to in the light of relevant secondary sources wherever possible. Hence, the study is empirical in nature and based on descriptive analysis using both primary and secondary source of data.

The concept 'border trade' has wide ranging connotation. At one extreme it could possibly be the country's international trade across its international border and for our present purpose the border of Arunachal Pradesh sharing the border of Bhutan, Tibetan region of China and Myanmar. On the other extreme it could be the trade practice among the neighbouring people of both sides of international border. In this case it would amount to a limited spatial mobility of locality produced goods. In between, the other possibilities could be (i) the trade practice of N.E. states as a single unit with neighbouring districts across the borders or (ii) trade practice between each constituent units of N.E. states and areas across its respective border.

Claims

The idea of cross-border trade has gained currency at different levels in all N.E. States. Even Shukla Commission Report and IIFT survey have recommended for border trade. Though the volume of legal and illegal trade along Indo-

Bangladesh and Indo-Myanmar borders is mentioned therein, these documents are conspicuously silent about the border trade in Arunachal Pradesh. This is because in Arunachal Pradesh such trade virtually does not exist. However, this does not mean to ignore small exchanges people of Changlang district and of Tali area in Lower Subansiri district near the border make with their counterparts across the border. The goods exchanged include vegetables, some items of traditional significance, etc.

The case for border trade in Arunachal Pradesh has been justified on various counts. The arguments have both general (as in the context of N.E. States following Shukla Commission Report) and state-specific significance. The arguments are summed up as the following:

1. The north-eastern region is bottled up with an outlet of about 33 kms. width which connects it with the rest of the country. On the other hand, it shares about 5,211 kms. of international borders with neighbouring countries. Transport and communication with mainland is very often disrupted because of natural calamities and terrorist activities. Obviously, therefore, external economic relations must be of special relevance to it in terms of obtaining essential items and marketing surplus products across the border at the time of crisis due to communication disruption.

2. Timber from Myanmar via Calcutta and silk from Karnataka are available in the markets of the region. Opening up border trade will be cost effective in terms of importing Myanmar timber and Chinese silk from across the border directly.

3. People along the border on both sides had the tradition of border trade and cultural ties because of cultural homogeneity. This could be the basis for opening up trade for greater mutual benefit to all concerned. Once the conventional type trade takes place, unconventional trade

will follow suit. For instance, electricity produced in Arunachal Pradesh probably could get a demand base in many places across the border.

4. Goods produced in small scale in places nearer to border area will get a market nearby across the border. In many interior villages, horticultural crops do not find a market nearby. Problem of transportation to markets of Assam and of finding suitable buyers by tribal farmers who do not have necessary market knowledge acts as a deterrent towards acceptability of horticultural crops as main source of income.

5. Productive activities will gear up consequent upon border trade. But large scale production will not be economically viable in view of backward industrial atmosphere and infrastructure (Barthakur: 1995) at the early stage. Production organised in a small scale probably could not be cost effective as externalities and economies of scale would not accrue. However, such products, if marketed in local markets, will not incur transport cost which are incurred when competitive goods are brought from outside N.E. region. These products also can not compete with outside products because of cost factors. Production in a small scale for local markets will ensure distributive justice and create conditions for a proper industrial atmosphere for undertaking large scale production subsequently. Initial productive activities following border trade will diversify industrial activities through forward and backward linkages.

6. Production organised at local and regional levels for border trade will take local demand into consideration. It will make use of local resource endowment and local skills. Production of locally demanded goods will have limited spatial mobility and hence will exert less pressure on resource base. Small scale production will use labour-intensive technology and thereby will provide employment opportunities for local labour force.

Counter Claims

The case for border trade has its justification in ensuring economic development. But the question arises, "Development for Whom?" The experience with development exercise in Arunachal Pradesh during plan period, though gives a rosy picture at macro-level in terms of indicators of development (Economic Review: 1996), the condition of the masses has rather worsened as compared to their rights on Common Property Resources (CPR). Commons are deprived of their rights over CPR because of the emerging process of privatisation of land resources. Benefit from development packages do not percolate down and a visibly rich class has emerged because of distributive inefficiency of economic benefits in the existing system. This consideration provides the base for counter claims which denounce border trade in following grounds:

1. National or regional (N.E. region) trade across the border of Arunachal Pradesh will not ensure the involvement of majority of Arunachalee workforce in the process. Because of the nature of economic diversification and shortage of Arunachalee workforce therefore (Arunachalee workforce has declined by 34.74 per cent while non-Arunachalee workforce has increased by 34.38 per cent during 1981-91 over 1971-81 as can be seen with reference to Census Report), economic activities are carried through non-Arunachalee workforce. Further, expansion of economic activities through border trade will increase the size of this short supply of workforce. As a result, influx of outside workforce will be encouraged. This will go against the spirit behind the philosophy of development in Arunachal Pradesh (Elwin 1960: xiii).

2. Even if few Arunachalee elites are involved at one or the other stage in the process of cross-border trade, they will be mere cogs in a wheel. They can not take independent decision solely keeping development perspective of Arunachal Pradesh in view. Rather Arunachal interest will be limited to

their individual interests which will be taken as the manifestation of the interest of Arunachal Pradesh. As we see today, mass interest melts down before the interest of the dominant group in the community (see Chambers: 1983) who are in fact the product of a system outside their own.

In case Arunachalee elites give priority to the interest of the people, they will fail in employment front. Because they will depend on non-Arunachalee workforce in the face of shortage in the supply of Arunachalee workforce at present Moreover, income and wealth have a tendency to concentrate at centre. The intensity of the ripples of spill over effects dies out as the ripples move away from the centre. Empirically it can be experienced with all the growth centres in India. This justifies economic backwardness in Bihar inspite of a large number of growth centres especially with large scale industries in the state.

3. Organising economic activities around trade and involving Arunachalee workforce therein will amount to withdrawal of workforce from other activities.

4. Trade in a small scale having limited spatial mobility along both sides of the border will lead to problems associated with difference in national currencies. Because of the present level of education and scattered settlements, people in these areas will not appropriate the benefit of foreign exchanges to be provided to them through some agencies or institutions which are to be located in selected places.

So far no study has been made to identity the demand base and surplus products available across the border of Arunachal Pradesh. Shukla Commission Report and IIFT survey are conspicuously silent on the issue.

5. Areas along the border are sparsely populated. Provision of transport facilities connecting scattered interior villages along the border and within the state will not be cost

effective for small scale border trade. Ginger produced in foothills and fruit crops in both foothills and middle belt can easily be transported to markets in plains than to markets across the border. This is because transportation is very slow in high hills. So far, all the districts of Arunachal Pradesh are not internally connected by road transport. In such a situation, the provision for a network of road transport as a pre-requisite for meaningful border trade will pose a serious challenge considering resource and time constraints.

6. Very often, the fissiparous tendency rocks many parts of the north-east. The rumble of its undercurrent is also heard in one form or the other in Arunachal Pradesh. Under such a situation there is no surety that guns will not enter in place of goods under the blanket cover of cross border trade. Insurgency problem will get an added fillip. Moreover, drug trafficking can possibly be another potential problem for the society.

7. Our relation with China blows hot and cold. Such uncertainty will be a deterrent towards a smooth cross-border trade.

8. After independence, economic life of the people of Arunachal Pradesh has undergone significant changes. The demand structure has changed. Earlier cross-border trade has also discontinued. Arunachalee people are used to get their requirements mostly through government endeavours directly or indirectly. Without creating proper motivation among the masses and providing a sound basic infrastructure for cross- border trade, any attempts by the government will not be meaningful in realising desired goals.

9. Many comparatively low cost foreign products like cosmetics, soft drinks, tooth paste, electronic products, etc will enter into Arunachal Pradesh through cross border trade. This will adversely affect industries producing such commodities in India.

10. In Arunachal Pradesh 'regimented planing' with government machinery as implementing agency could not ensure economic growth with distributive justice. For this failure, corruption at administration level is held responsible. A few years back, a BBC news broadcast also pointed out rampant corruption in Arunachal Pradesh. With wide spread corruption in the state, the best plan for deriving benefit from cross- border trade will end up in futile exercises.

Trade Off

In the era of globalisation when India herself is a party to it, Arunachal Pradesh can not be closed to cross-border trade for a long time. Therefore, a timely move in this direction needs to be initiated. The main thrust of such a move will be on development around the people rather than people around the development. The following points may be considered as break through while dealing with the issue of cross-border trade in Arunachal Pradesh.

1. A proper survey of demand structure, surplus products and existence of complementary goods in both sides of the border has to be conducted before any concrete step towards cross-border trade in Arunachal Pradesh.

2. Road transport and railway transport linking border areas of either side and with nearest commercial centres in respective countries have to be developed after survey. International trade, regional trade and border trade by neighbouring people have to be so planned and integrated that the advantage to the nation as a whole shall be to the tune of cost of providing transport and other necessary infrastructure.

3. A regional body like NEC shall have to coordinate and monitor regional trade across the borders of N.E. states. This body shall also have to look after interstate transport facility to ensure efficient movement of goods. Departmental coordination has to be worked out for providing necessary

infrastructure. For example, the provision for road transport shall have to be the joint work of Forest Department. Trade and Commerce Department, Surface Transport Department, etc. Besides, wage-employment schemes shall have to be designed to supplement the efforts of normal departments.

4. Community resources in the process of cross-border trade shall have to be used only for common good and that too in a way such that it may not lead to concentration of economic power (Sharma: 1995: 11 & 54).

5. All possible measures have to be taken to prevent inflow of goods other than agreed upon.

6. Initially few places in the districts of Changlang, Lower Subansiri and Tawang, where cross-border trade is believed to be taking place, may be opened up for such trade on trial basis. Action plan for the entire state may be formulated basing on the experience from the above trial.

7. As far as practicable trading of processed food items in place of fruits and other horticultural crops have to be encouraged to ensure added employment in secondary sector activity.

In short, the issue of trans border trade in Arunachal Pradesh has to be considered in a long term perspective keeping economic development with distributive justice in view. At the same time, development must be sustainable in terms of resource use consequent upon resource mobility due to cross- border trade.

REFERENCES

Barthakur, I.K. (1995), *The Report of the Group on Industrial Development of the North Eastern Region including Sikkim, and the Andaman and Nicobar Islands*, Dept. of Economic Affairs, Ministry of Finance, New Delhi.

Census of India, 1971, 1981 and 1991 reports.

Chambers, R., (1983), *Rural Development: Putting the Last First;* Longman Scientific & Technical, England

Cooper, T.T. (1873), *The Mishmee Hills, Mittal Publications,* New Delhi, 1992 Reprint

Economic Review of Arunachal Pradesh, (1996): Directorate of Economics and Statistics, Itanagar.

Elwin, V., (1959), *A Philosophy for NEFA,* 2nd Edition, 1960, Shillong.

Gazetteers of Arunachal Pradesh : Lohit, Tirap, Siang, Subansiri and Kameng districts.

Human Development Report (1993): Oxford University Press, New York (USA).

Sacks, H. (1992), *Lectures on Conversation,* Vol. 1 & 2, Blackwell, Oxford.

Sharma, B.D. (1995), *Globalisation: The Tribal Encounter,* Har Anand Publications, New Delhi.

Shukla, S.P. (1997), *Transforming the North-East, High Level Commission Report to the Prime Minister,* Planning Commission, N. Delhi.

Survey of Export Opportunities in Myanmar, (1995): The Indian Institute of Foreign Trade (IIFT), N. Delhi.

23

A Note on Border Trade in Arunachal Pradesh

—Anup Saikia

Arunachal Pradesh's location at India's north eastern margins may often be seen as a disadvantage, and this may be true in many respects, however considering her location in close proximity to Tibet (China), Myanmar and Bhutan, the location can hardly be considered disadvantageous, at least in terms of trade possibilities. Given such a location it is not surprising that the rugged topography notwithstanding, numerous tribal communities of Arunachal had trade links across the international border. Historical studies point out that since pre-British days various communities such as Mishmis, Monpas, Sherdukpens, Apatanis, the various Adi sub tribes, Khamptis and the Nishings had trading contact with Tibet, Bhutan and Burma via trading routes.

The position of Arunachal Pradesh in terms possibilities for border trade given its past links looks encouraging. At present no official trade is carried out (though 'unofficial trade' in some places is carried out), however with the necessary planning from the state government and with the concurrence of the centre trade could serve as an engine for growth. The state government is currently in the process of identifying centres that could be developed for border trade. Zeminthang (Kanzamane), Bumla, Gelling and Kebitho have been so identified on a preliminary basis (i.e. the matter is at the proposal stage) for trade with China. However the status of these four centres as trading points is still uncertain and clearance from the Ministry of External Affairs, Government of India is awaited before steps toward creation of physical and associated infrastructure necessary for a trading centre can be initiated. All four centres had trading traditions in the past and all of them are high altitude locations. As the proposal notes, none of them are thoroughly linked by motorable roads and 10-15 kms of roads require maintenance. Gelling and Kibitho are air-fed. In terms of infrastructure development, roads, water supply and power supply need to be developed. The proposal states that areas potentially suitable for trading activities could be piggery, poultry, goateries, meat processing & packing in addition to the horticultural sector, etc.

There are, of necessity, security considerations involved particularly with trade considerations with China since the latter not infrequently lays claim to a large tract of Arunachal Pradesh. Against such a background, the Government of India, at least during the initial stages, may move along the lines of its border trade policy in Manipur in which one centre is opened. Though plans are at an initial stage, it appears that if this is to be the case then Kanzamane could be the initial trade point for border trade across Arunachal Pradesh.

The possibilities for trade with Myanmar and China are theoretically limitless. However considering the nature of the Arunachalee economy which relies heavily - almost predominantly — on the primary sector, a small but rapidly growing tertierisation (mainly in the white collar services) of the economy and a negligible secondary sector, there are limits to the trade story.

Trade Possibilities: trade from the primary or secondary sector

There are two trade possibilities. Given the current nature of the economy, trade could be confined to the primary sector.

This is one alternative. There is of course considerable variety involved. Arunachal Pradesh, climatically akin to Himachal Pradesh or Kashmir more than the other north-eastern states, has strength in the horticultural sector. Fruits range from apples (in East Kameng, Tawang, and Lower Subansiri areas; and here Bhutan comes across as the closest market) to oranges (in places like Yinkiong, Tuting, Boleng, Pangin) and pineapples (Along) or bananas (fairly ubiquitously distributed). Other agro products range from ginger (found in the Lohit and Changlang districts and in Dibang Valley near the Anini area), cinnamon (found to grow in West Siang in the Tato area and in the Tirap district in and around Khonsa). High value items such as orchids and medicinal plants are found fairly well distributed.

The other alternative would lie in developing the secondary, particularly in those areas which could be exported to China or Burma. Of course in depth studies would be a pre-requisite to ascertain whether guns or butter would find a market in the destination countries. A host of related questions come into play with this second proposition. Can the state of Arunachal Pradesh overcome several hurdles so as to start production of industrial items ? Would these meet the quality standards required by the importing countries. Can the manufacturing and production be economic ? Fortunately there is room for optimism here. Tea is an illustrative case. The Oyan and Sang tea gardens are producing good quality CTC tea, and with cultivation being extended to areas like Mebo, Namsang, Namsai and Chowkkham prospects look encouraging. It is said that coffee cultivation has started in the Tirap (Deomali) and Changlang areas.

Nonetheless if there is a toss up between trading in primary products or initiating export oriented secondary production, the former would appear the more viable of the two; at least if trade is to start in the next few years. The reasons behind favouring the primary sector are not far to seek: the secondary sector in Arunachal Pradesh is virtually non existent, it could be years altogether before a manufacturing sector becomes an important part of the economy, gets entrenched into the system and moves into the exporting category. This is, however, not to imply that export from the secondary sector is out of bounds for Arunachal Pradesh. In the long run, it would be this sector that would emerge as important; however in the immediate future Arunachal's trade prospects must be sought in the primary sector and it would be unrealistic to seek trade items from a currently non-existant secondary sector.

Within the primary sector, depending on the item, outputs could be categorised into perishable and non-perishable. Various horticultural and dairy products would need minimal treatment with preservatives and some sort of packaging (this could be bottling or canning as well) to increase their 'shelf life' for export. Arunachal Pradesh needs to take a leaf out of the examples of neighbouring states. While products like 'Meg' and 'Goldpine' (from Meghalaya) or 'Frutos' (from Assam) and 'Druk' (from Bhutan) are performing creditably, the 'Aap Aase' that Arunachal produced a few years back has now run aground. With the necessary spadework there is no reason why this sort of product cannot be profitably marketed, whether for the market across the border or within the state, and even the nation's borders. It is in this direction that border trade needs to be directed : primary products with a minimal of processing and packaging.

Conclusion

From a preliminary analysis it appears that for border trade Arunachal Pradesh's best options would lie in the primary processing sector. In view of the interior and inaccessible locations of the potentially developable trading centres investments in the transport will be a primary concern. And along with development of other physical infrastructure sectors, the human resource development will need to be taken up for the local people to benefit. Related aspects such as export marketing will also have to be planned with foresight. Border trade could boost the local economy and then the dilemma of some primary producers (e.g. orange growers of Along or Basar) in finding a market, would hopefully be a thing of the past.

ACKNOWLEDGMENTS

Thanks are due to the Directorate of Industries, Govt. of Arunachal Pradesh for making available the List of Approved Items for Exchange and the Proposal for establishing Indo-China Border Trade Centres in Arunachal Pradesh.

REFERENCES

Govt. of Arunachal Pradesh (1998), Proposal for establishing Indo-China Border Trade Centres in Arunachal Pradesh, Directorate of Industries (mimeo).

APPENDIX

LIST OFF ITEMS LIKELY TO BE TRADED

Anticipated items likely to be exported to Myanmar

Medicines & pharmaceuticals, medical equipment.

Consumer goods.

Textiles & various types of yarn.

Tools & spare parts, machinery & equipments for industries.

Construction materials, electricals, cement, CGI sheets etc.

Various types of vehicles including motor cycles, bicycles & spare parts.

Stationery & printing materials.

Agricultural & horticultural tools & implements including tractors, fertilizers & chemicals etc.

Anticipated items likely to be imported from Myanmar

Valuable timber including rose wood, Mahogany, teak & other forest resources.

Minerals like tin, zinc, gold, silver, coal, bauxite & dolomite precious stones.

Agricultural products like rice, wheat, beans, pulses, oil seeds, jute, rubber etc.

Anticipated-items likely to be imported from Bhutan

Mushrooms, cattle, animal fats, ghee & ghee products ('churpi'), vegetable dyes & shellac, oranges, peanuts & red chilis, spices from Nepal, ornaments—gold, coral pearls, turquoise, Bhutanese rum & whiskey, blankets & woollen garments, crockery, electronic & electrical items.

Anticipated items likely to be exported to Bhutan:

Rice, salt, handicrafts including carpets, garments (local items such as 'Alipodung'), dry maize, millet.

Source: Directorate of Industries, Government of Arunachal Pradesh.

PROPOSED/ANTICIPATED ITEMS LIKELY TO BE TRADE IN THE INDO-CHINA BORDER

To be Exported	*To be Imported*
1. Wooden bowl	1. Salt
2. Soyabean.	2. Wool
3. Dry Chilli	3. Dry Meat
4. Local handmade paper	4. Woollen garments
5. Rice	5. Ghee
6. Hydes & skin	6. Cheese
7. Bee Wax	7. Earthen pots
8. Salt	8. Carpet
9. Potato	9. Electronic items
10. Chitranalla	
11. Ginger	
12. Maize	
13. Millet	
14. Tea	
15. Apple	
16. Papaya	
17. Guava	
18. Banana	
19. Bamboo chopsticks	
20. Bamboo Shoots & Chips	
21. Toothpick	
22. Various kinds of ethnic traditional Handicraft items	
23. Various cane products	
24. Mushroom	
25. Churpi	
26. Various grades of oil & natural gas	
27. Coffee	
28. Rubber	

Source: Directorate of Industries, Government of Arunachal Pradesh.

24

Prospect of Border Trade in Arunachal Pradesh

—R.P. Bhattacharjee

Strategic-Position of Arunachal Pradesh

Arunachal Pradesh is the largest state in North East India. It lies between latitude 20°28′N and 29°30′N and longitudes 91°30′E and 97°30′E. The State has a population of 864558 (1991) with a density of 10 persons per sq. km. and 63.66% of its population indigeneous.

The State is surrounded by Bhutan on the West, China on the North, Myanmar on the East and the States of Assam and Nagaland on the south. The geo-strategic importance of the State becomes evident from the fact that it has 1628 km. of International border of which 1030 km. is with China. 441 km. with Myanmar and 157 km. with Bhutan.[1] However the border is disputed particularly with Tibet Region of China. Let us now trace out the historical incidence of border trade in Arunachal Pradesh.

History of Border-Trade

We have hardly any information about this state before the advent of British in Assam (1826). But in respect of border trade, it is Thomas Throunil Cooper who made an attempt to travel through Tibet to India. At the beginning of 1868, he left Hankow for Batang. At the end of six months, after passing safely through the Chinese empire from east to west, traversing the almost impassable snowy ranges of Eastern Tibet he found himself at the town of Batang some two hundred miles from Sadiya. From Batang Cooper attempted to reach Sadiya.[2] The Chinese authorities, however, refused to let him proceed and he went instead south to Bhamo. Cooper's journey demonstrated the impracticabilities of a trade-route over the rugged mountains.[3] But recognising the potential rivalry with France and Italy, pressure among British-officials were mounting to open trade route through Myanmar (Burma).

Infact, it was Sir Amther Cottan, an Engineer, who commented that the missing link of communication was between the Irrawaddy and the Brahmaputra. If this distance of only about hundred miles could be linked then the produce of South-West China could flow down to Calcutta as well as Rangoon.[4] Prospect of this brightened after the annexation of upper Burma in 1885 by the British.

Even after the annexation of upper Burma, British official posted in Assam were still arguing the merit of opening up of a practicable route between northern districts of Assam and Burma.[5] It was F.J. Needham, Asstt. Political Officer of Sadiya who explored two routes from the river Dihing in upper Assam towards Hukang Valley. Though he failed to reach Hukang Valley, explored to a considerable extent two routes, one of which after learning the Dihing river crossed the Patkoi at an elevation of 4650 feet, and going up the Nangyong Lake and Longlai river reached to Singpho village called Nangong. The other of which going through the hills south of Margherita via Yogli and Namchik river, crossed the Patkoi at an elevation of 7300 feet and after passing through the villages of Phoong, Morang, Shangye, Hashan, Khulluk, reached a village in Hukong, inhabited by a Singpho Chief called Sumbaynang. This village was at a distant of two days journey from Khulluk and was the farthest point reached by Needham. In a letter written to the Secretary to the Govt. of India, the Secretary to the Chief Commissioner of Assam expressed the view that since upper Burma had become British territory, the belt, inhabited by 'wild tribes' must instead of being left alone as a convenient barrier, gradually brought under control from our side or other and wherever the boundary between two provinces was to be ultimately fixed, whether of Patkhoi or else where it was for the interest of both the provinces that the country should be explored and communication established.[6]

Thus we find in the process along the old Burmese route through Singpho territories, some traffic went on in Indian tea, blanket, matches etc.[7] *Bhamo,* the great trade centre on the Irrawaddy river, attracted a large number of hill tribes from Tirap district of Arunachal Pradesh. Through them, some of the articles that were imported from Assam found way to Burma.[8] The actual trade was not voluminous because any one making the journey had to carry such a large stock of provisions, as to preclude the possibility of carrying much merchandise.

The route to Tibet was explored by Lt: Neufville in 1825, Captain will Cox (1826), W. Griffith (1836), EA. Rawlatt (1844), T.T. Cooper (1869, 1870), Nain Singh (1865-66). Singh's explorations yielded valuable results. Beside the above, Captain Woodthrope (1876-77), had penetrated in Arunachal Pradesh and became known to the tribes who traded with China on the one hand and Assam on the other.

The items traded across the border were Assam fabrics, raw coarse, silk cloth etc. and there was large prospect of trade of Indian tea.

Colonial Achievements

The attempts of the nearly whole of the century to penetrate into central Asian markets was not crowned with much success. The hostile attitude of the Tibetans and the events that followed stood on the way of promotion of direct trade with Tibet. The

Tibetan Govt. opposed to closer intercourse with India for they were suspicious of British activities in India.[9]

The direct trade with Tibet was possible only at Udalguri fair where Tibetans continued to come down annually to trade. There were also some Tibetans who resorted to Dewangiri via Bhutan. The introduction of cheap Liverpool salt pushed Tibetan salt out of market. In 1875-76 the quantity of Tibetan salt imported into Udalguri fair was 1889 mounds and at Doimara 225 mounds.[10] In 1876-77, the quantity imported in Udalguri and Doimara fairs was 1764 mounds 19 seer and 258 mounds respectively. The salt was bartered for Assamese cloth and other articles of local produce. In Lakhimpur district, the Tibetan rock salt was imported by the people of Assam for medicinal purpose only.[11] Eventually rock salt failed to compete with cheap Liverpool salt. Thus slowly the border trade in trade-fairs died down.

This shows some sort of commercial inter-course was there with Tibetans though in a limited extent. With slowing down of intensity of trade fairs, the trade also declined.

Prospect of Border Trade

Compared to pre-independent era, the communication network is far better today. With improvement of road, hotel and restaurant, and other basic amenities, the State can have border trade with neighbouring countries. It is true that the State is strategically sensitive. But as per SAARC nations decision towards a South Asian Free Trade Area (SAFTA) by the end of 2000 AD, we can expect that Arunachal Pradesh will have immense scope of border-trade with Bhutan. The relation with Myanmar and China has improved and friendly relation with South-East Asian Countries has brightened the prospect of border trade in the State.

For Socio-economic development of the State, it is essential to open her border for trade. A few circles and it's headquarters could be prospective trade centres in the State. These are shown below:

Name of Circle: District: Adjacent Country

1.	Zemithang	Tawang	China
2.	Thingbu	Tawang	China
3.	Lumla	Tawang	Bhutan
4.	Kalaktang	West Kameng	Bhutan
5.	Balemu	West Kameng	Bhutan
6.	Taksing	Upper Subansiri	China
7.	Limeking	Upper Subansiri	China
8.	Mechuka	West Siang	China
9.	Monigong	West Siang	China
10.	Gelling	Upper Siang	China
11.	Tuting	Upper Siang	China
12.	Singa	Upper Siang	China
13.	Chaglagaon	Lohit	China
14.	Kibitho	Lohit	China
15.	Waleng	Lohit	China
16.	Vijoynagar	Changlang	Myanmar
17.	Nampong	Changlang	Myanmar
18.	Khimiyong	Changlang	Myanmar
19.	Laju	Tirap	Myanmar
20.	Wakka	Tirap	Myanmar
21.	Pongchou	Tirap	Myanmar

The above stated 21 circle/head quarters are identified by the author as prospective centres of border-trade. Historically, the state had border trade through Tawang and Tirap districts and these trade could be termed as illegal trade as there were no proper administration. Today also, some sorts of illegal trade exists and this can be observed from the availability of foreign goods specially in North-West and Eastern parts of the State. The state can earn huge revenue if these are legalised. Beside that, the State can export agricultural products, horticultural products, diary products and forest products. Some of these items are butter/cheese from Yak's milk, timber, medicinal plants, fruits and spices. Even the traditional handloom and handicraft items like gale, marrigin, cane chairs and tables, musk, etc. The state has immense scope of supplying skins and other hydes if the people are taught to preserve the skins and tanner is introduced in the state.

The state has about 44000 MW (26,400 MW at 60% load factor) of hydel power generation potentiality but it hardly produce 23 MW at present. This power resource, if tapped, can earn huge revenue for the state. A SAARC power grid will be operational within a year as per the ministry of power. Thus with high potentiality of surplus power the state can dream of surplus revenue and can have huge capital receipt for investment in all sectors. From large hydel projects, the state's Agriculture and pisciculture sectors also will improve specially in catchment areas.

The State can import rice and teak from neighbouring countries specially from Myanmar. Even the easily accessible mineral resources of Myanmar can be utilised for industrial development of the state.

Beside the above, the finished goods of other states like cycle, machine-tools, computer-software etc. can find way to neighbouring countries and South-East Asia through this State and perhaps this will be economical compared to sea-route. If railway link is connected through eastern part of the state, the communication facility will boost the border trade.

The Govt. of India has earmarked Rs. 4 crores in the current financial year for development of the Indo-Myanmar

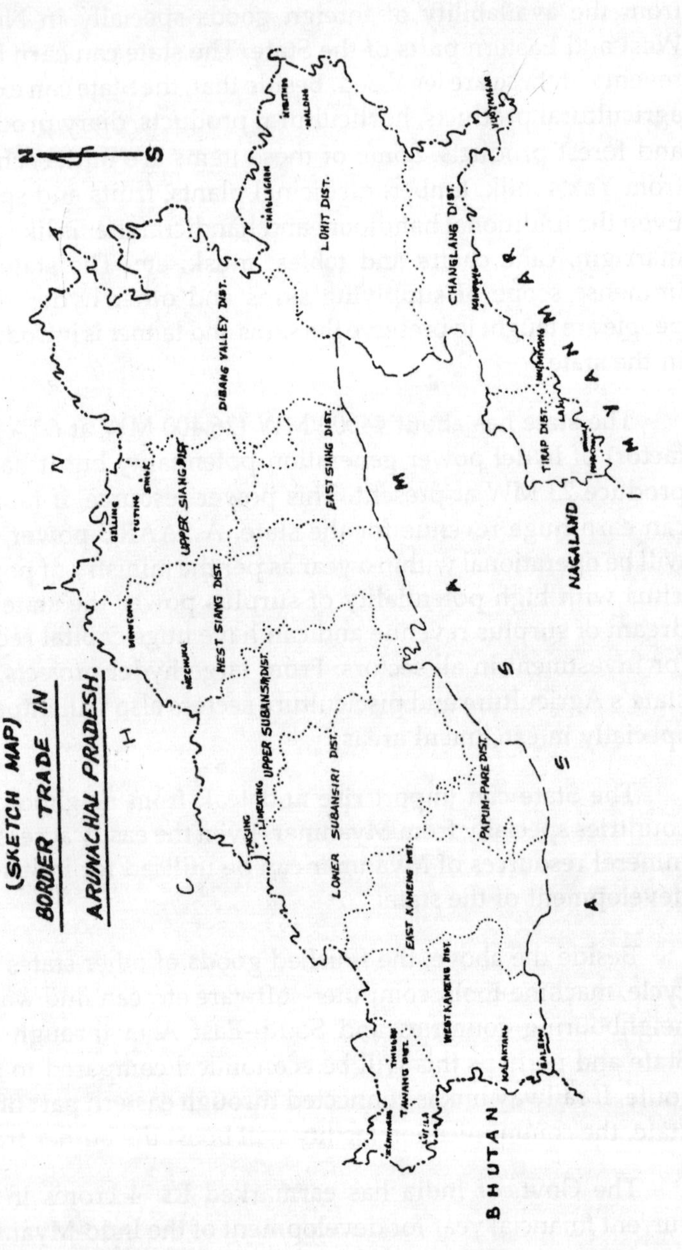
(SKETCH MAP)
BORDER TRADE IN
ARUNACHAL PRADESH.
CHINA
MYANMAR
BHUTAN
ASSAM
NAGALAND
TAWANG DIST.
WEST KAMENG DIST.
EAST KAMENG DIST.
PAPUM-PARE DIST.
LOWER SUBANSIRI DIST.
UPPER SUBANSIRI DIST.
WEST SIANG DIST.
UPPER SIANG DIST.
EAST SIANG DIST.
DIBANG VALLEY DIST.
LOHIT DIST.
CHANGLANG DIST.
TIRAP DIST.
N
S

Figure 24.1

border area under the Border Area Development Programme.[12] Though the amount is nominal but it is perhaps a good beginning towards future border-trade with Myanmar.

Suggestion

The border-trade in the state could be expedited and subsequently the economic development of the region could be enhanced if proper road is constructed upto the border as identified earlier. The still-well Road which was from Ledo in Assam to Pangsau Pass in Tirap Myanmar border could be opened again by the Govt. of India. This will facilitate access upto Wauling at Mongyu in China. In order to boost trade with neighbouring countries and to contain illegal trade along the border—a comprehensive policy should be taken up by the Government. This will improve the living condition of the people in border-areas and relationship with neighbouring countries will improve further.

REFERENCES

1. R.P. Bhattacharjee (1997) "Economic Development of Arunachal Pradesh," Unpublished Ph.D. Thesis, Guwahati University, pp. 1-14.
2. A.S.R., General Dept., File No. 167J of 1978, Series No. 1. (Cited from Sudatta Sikdhar (1984) "The Eastern Himalayan Trade of Assam in the Nineteenth Century; A study of British Policy," Unpublished Ph.D. Thesis, NEHU, P-201).
3. *Ibid.*
4. D. Woodman (1962); *The Making of Burma*, London, pp. 173-194.
5. A.S.R., File No. 5475 of 1887, From the commissioner of Assam, Letter No. 33,90, dated Gauhati 18, July 1887.
6. Sikdhar, *Ibid*, p. 206.
7. E.C. Young, "A journey from Yunan to Assam" *Geographical Journal*, Vol. XXV, July to December 1907.
8. S. Duttachowdhury (Ed.), *Tirap Dist. Gazetteer*, Shillong 1980, p. 133.
9. C. Bell (1924), *Tibet, Past and Present* London, B. Nand (1975), "British India and Tibet", New Delhi, p. 4.

10. A.S.R., R.P., June (1878, from the Secretary to the Chief Commissioner of Assam to the Secretary to the Govt. of India, letter No. 1585 dated Shillong 8 June 1878. Cited from Sikdhar *ibid*, p. 225.
11. *Ibid*.
12. *The Times of India*, dated 19.1.99.

PART VI

INDO-NEPAL TRADE

25

Indo-Nepal Trade: Some Reflections

—Ramesh C. Arya

Third Country Imports

Nepal opened up its international business in the '60s. Till then, India was its sole trading partner except for the small business that people in the north had with their Tibetan neighbours. In absence of adequate infrastructure linking the northern region with the south, the people there were more or less isolated. After the formal transit arrangement with India, Nepalese market attempted to diversify its export and import. India was still its majority partner till 1980. In 1974/75, for example, the third country import was at NRs 339 million, while that from India was NRs 1476. But in 1979/80, it was NRs 1694 million and NRs 1786 million. The Indian share in the total volume of trade came down from 82 per cent to 22.5 per cent in 1989/90. It is now at around 28 per cent. In 1989-90, the trade and transit treaty was expired and the new one was not yet effective for more than a year.

Though the trade with India has come down over the years, the import from India is still significant, as the items are essential items for the Nepalese consumers. It is the non-essential high value products from the third countries that have in toto raided the third country component.

Also, as common phenomena in the open border, significant volume of trade goes unrecorded. In the case of Nepal-India border trade, it may be well in the range of 30 per cent over the normally recorded.

Nepal-Indian Market

Trade basically deals with the products that are in demand and their availability. Traditional items traded between the two countries, have been the primary products like jute, rice, timber etc. It has not changed. But with the industrialisation, several manufactured goods, earlier being imported from the third countries, are being locally manufactured and traded.

Indian Entrepreneurship

India has opened up its market gradually over the last twenty years. The export of Nepalese manufactured goods had been based earlier on content limitations. The first agreement opened the goods consisting of not less than 80 per cent Nepalese and/or Indian content in the form of men and material. It was gradually relaxed to 50 per cent. Besides the content clause there was a long negative list. The agreement in 1996 was a milestone when the content clause was entirely removed. The negative list was brought down to just three groups: (i) Alcoholic liquors/Beverages and their concentrates except industrial spirits, (ii) Perfumes and Cosmetics with non-Nepalese, non-Indian brand names and (iii) Cigarettes and tobacco. The earlier negative list also included precious stones, synthetic/blended yarn and fabrics unless the yarn and fabric is imported from India.

The content clause encouraged Indian entrepreneurs to go for joint-venture investments in Nepal. Till 1986, Nepal had been permitting joint ventures with a foreign collaboration of up to 90 per cent in the large-scale industries. But later even 100 per cent foreign owned investment was permitted. This encouraged many Indian to come for the direct investment. The number of Indian joint ventures in Nepal outnumbers the others taken together. But still, they had to receive clearance from the Reserve Bank of India on money transfer etc. Recently in the Tenth SAARC Summit, the Indian Prime Minister announced a fast track clearance for Indian investment of up to IRs 60 crore in Nepal. This will definitely accelerate Indian investment in Nepal.

Nepal already has establishments of some of the reputed industrial houses of India. These include the Colgate-Pamolive, Hindustan Lever, Dabur, Asian Paints, State Bank of India, Punjab National Bank, Taj Group of Hotels, Jenson and Nicholson, number of Indian students have joined medical and engineering courses in the Nepalese Colleges.

Balance of Trade

The negative balance of trade may be reduced by promoting exports to the Indian market. The joint venture companies have a significant role in this regard. Dabur, Hindustan Lever and Colgate together are exporting Rs. 150 million worth of their products to India. The Colgate-Pamolive joint venture has targeted markets in Myanmar and Bangladesh as well.

Relaxed export conditions have helped other Nepalese products find market in India. Iron rods, Blue and Finished leather, Biscuits and Noodles etc. are being exported to India. In the recent past, when there was a shortage of vegetable ghee in the nearby Indian market, the Nepalese manufacturers filled up the demand.

Export of Energy

Nepal has rich water resources. India and Nepal have agreed to meet their power shortages from the nearby hydroelectric supply sources of the two countries. A number of such projects may be completed within the next five years when once again Nepal will have surplus power available for export. The big projects on the Mahakali River, bordering western Nepal with India is being discussed. The construction work may be started after the two countries finalise the Detailed Project Report (DPR). The power, supplied from India or Nepal, through its linking with the national grid, may supplement power needs for the region. The matter for seeking regional utilisation of the resource has been seriously discussed in several SAARC forums.

Tourism

Tourism holds very important position in the Nepalese economy. Indian tourists have been an important source of foreign exchange earning. But unfortunately, the country is keeping account of hard currency earning only. In the recent years, several Indian companies and groups have been holding their regional meetings and conferences in Nepal.

Potential

The world narrowing down. The membership of the WTO may reduce the national boundaries. In fact several countries are liberalising their trade restrictions. It is an international need, which some countries take it as a pressure that may affect their national enterprises. A regional cooperation in harnessing their resources may go a long way in surviving the global competition. Already several economic co-operation arrangements, such as NAFTA, ASEAN etc. have come into existence. Strategy to develop bi-national bondage may supplement the regional feelings. Even in the SAARC, Nepal has proposed quadrangle approach of co-operation in the sub-region consisting of Nepal, India, Bangladesh and Bhutan. The proposal has been favourably taken by the member states. The earlier it gathers momentum, the more advantageous the region would be in meeting the global challenges.

Export of Major Commodities to India

(NRs in Million)

Description	*1974-75*	*1984-85*	*1992-93*	*1996-97***
Total	512.5	722.2	740.1	1332.6
Others	234.2	879.5	943.8	2748.5
Grand Total	746.7	1601.7	1683.9*	4081.1
Total Export (FOB)	889.6	2704.6	17266.5	16821.4

Note: * The revised data, as per the economic Survey 1994-95, for certain products and the total slightly different.

** Estimated for the first nine months.

Exchange Rates: 1974/75 IRs 100 = NRs 139;

1984/85 IRs 100 = NRs 145;

1992/93 IRs 100 = NRs 160;

1994/95 IRs 100 = NRs 160;

Direction of Foreign Trade

(NRs in Million)

Description	*1974-75*	*1984-85*	*1992-93*	*1996-97***
Export FOB	746.7	1601.7	1621.7	4081.1
Import CIF	1475.7	3695.8	12542.1	19399.3
Trade Balance	- 925.0	- 5001.5	109260.4	–15318.2
(India)				
Total Volume	2704.2	10482.7	14163.8	23480.4
Share of the Total Trade	82.2%	52.4%	25.1%	27.3%

**Estimated for the first nine months.

26

VAT and Its Effect on Indo-Nepal Trade

—Raghu Bista & Ramesh C. Arya

VAT is a brief form of Value Added Tax. It is a commodity-based tax. In general, it means a tax on the value added by the firm. It is defined as a tax levied on the difference between the price of output and the cost of input.

In other words, in the path of commodity from the production to the distribution there are three stages. They are the importer/manufacturer, the wholesaler and the retailer. When the commodity passed through each stage to the consumer, each stage adds the value with the margin. A tax which is levied on the value added by each stage is called VAT. It may be illustrated below:

The Operation of VAT

VAT Rate 10%

Sl. No.	*Stage*	*Output cost*	*Output price*	*Value Add*	*VAT*	*VAT collect*
1	Manufacture	0	100	100	10	10
2.	Wholesaler	100	120	20	12	2
3.	Retailer	120	150	30	15	3

Total VAT-15

Let's suppose there is 1 unit of commodity to which the

manufactured industry's input cost is zero rupee. The industry add itself a value with a margin. Its output price is Rs. 100. There is Rs. 100 value added. If VAT rate is 10 per cent. VAT is Rs. 10 and VAT collection is Rs. 10.

The output price of a commodity is a input cost of the wholesaler. Its input cost is Rs. 100. If the wholesaler adds itself a value of Rs. 20, the output is Rs. 120. Then the value added is Rs. 20. VAT is Rs. 12. According to the tax credit method, VAT is Rs. 2.

Similarly, the output price of a commodity of the wholesaler is the input cost of the retailer that is Rs. 120. If the retailer adds value of Rs. 50, its output price is Rs. 150. Value added is Rs. 30. VAT is Rs. 15 and VAT collection is Rs. 3. In this way, total VAT collection is Rs. 115.

VAT has a long history. Dr. William Von Simen, industrialist, in 1919 first of all recommended VAT to the Government of Germany to levy it, in lieu of the existed Turnover Tax. There wasn't a good pace in the process of evolution of VAT until France introduced in 1954. Thereafter, the VAT picked up a good speed. Then, Ivory Coast and Sinegal followed in 1960;s. Thereafter, European countries including Germany, Netherlands, Luxemburg, Ireland, Finland, Italy adopted it. In this way its popularity got momentum and Vietnam, South Korea, Bangladesh, Pakistan followed the VAT.

In context of Nepal, the restoration of Democracy in 1991 that was a political revolution in Nepal after 30 years long Kingship Panchayat system had made the general people over-excited and over-aspirant for a radical change in Nepalese Economy.

In 1992, Nepali Congress (NC), a 50 years old and historic party, formed the majority government. The government liberalised Nepalese Economy not only for the global market but also for the foreign and private investment so that the economic development could be achieved as a fruit of Democracy, while the government introudced VAT on the seven commodities as an experiment through the budget speech.

Because of the inter party power struggle among leaders inside the NC party, the country had a mid-poll in 1994 as a bitter experience, although the country wasn't prepared to embrace it. The result was the hung parliament. In 1994, United Marxist and Leninist (UML) formed the minority government. The government reversed the sales tax as before instead of VAT. After 9 months, in 1995, NC-led coalition government decided to introduce VAT in Nepal. Despite the political instability, each new government followed the decision of the NC-led first coalition government relating the VAT.

After a long suffering, now VAT is implemental in Nepal. The question as to what kinds of effects VAT will have on the foreign trade, especially on the Indo-Nepal trade, has been arising in Nepal since the implementation of VAT. This is very sensitive and significant to both India and Nepal, while both countries have been suffering from the smuggling trade of manufactured commodities and contraband goods in the side of Indo-Nepal open border.

Nepalese Tax Structure and Indo-Nepal Trade

Nepal had followed the system of sales tax at the importer and manufacture level until the tax reformation. Since Nepalese tax structure is import based, the share of the import based revenue is more than the share of the manufacture based revenue. In terms of the revenue mobilisation, the growth of import inflow is beneficial to the Nepalese Economy. However, it increases the trade deficit due to the under developed industrialisation process. The growth of trade deficit is never considered as a good sign in economy.

In the import based revenue, there are two potential

sources. They are the import trade from the third countries and the import from India. In relation with the import trade, its growth per annum is decreasing due to the trade diversification policy adopted by Nepal. But the growth of the revenue mobilisation to Nepal is continuous. Although the smuggling trade flow from India and the under valuation have been eroding the correct number of import duties since a long back. Therefore, the import trade from India is a significant and sensitive matter not only for the revenue mobilisation but also the economic development of Nepal.

Problems and Challenges

Indo-Nepal open border is a sign of historical and cultural relation and also a knot of good neighbour between these two countries. However, it is not ever fruitful in terms of Indo-Nepal trade because the open border has been facilitating to the smuggling business of manufactured goods and also of contraband goods. Therefore, many complicated problems are arising so that are challenging not only for the fiscal policy and structure but also for the national security and peace.

Possible Effects of VAT on Indo-Nepal Trade

Since VAT is the best one fiscal measure in the world, its possible effects should be positive, productive and effective as well as efficient However, its possible effects may be different due to the different socio-economic and geo-political circumstances and other constraints. Therefore, its possible effects on Indo-Nepal trade may be projected as follows:

Possible Effects on Trade Deficit

1) since VAT is a transparent tax policy, there is no chance to follow the undervaluation of the imported goods, on the one hand and the importer, if they exibit dislike the undervaluation of the imported goods to have the tax rebate facility, while the imported goods passes through the custom

office value can be revaluabled. It means the trade deficit will grow, although the revenue collection will grow immensely. But, VAT simplify the existed trade barrior between India and Nepal, and VAT follows the destination Principle (tax import, exempt export) and VAT is an export intensive policy. These reasons will attract the foreign investment on the export intensive industries will increase enormously. Ultimately, the trade deficit will not be unmanageable in Indo-Nepal trade.

Possible Effects on the Smuggling Trade

since VAT is account based and invoice based system, and it is having the cross-checking and self-policing mechanism, the smuggling goods may be easily verified and caught. So the smuggling trade may be discouraged.

In general Nepalese industries which are located in the side of Indo-Nepal border always export the manufactured goods illegally to India. Therefore, there is a tax leakage, since the provision of tax rebate and exemption to the exporter, such industries may register in the VAT office. Consequently, the legal export will increase to India. This component will also contribute to improve the trade deficit.

Like an invisible export trade, the re-export trade of the imported goods from the third countries is diverted to India VAT totally restricts such business through the destination principle.

Possible Effects on Investment

VAT which is a clear tax policy and also an export intensive policy attract the foreign investment like the Indian investment. The investment comes in order to get benefit from the export intensive policy, and also the large Indian market. The process of industrialisation will be accelerated. It is a good and positive sign to the Nepalese Economy.

Possible Effects on the Revenue Mobilisation

since VAT reduces the smuggling trade and the under valuation, the revenue mobilisation will tremendously and optimally grow. Nepal will then get good financial resources in order to construct the infrastructure and to eradicate the massive poverty.

Observations and Recommendation

1. There is a growing realisation that much of the perennial socio-political problems of the region are because of its stunted economic development. Economic development is, thus, viewed to be the major panacea for socio-political unrest in the region.

2. As the region is having 98 per cent international border with the neighbouring countries of Bangladesh, Bhutan, China and Myanmar, and only 2 percent border with the mainland of our country, the need to situate the region within the larger setting of South and South-East Asia is increasingly being felt to be the precondition for any successful development strategy.

3. The markets of neighbouring countries, because of their proximity, may act as both time & cost effective vents' for region's surplus as well as sources of supply of many a demand.

4. As a result, any development strategy for the region needs to be accompanied by a complementary trade policy.

5. We appreciate the recent decision of the Central Government to open up a free trade centre at Sutarkandi, Assam. We also appreciate the achievements of the Indo-Bangla Trade Review Meeting held in Dhaka during 8-9 December and welcome the decision to open up multi-model transportation facilities for the region through Bangladesh. A special note may be taken of the keen interest of Bangladesh in forging and strengthening the economic ties with India's land locked north-eastern region.

6. The region is presently having bilateral trade with Bangladesh, Bhutan and Myanmar through the Land Custom Stations along the border with these countries and also 'border trade' with Myanmar. In spite of having a long border with China, there is no land border trade. Efforts may be made in order to identify probable centres for trade along the Arunachal Pradesh-China border as well as North East India-Bangladesh border and initiative may be taken to open up these centres for trade with their counterparts across the border like Indo-Myanmar border trade agreement.

7. As the lion's share of North East India's trade with Bangladesh, Bhutan and Myanmar flows through Meghalaya, Assam and Manipur respectively, Shillong, Guwahati and Imphal may be chosen as the centre of NER-Bangladesh, NER-Bhutan and NER-Myanmar trade respectively.

8. Necessary institutional framework including banking consultancy, market intelligence, training, research, commodity specific export promotion boards, etc., may be created in all these three centres.

9. Issues relating to the promotion of border trade between North East India and neighbouring countries may conveniently be divided into five types, viz.,

i) there are some issues, the settlement of which require joint efforts from both the Government of India and that of neighbouring countries.

ii) there are some that require joint efforts from Government of India and the State Governments in the region,

iii) inter-state issues that need to be settled between the State Governments in the region,

iv) issues need to be settled between NEC and the State Governments, and

v) issues which are to be looked into exclusively by the State Governments.

10. In order to sort out all the issues and to carry out subsequent follow-up with different agencies at different levels on a regular basis, an institutional device in the form of an organisation may be conceived of. This organisation may be constituted of drawing people from both the Central and State Government officials associated with the promotion of trade like DGFT, Customs, Industry and Commerce, etc., banking officials, exporters and importers, members of the state Planning Boards, marketing professionals,. NEC officials, academicians, geologists, environmentalists etc. A marketing professional may be appointed as the Chairman of this organisation.

11. It has been observed that inadequate infrastructural support in most of the authorised trade outlets has been the immediate cause of low volume of trade and which has also made many of them defunct. A study may be made to identify the important trade outlets on the basis of their quantum of annual volume of trade following which a priority list may be prepared for immediate supply of the required infrastructural inputs like road, dumping ground, guest house, weigh bridge, trade permit centre, banking, etc. As the forces of market take a long time to provide public goods, State Governments have to take initiative in providing them through a 'Pay and Use' mechanism.

12. While the trade between North East India and Bangladesh involves exchange of commodities largely produced within the respective areas, North East India-Myanmar trade is essentially transit trade involving the exchange of goods mostly produced outside North East-India as well as Myanmar.

13. Exports from North East India to Bangladesh mainly consist of raw materials, i.e. coal and limestone. This is a trade between two regions where raw materials are available in one region and not available in the other. It has nothing to do with the comparative advantage notion of trade. Exports

of raw materials, in a sense, weaken the industrial potential of the region. In absence of diversification, the time horizon of such trade will coincide with the time required for the reserves of non-renewable natural resources to exhaust. As a result, it is important to have a long term perspective involving a shift in commodity structure of exports from raw materials to value added manufactured goods.

14. It has been observed that trade along the Bhutan and Myanmar borders is essentially transit trade. Although transit trade has its own importance, the gains from trade is likely to go to the distant operators leaving only a marginal sum for the local agents in the form of commission. As a result, efforts should be made to link up the border trade along these stretches to the local economy. Otherwise the growth effect of trade in terms of production, income and employment generation will not be felt in the region in general and the border states in particular.

15. It has been observed that neither the State plans nor the NEC Plan have tried to synchronise their area development projects with the programmes for the promotion of border trade. In order to establish a link between trade and production structure, both agricultural and industrial programmes in north eastern states have to have an export orientation to cater the external demands across the border.

16. It has been observed that a large scale unofficial trade exists along the Myanmar border. A regulatory framework needs to be devised so that the unofficial trade can be diverted through legal channels.

17. For all these years, border areas have been viewed as liabilities. As a result, these areas and the people therein were left to themselves and developmental programmes, by and large, have bypassed them. In an era of globalisation, we need to view our international borders not as liabilities but as assets as they provide the arteries to the markets of neighbouring countries.

A large part of our international border between North East India and neighbouring countries is unmanned, and in many places, ill demarcated. Border trade, as a result, cannot flourish without a good border management.

Contributors

Arya, Ramesh C., Nepal Yearbook, Kathmandu, Nepal.

Baruah, Srinath, Department of Economics, Guwahati University, Guwahati.

Behera, M.C., Department of Tribal Studies, Arunachal University, Itanagar.

Bezbaruah, M.P., Department of Economics, Guwahati University, Guwahati.

Bhattacharjee, N.N., Department of Geography, Guwahati University, Guwahati.

Bhattacharjee, R.P., North-Eastern Regional Institute of Science and Technology, Arunachal Pradesh.

Bhuyan, Dulal, Town and Country Planing, Govt. of Assam, Tezpur

Bista, Raghu, Kathmandu, Nepal.

Chakraborty, Atri, Laban, Shillong.

Das, Gurudas, Department of Economics, St. Anthony's College, Shillong-1.

Datta, P.C., Department of Statistics, S.S. College, Hailakandi, Assam.

Dhar, Bibhash, Anthropological Survey of India, Shillong.

Dutta, Rajesh, Department of Economics, St. Edmund's College, Shillong.

Dutta, Sukhendu Shekhar, M.L.A., Assam State Assembly, Guwahati.

Ganguly, J.B., Calcutta.

Goswami, S.N., ICAR, Umiam Meghalaya.

Husain, Zahid, Department of Geography, North-Eastern Hill University, Shillong.

Kumar, B.B., Officers Colony, Katihar.

Laskar, Harun Rashid, Research Fellow, Silchar.

Marak, S.C., Chairman, State Planning Board, Meghalaya.

Medhi, G., North-Eastern Council, Shillong.

Mero, M.K., Office of the DGFT, Guwahati.

Prassain, G.P., Department of Commerce, Manipur University, Imphal.

Roy, N., Department of Economics, Karimganj College, Karimganj, Assam.

Saikia, Anup, Department of Geography, Arunachal University, Itanagar.

Sarma, B.K., ICAR, Umiam, Meghalaya.

Sengupta, Keya, Department of Economics, Assam University, Silchar.

Singh, Rajmani, Department of Commerce, Manipur University, Imphal.

Singh, S.B., ICAR, Umiam, Meghalaya.

Thomas, C.J., ICSSR-NERC, Shillong.

Index